Welfare
& the Poor

Welfare
& the Poor

Edited by Lester A. Sobel

Contributing editors: Joseph Fickes, Chris Larson,
Stephen Orlofsky, Gerry Satterwhite, Barry
Youngerman

Indexer: Grace M. Ferrara

FACTS ON FILE, INC.   NEW YORK, N.Y.

Welfare
& the Poor

Library of Congress Catalog Card No. 76-41985
ISBN 0-87196-293-4

9 8 7 6 5 4 3 2
PRINTED IN
THE UNITED STATES OF AMERICA

Contents

Welfare & the Poor

POVERTY IS A CONDITION that appears to have come into existence almost simultaneously with civilization. And while not quite the world's oldest profession, the effort to relieve the poor seems to be nearly as ancient an activity as the problem of poverty itself. The issue has been attacked by moral, religious, political and economic thinkers and doers for millenia, yet their labors have ended in failure at least as frequently as in success. Kind and intelligent people have done their best, but "the poor are always with us."

Welfare Program in Trouble

Programs to relieve the poor in the United States have been varied, extensive and costly and usually controversial. They have also been denounced often as ill-devised, inefficient, wasteful, corruption-ridden failures. Sen. Hubert H. Humphrey (D, Minn.), addressing a welfare-reform conference of the Institute of Socioeconomic Studies of White Plains, N.Y. May 25, 1976, asserted that "despite the sincere efforts of the past to devise a fair, efficient and compassionate system of support for the poor and the needy, we have not done so. And well-known deficiencies in our current patchwork of federal and state income-support programs have been severely worsened by poor management of the economy in the last six years."

Detailing the problems of the welfare program, Humphrey noted that inflation and recession had "sharply increased the number of families requiring welfare, raised the cost of providing families with welfare, and drastically reduced the ability of state and local governments to meet these increased demands.'' Humphrey continued:

The wide disparities among income support levels in various states have encouraged the movement of the welfare population, often to areas where future job prospects are no better or are actually worse than in their home state. This continuing movement threatens financial collapse in progressive states and inner cities and is beyond their ability to control without betraying their citizens.

Intact families are penalized compared to those in which one parent has abandoned the family. [Thus] our income support system encourages the break-up of low-income families. . . .

In some parts of the country, the combination of cash and in-kind benefits to some families exceed the after-tax income of working families. This, combined with the sharp benefit reduction generally for any earned income, creates severe disincentives for welfare recipients to return to work.

Some programs fail to target our limited resources on those most in need and, at the same time, create a bureaucratic nightmare for those who need help.

High unemployment over a prolonged period has increased the number of individuals and families in need of income support. As a result, we have had to lengthen and broaden the coverage of Unemployment Insurance, making the U.I. system as much a welfare program as an insurance system against short spells of unemployment. . . .

A serious problem of the welfare system was pointed out by Dr. Andrew F. Brimmer of the Federal Reserve Board. Brimmer had said in a commencement address at San Francisco State College June 3, 1971 that "the accelerated growth of dependency on public welfare is creating a permanent 'underclass' in America. . . . Moreover, the problem of welfare is increasingly acquiring racial overtones. The representation of blacks and other minorities in the welfare system is expanding at an accelerated rate—with a disproportionate share of the growth being accounted for by families headed by black females. . . . Furthermore, the increased association of the welfare program with blacks has implications that are farreaching. It has strengthened the distorted image . . . of the black community as a subculture of American society with little capacity to support itself . . . [although] the facts belie such a view. . . .''

Over the years, considerable resentment has developed against welfare programs as benefiting people who refuse to work at the expense of hard-pressed taxpayers, who, it is said, often live less well than the welfare recipients their taxes support. To answer this charge and other "myths" about welfare, the National Welfare Rights Organization in 1971 published a brochure listing six welfare "myths" and refuting these charges with the "facts." The brochure said:

Myth No. 1: Hard work is the answer to the welfare problem.

Fact: Most welfare recipients cannot work. According to a recent HEW [Health,

Education & Welfare Department] survey, 24% of the welfare recipients are old-age recipients, 8% are permanently and totally disabled, 1% are blind, 2.9% are incapacitated parents in the home, 50.3% are children, and 13% are mothers. Of the mothers, one-fifth are in job training or so underemployed as to remain eligible for assistance. The possibilities of many others are limited by the unavailability of day-care facilities. While some five million children needed day care in 1969, only 640,000 spaces were available. This situation continues today.

Myth No. 2: Most welfare recipients are blacks who have moved to northern cities just to get on welfare.

Fact: The majority of welfare recipients are white—about 55%. 39% are black and 6% are American Indian and others. Of the 20 million people who moved to urban areas since World War II, only one-third were nonwhite. In the 1950–60 period when black migration to the North was greatest, welfare rolls increased by only 17%. Significant increases in welfare rolls (103% from 1960 to 1968) did not occur until after the peak period of black migration had passed. Most blacks moved north to find better jobs, better education, and less oppressive discrimination, not to sign up for welfare.

Myth No. 3: Welfare mothers have large numbers of illegitimate children.

Fact: The average welfare family has only three children. While 30% of AFDC [aid to families with dependent children] children are "illegitimately" born, HEW data shows that one-third of all first-born children in this country born between 1964 and 1966 were conceived out of wedlock

Myth No. 4: Welfare is the good life of color TV's and Cadillacs.

Fact: According to the Bureau of Labor Statistics a family of four needs a monthly income of $458 to live at a minimally adequate level of health and nutrition. New Jersey, the most liberal provider of welfare benefits, fails to reach that level by $117. Only a few states even provide benefits that would bring families of four up to the poverty level, the absolute minimum at which life can be sustained. This is hardly the "good life."

Myth No. 5: Most welfare recipients are welfare cheaters.

Fact: A 1969 HEW investigation revealed that only four-tenths of one percent—or 4 out of every 1,000—of all welfare cases were fraudulent. . . .

Myth No. 6: Welfare takes most of our taxes.

Fact: According to Budget figures for fiscal 1971, public welfare payments . . . amount to $4.2 billion out of a $201 billion budget or 1.9%. Military programs account for 36.7%, space programs for 1.7% and farm subsidies for 2.7%.

Frustration and anger at the welfare problem are sentiments expressed by many well-informed officials who are perfectly aware of the "facts" of the situation. In a special message to the Illinois General Assembly May 20, 1971, Gov. Richard B. Ogilvie said: "The failures of this nation's welfare system are failures of historic magnitude. The example of imperial Rome may prove to be prophetic for us. Welfare is warping our nation. . . . It is a human outrage and a fiscal monster. It robs the poor of their dignity and the taxpayers of their hard-earned dollars. The welfare system embodies all the worst of our failures—moral, fiscal, administrative and legal. Where in the system do we find charity, service, work, dignity, respect and responsiveness? Think of the children whose lives are

being distorted by this hopeless environment and what that means
for the future. . . . ''

Professors Frances Fox Piven and Richard A. Cloward, leaders in
the "welfare rights movement," are infuriated at the welfare system
for another cause. The title of one of their books, *Regulating the
Poor: The Function of Public Welfare* (Pantheon, 1971), indicates
the reason. They assert in the book: "Relief arrangements are not
shaped by the impulse to charity. . . . [they are] created and sustained to help deal with the malfunctions inherent in market
economies. Relief arrangements are usually initiated or expanded in
response to the political disorders that sometimes follow from the
sharp economic downturns or dislocations that periodically beset
[capitalistic] market systems. The purpose of relief-giving at such
times is not to ease hunger and want but to deal with civil disorder
among the unemployed. Once stability is restored, however, the relief system is not ordinarily eliminated. Instead, it is reorganized to
buttress the normal incentives of the labor market. This is done in
two ways. The main way is by cutting the 'able-bodied' off the
rolls, whether or not there are jobs, and whether or not the wages
offered are sufficient for survival. Second, some of those who cannot work or who are not needed in the labor market are allowed to
continue on the relief rolls, but they are treated so barbarously as to
make of them a class of pariahs whose degradation breeds a fear
and loathing of pauperism among the laboring classes.''

Views on Poverty Vary

Poverty is a plight that, it has been said, exists as much because
it is perceived as because it is suffered. It is not the same in every
country. The poor of America may be regarded by inhabitants of
some Third World countries as economically fortunate. An American welfare recipient might look upon an Asian or African worker
as a victim of intolerable deprivation, but the foreign worker could
perceive his own situation as comfortably above average in his own
country. In the United States, a family of four with an annual income of less than $6,550 would be considered officially to be living
in poverty. Families earning even two or three thousand dollars
more than this figure would be regarded by many fellow
Americans—and probably by themselves—as poor. In some countries, such income would seem to be an almost impossible dream.
Poverty, however, is a relative condition. Measured against the rich,
the middle class and the working class of America, the American
poor indisputably are poor.

Commenting on the perception of poverty, Lee Rainwater noted in a study published by the Fiscal Policy Committee of the Congressional Joint Economic Committee Dec. 3, 1973 that "reflection on the past decade of the war on poverty reveals many paradoxes. The most central is that while 'poverty' has been reduced by almost half, we have no sense of a reduction in the prevalence of human problems associated with poverty. The proportion of all persons living below the poverty line decreased year by year from 1959 to 1969. . . . Reductions in the poverty population seem to go hand in hand with increases in per capita personal income. No more elaborate explanation of the decline in poverty over the past decade is necessary than to say that the people at the bottom of the heap got their share of increasing affluence, and that this shift in their income moved almost half of them above the poverty line."

Rainwater continued:

If economic growth continues at its long-term rate, it is not overly risky to predict the virtual elimination of poverty by around 1980. But we know this is ridiculous. Any speaker is likely to meet with audience disbelief if he argues that in 1972 the poverty problem is almost half of what it was in 1959. His listeners will be quick to point to the undiminished intensity of a broad range of human and social problems.

If one leaves aside the statistical indicators of problems and looks instead at the quality of life of families at the lower end of the socioeconomic scale one is impressed by the extent to which it seems hardly to have changed over longer periods of time than a decade. The people who would have been considered poor on an "eyeball to eyeball" basis in 1959 still seem poor today. The people who felt themselves poor, deprived, oppressed, and wasted by society in 1959 still seem to feel poor, deprived, oppressed, and wasted today. Indeed, a reader who systematically compares studies carried out in low income slum or ghetto communities in the 1930s with recent ones is struck by the tremendous similarity across that timespan in the style of life and in the kinds of human difficulties and problems confronting people. No one who was acquainted with the lower-class described in the 1930s studies by such researchers as [W. Lloyd] Warner, [Allison] Davis and [Burleigh B. and Mary R.] Gardner, or [William Foote] Whyte would feel at all surprised by the style of life in Boston's white slums of today. And no one acquainted with Negro lower class life as dealt with by authors such as [Horace] Cayton and [Sinclair] Drake or Allison Davis would find basic change in the conditions of life of today's ghettos (although he might be surprised by the nature of ideological and political expression).

Yet the material base for life would have changed dramatically. Today's low income person has available to him perhaps two-and-a-half times as much in the way of goods and services.

To find what has not changed in the economic situation of the poor, we do not have far to look. Although the incomes of people at the bottom of the income hierarchy (as in the middle and at the top) have changed dramatically, the pattern of inequality in income distribution has varied only marginally since before World War II. There is some reason to believe that there has been a slight shift toward a more equal distribution during the depression and through World War II. Since

1947, however, there seem to have been hardly any changes in the income distribution. The proportion of the population with incomes less than half the median family income was 18.9% in 1947—it was 18.9% in 1970. (It had reached a high of 20.9% in 1954 and a low of 18.3% in 1968). The post-World War II economy was capable of practically eradicating poverty in a generation—if poverty is defined as having to live on less than half of the median family income at the generation's beginning. But the post-World War II economy does not seem to contain anything approaching automatic mechanisms to significantly change the share of the income that people on the bottom receive.

. . . [However,] *only a relative definition of poverty has any relevance for the human concerns that lie behind Americans' interest in poverty as a public policy issue.*

Poverty can be defined in several ways. But in a national campaign against poverty, a statistical definition seems necessary—if only to help set targets and determine the limitations of antipoverty programs being devised. A "poverty line" was, therefore, developed in the mid-1960s on the basis of these two measurements: (1) the amount of money poor families spent for food (in relation to their total expenses) and (2) the cost of what was considered a temporary but at least minimally adequate diet. (Federal officials described such a diet in their Economy Food Plan, which was heavy on starches and light on meat and which eliminated everything considered unessential.) The poverty line, which obviously produces a different income figure each year, is used to show whether the number and percentage of people living in poverty—that is, having less than even barely adequate income—is increasing or decreasing.

Using the poverty line as the gauge, there seemed to be a steady annual reduction in poverty, both in numbers and in percentages, throughout the 1960s. The trend ended, however, in 1970, when a slight rise in poverty was recorded. (In 1970, a family of four with a yearly income exceeding $3,968 was considered, statistically, to be above the poverty level.) The following figures (as compiled for the Senate Select Committee on Nutrition & Human Needs) show the numbers and percentages of people in the U.S. reported to be living in poverty during the years 1959 through 1971:

1959	39,500,000	22.4%	1966	28,500,000	14.7%
1960	39,900,000	22.2%	1967	27,800,000	14.2%
1961	39,600,000	21.9%	1968	25,400,000	12.8%
1962	38,600,000	21.0%	1969	24,300,000	12.2%
1963	36,400,000	19.5%	1970	25,400,000	12.6%
1964	36,100,000	19.0%	1971	25,600,000	12.5%
1965	33,200,000	17.3%			

The 1970 Census Employment Survey (CES), for the first time, provided hard information (rather than the estimates previously used) on employment, incomes and poverty in the central cities of the nation's 51 large urban areas. According to the findings, 31% of Americans lived in cities with population over 50,000, but these cities had 34% of the nation's poor. Comparisons of the 1970 CES with the Decennial Census indicated that, nationally: 14% of Americans lived in poverty in 1970, but 23% of the residents of the inner cities were poor; 11% of all families lived in poverty, but 23% of inner-city families were poor; 32% of all families headed by a woman lived in poverty, but 45% of inner-city families headed by a woman were in poverty; 57% of elderly unrelated individuals lived in poverty, but 55% of such inner-city individuals were poor.

It was found that full-time employment was no guarantee against poverty in the inner city: 7.3% of all inner-city families with at least one year-round, full-time worker lived in poverty; 8.7% of all black inner-city families with at least one year-round full-time worker were in poverty, and 13.9% of inner-city families headed by a female and with at least one year-round full-time worker were in poverty.

"Mainstream economists" and government policymakers "typically cite fluctuations in the economy and low individual productivity as the primary cause of poverty in the United States," Professor Rick Hurd asserts. Hurd, a member of the economics department of the University of New Hampshire and an economic policy fellow of the Brookings Institution, presented an "alternate view" in a 1975 paper prepared for the Institute for Policy Studies. According to Hurd, "in the United States, poverty is a product of the economic system."

Hurd reported these opinions of those holding the "mainstream" view:

The amount of poverty expands during down-swings [of the business cycle] and contracts during up-swings, primarily because of cyclical variations in unemployment. During peak business periods unemployment is low, while during troughs of the business cycle unemployment is high. Those on the margin of poverty are hit hardest by increases in unemployment, and the resulting reduction in their income causes many families to fall into poverty.

The accepted remedy for the elimination of business cycle related poverty is continuous economic growth. During the economic euphoria of the late 1960s continuous growth seemed to many to be an attainable objective. To quote a leading manpower expert writing in 1969: "The quest for measures to expand the total supply of economic opportunity can probably be pronounced complete . . . . The prospects for the future are for general levels of unemployment fluctuating between 3.5 and 4.5%. Given the knowledge and tools available, political pressures will not accept higher levels of unemployment." The recent downturn has reaffirmed the inevitability of business cycles under capitalism, and has necessitated a resort to special policy tools such as PSE [Public Service Employment] and TEA [Temporary Employment Assistance] . . . .

"The human capital approach" of the "mainstream economists" and policymakers "sees poverty as a result of low productivity," Hurd wrote. "The low productivity of individuals [as seen in this light] may result from lack of information, lack of training or lack of opportunity." "The uninformed poor are those who are unemployed or work at low-wage jobs even though there are vacancies in relatively high-wage positions for which they are qualified," Hurd continued, and he said that the solutions of the policymakers were the government programs of placement and information. "Quantitatively more important," however, Hurd said, "is the low productivity resulting from inferior education and low skill levels. The adopted cures for this type of poverty, manifested in [government-proviced] manpower training programs, are more accessible education (especially vocational education) and special training to improve skill levels."

Hurd said "liberals recognize that institutions are a partial cause of poverty. Discriminatory employment practices exclude women and minority group members from high wage markets, flooding the markets where they are allowed to participate, thus forcing wages down. Further, discrimination results in underemployment for many women and minorities; they are hired for jobs where productivity is low even though they are capable of performing jobs with much higher productivity. The policy response to discrimination is the activity of the Department of Labor to insure equal employment opportunity. If low productivity is accepted as the *cause* of poverty, then the implicit solutions are improved skill levels for the poor, the elimination of discrimination, and more smoothly functioning labor markets. Current manpower policy is based on this low individual productivity explanation of poverty."

By contrast with "mainstream economists," Hurd noted, "radical economists contend that the capitalist economy is responsible for poverty." Arguing for this "alternate view," Hurd said:

Poverty is more appropriately viewed as a consequence of societal characteristics than as the result of individual attitudes. Specifically, the operation of labor markets profoundly affects the incidence of poverty. Those with low-labor income (the unemployed and those who work at low-wage jobs) are likely to be poor. Because they have concentrated on the effects of individual characteristics on employability and productivity, policymakers have ignored the effects of labor markets on labor force status. Individuals who reside in areas where the unemployment rate is unusually high are more likely to suffer loss of labor income because of unemployment. In markets where the structure of labor demand is shifting, workers whose skills are no longer appropriate may become unemployed or be forced into low-skill, low-wage jobs. In areas where the economy is stagnating, or growing too slowly to accommodate labor force increases, workers may be unable to find jobs or be forced to compete for low-wage jobs. To a great extent, then, the worker is at the mercy of the local labor market. This situation persists throughout the business cycle, although during recessions even more workers suffer from the vagaries of the labor market.

Expanding on the assertion that the system was the primary cause of poverty, Hurd pointed out that many of the poor were full-time workers. He said:

Related to failures of local labor markets is the failure of some industries to pay a living wage. In 1973 approximately 20% of all families living in poverty were headed by persons who worked 50–52 weeks at full-time jobs. These "working poor" are typically employed in non-unionized industries characterized by low productivity, low profits, and fierce product market competition. The inadequate incomes of the working poor result not from personal deficiencies but from the economic system—competition is the free enterprise ideal, but highly competitive industries generally can afford to pay only very low wages. In a capitalist system, whether an individual has a job and what kind of job he or she has is determined primarily by the labor market. Labor markets cause unemployment and low-wage jobs, and thus cause poverty. Individual characteristics, many of which cannot be controlled by the individual (such as age, race, and sex), only determine who it is that will suffer the poverty imposed by the economic system.

Current manpower policy attempts to counteract market imperfections. Through labor market services, manpower training programs, and anti-discriminatory measures the government will supposedly equalize opportunities and poverty will be erased. Appealing though this view may be, it is not a realistic one. As long as it remains devoted to capitalism there is little the government can do to eliminate poverty. Programs to assist the poor within the framework of the economic system can have only limited short-run impact. . . .

If the federal government were interested in adopting a manpower policy that would strike directly at the labor market problems of the poor and unemployed, it would shift the emphasis of its programs from the supply side of labor markets to the demand side. The central goals of manpower policy would become the elimination of unemployment and the upgrading of low-wage labor markets. In short, the government would commit itself to guarantee every person the right to a decent job at reasonable pay. Attainment of a true full employment economy could not be accomplished with traditional expansionary policies but would require a massive job creation effort.

THIS BOOK IS INTENDED TO SERVE as a record of events surrounding the controversy over the various programs for helping the poor in the U.S. during the final years of the 1960s and the first half of the 1970s. The material that follows consists largely of the developments chronicled by FACTS ON FILE in its weekly reports on

current history. As in all FACTS ON FILE works, there was a consci-
entious effort to keep this volume free of bias and to make it an
accurate and useful reference tool.

LESTER A. SOBEL

New York, N.Y.
November, 1976

Johnson & the War on Poverty

War on Poverty Declared

In January 1964, a bare month and a half after he was elevated to the Presidency, Lyndon B. Johnson set in motion one of the programs with which his Administration has become identified—the War on Poverty.

LBJ's call for antipoverty action. President Johnson, speaking Jan. 8, 1964 before a joint session of Congress, said:

"This Administration today here and now declares unconditional war on poverty in America, and I urge this Congress and all Americans to join with me in that effort."

With these words Johnson introduced to Congress and the public the concept of an all-out governmental attack on poverty.

"It will not be a short or easy struggle—no single weapon or strategy will suffice—but we shall not rest until that war is won. The richest nation on earth can afford to win it. We cannot afford to lose it.

"One thousand dollars invested in salvaging an unemployable youth today can return $40,000 or more in his lifetime.

"Poverty is a national problem, requiring improved national organization and support. But this attack, to be effective, must also be organized at the state and the local level and must be supported and directed by state and local efforts. For the war against poverty will not be won here in Washington. It must be won in the field—in every private home, every public office, from the courthouse to the White House. The program ... will emphasize this cooperative approach to help that one-fifth of all American families with incomes too small to even meet their basic needs.

"Our chief weapons in a more pinpointed attack will be better schools, and better health, and better homes, and better training and better job opportunities to help more Americans—especially young Americans—escape from squalor and misery and unemployment rolls where other citizens help to carry them. Very often a lack of jobs and money is not the cause of poverty, but the symptom.

"The cause may lie deeper—in our failure to give our fellow citizens a fair chance to develop their own capacities—in a lack of education and training, in a lack of medical care and housing, in a lack of decent communities in which to live and bring up their children.

"But whatever the cause, our joint federal-local effort must pursue poverty—pursue it wherever it exists—in city slums and small towns, in sharecropper shacks, or in migrant worker camps, on Indian reservations, among whites as well as Negroes, among the young as well as the aged, in the boom towns and in the depressed areas."

Johnson had indicated previously that

11

the problem of poverty would be a major concern of his administration. He had told reporters Dec. 18, 1963, at an informal, unannounced news conference, that "poverty legislation for the lowest income groups" would be "high" on the "agenda of priority." "Any kind of poverty will be a concern of this Administration," he said. "All of us know enough about it to not want the people to have to experience it any more than is absolutely necessary."

Magnitude of the problem. In his first annual Economic Report, submitted to Congress Jan. 20, 1964, Johnson reiterated his intention of waging war on poverty. He pointed out that 35 million of "our fellow citizens" live "without hope below minimum standards of decency," having had only $590 per capita income in 1962 compared with the national average of $1,900. He recommended that a "concerted attack on poverty" concentrate on education, health, skills and jobs, community and area rehabilitation and equal opportunity.

The Council of Economic Advisers' annual report, sent to Congress Jan. 20 with the President's Economic Report, included a chapter describing the scope of American poverty and declaring the eradication of poverty to be a national goal. (The report considered a family of four to be poor if its annual income was under $3,000; an individual was classed as poor if his income fell below $1,500 yearly.) According to the report: "The poor inhabit a world scarcely recognizable, and rarely recognized, by the majority of their fellow Americans. It is a world apart, whose inhabitants are isolated from the mainstream of American life and alienated from its values. It is a world where Americans are literally concerned with day-to-day survival—a roof over their heads, where the next meal is coming from. It is a world where a minor illness is a major tragedy, where pride and privacy must be sacrificed to get help, where honesty can become a luxury and ambition a myth. Worst of all—the poverty of the fathers is visited upon the children."

The Council of Economic Advisers found these six groups especially susceptible to poverty: (1) families headed by persons 65 or older, (2) nonwhite families, (3) families headed by women, (4) families headed by unemployed persons, (5) fami-

lies containing no wage-earners and (6) rural farm families.

Among apparent causes of insufficient income pinpointed by the council's report: (a) The family wage-earner was poorly paid, either because of his low productivity or because of the nature of the work. (b) The wage-earner was relatively uneducated; 37% of poor families in 1962 were headed by persons with eight or fewer years of education. (c) The wage-earner was nonwhite; "the incidence of poverty among nonwhites," according to the report, "is almost invariably higher than among whites, regardless of age, family type or level of educational attainment." Forty-four percent of nonwhites were poor in 1962. (d) The wage-earner's family responsibilities were especially time-consuming, as in the case of a woman with small children. (e) Retired persons who had had low incomes during their working careers suffered from the fact that pensions and Social Security were related to their previous earnings. (f) "Poverty breeds poverty." The culture of poverty was characterized by lack of motivation and incentive as well as by insufficient income, and "inadequate education is perpetuated from generation to generation."

The council's conclusion: "The tasks for our generation are to focus and coordinate our older programs and some new ones into a comprehensive long-range attack on the poverty that remains. A new federally led effort is needed, with special emphasis on prevention and rehabilitation." Even at the current rate of poverty's decline, in 1980 13% of the nation's families would still be poor. "We cannot leave the further wearing away of poverty solely to the general progress of the economy. The nation's attack on poverty must be based on a change in national attitude. We must open our eyes and minds to the poverty in our midst. Poverty is not the inevitable fate of any man. The condition can be eradicated; and since it can be, it must be."

Among measures recommended by the Council of Economic Advisers as means of carrying out the War on Poverty: tax reduction, rapid economic growth, a program to eliminate racial discrimination, programs to rehabilitate urban communities and distressed rural areas, educational programs including adult literacy training and improved educational services to children of the poor, and increased job opportunities for young people.

Congressional reaction. The Joint Congressional Economic Committee filed majority and minority reports on the President's Economic Report March 2, 1964, and both reports took a position on Johnson's proposal for a War on Poverty. The Democratic majority found the poverty war a "most welcome" proposal, although it felt that a large group of low-income persons (the aged and disabled) could "be helped only by improved public and private provision for insurance."

The minority report said: Antipoverty efforts were fine, but the Administration's proposals were "inadequate to the task," and the federal government's role should be "far less" than state and local efforts. "Carefully selected" children should be removed from poverty areas and placed in state-operated "residence schools" outside slum areas. Research should be done on the relationship between birth control and the reduction of poverty.

An individual report filed by Sen. Jacob K. Javits (R, N.Y.) gave particular emphasis to the need for more local and state antipoverty action.

Johnson Submits Program

Presidential message proposes legislation. A special Presidential message on poverty, transmitted to Congress March 16, 1964, proposed enactment of an Economic Opportunity Act of 1964. Pointing out that "one-fifth of our people ... have not shared in the abundance which has been granted to most of us," the President said the nation must "strike down all the barriers" that kept the poor trapped in their poverty. He said:

"The War on Poverty is not a struggle simply to support people, to make them dependent on the generosity of others. It is a struggle to give people a chance. It is an effort to allow them to develop and use their capacities, as we have been allowed to develop and use ours, so that they can share, as others share, in the promise of this nation.

"We do this, first of all, because it is right that we should. From the establishment of public education and land grant colleges through agricultural extension and encouragement to industry, we have pursued the goal of a nation with full and increasing opportunities for all its citizens. The War on Poverty is a further step in that pursuit.

"We do it also because helping some will increase the prosperity of all. Our fight against poverty will be an investment in the most valuable of our resources—the skills and strength of our people. ... If we can raise the annual earnings of 10 million among the poor by only $1,000 we will have added $14 billion a year to our national output. In addition we can make important reductions in public assistance payments, which now cost us $4 billion a year, and in the large costs of fighting crime and delinquency, disease, and hunger...."

The message proposed legislation that would provide "five basic opportunities":

"It will give almost half a million underprivileged young Americans the opportunity to develop skills, continue education, and find useful work.

"It will give every American community the opportunity to develop a comprehensive plan to fight its own poverty—and help them to carry out their plans.

"It will give dedicated Americans the opportunity to enlist as volunteers in the war against poverty.

"It will give many workers and farmers the opportunity to break through particular barriers which bar their escape from poverty.

"It will give the entire nation the opportunity for a concerted attack on poverty through the establishment, under my direction, of the Office of Economic Opportunity, a national headquarters for the war against poverty."

The proposed Economic Opportunity Act was to establish these programs:

(1) *Youth programs.* These were to comprise a Job Corps, a Work-Training Program and a Work-Study Program. The Job Corps was to "build toward an enlistment of 100,000 young men" who would come from "those whose background, health and education make them least fit for useful work." In "more than 100 camps and centers around the country" the volunteers were to be divided into two programs: Half would work "on special conservation projects to give them education, useful work experience and to enrich the natural

resources of the country"; the other half would receive "a blend of training, basic education and work experience in job training centers."

The Work-Training Program would "provide work and training for 200,000 American men and women between the ages of 16 and 21" through programs developed by state and local governments and nonprofit agencies. The Work-Study Program was to "provide federal funds for part-time jobs for 140,000 young Americans who do not go to college because they cannot afford it."

(2) *Community action program.* This phase of the War on Poverty, intended "to strike at poverty at its source;" called for the creation by "men and women throughout the country" of "long-range plans for the attack on poverty in their own local communities." The President emphasized that "these are not plans prepared in Washington" but were to be plans "based on the fact that local citizens best understand their own problems and know best how to deal with those problems." Such plans were to be submitted to an Office of Economic Opportunity; if approved, the federal government would finance up to 90% of the cost for the first two years and 75% thereafter.

(3) *Volunteer programs.* Volunteers were to be recruited among the "many Americans" of all ages "who are ready to enlist in our war against poverty. ... If the state requests them, if the community needs and will use them, we will recruit and train them and give them the chance to serve."

(4) *Programs for poverty-stricken groups.* Intended "to create new opportunities for certain hard-hit groups to break out of the pattern of poverty," these programs would provide loans and guarantees to furnish "incentives to those who will employ the unemployed," opportunities for "work and retraining for unemployed fathers and mothers" and funds to rural families "to purchase needed land, organize cooperatives and create new and adequate family farms."

To administer the War on Poverty, Johnson proposed the creation of an Office of Economic Opportunity (OEO) in the Executive Office of the President. He announced his intention of appointing Peace Corps Director Sargent Shriver (Robert Sargent Shriver Jr.) to head the OEO and serve as his "personal chief of

staff in the war against poverty." (Shriver had been sworn in Feb. 18 as a special Presidential assistant to draft the antipoverty program; a task force under Shriver had prepared the President's message.)

The funds for the program were already included in the fiscal 1965 budget, and the program as presented was to go into effect July 1; the President added to his original $500 million antipoverty request a $462½ million request for several pending (and budgeted) programs.

Congress Approves Compromise Program

Economic Opportunity Act of 1964. The Johnson Administration's draft legislation was introduced March 16, 1964 in the House of Representatives (as HR10440) by Rep. Phil M. Landrum (D, Ga.), and an identical bill was introduced by Rep. Adam Clayton Powell (D, N.Y.), chairman of the House Education & Labor Committee. The Senate bill (S2642) was introduced by Sen. Pat McNamara (D, Mich.). A compromise Economic Opportunity Act of 1964 was finally enacted in August.

House hearings were conducted Mar. 17–Apr. 28 by an Ad Hoc Subcommittee on the Poverty War Program, a unit of the Education & Labor Committee. The subcommittee was headed by Rep. Powell.

Administration officials testifying in support of the bill at the House hearings included Sargent Shriver, the poverty program's director-designate, Defense Secretary Robert S. McNamara, Labor Secretary W. Willard Wirtz, Health, Education & Welfare Secretary Anthony J. Celebrezze, Commerce Secretary Luther H. Hodges, Attorney General Robert F. Kennedy and Interior Secretary Stewart L. Udall.

AFL-CIO President George Meany, testifying April 9, endorsed the bill as a "step forward" but said it should be supplemented by such measures as public works programs and extension of minimum-wage coverage. United Auto Workers President Walter Reuther told the subcommittee Apr. 9 that the bill was "wholly inadequate." He urged national economic planning and massive federal spending as necessary to eliminate poverty and unemployment.

Harry L. Brown, speaking for the American Farm Bureau Federation, opposed the bill April 13 as "unnecessary and unwise"; he contended that it would result in "stabilized, government-directed and subsidized poverty." But spokesmen for the National Farmers Union, the National Grange and the National Sharecroppers Fund all supported the bill in April 13 testimony.

National Urban League Director Whitney M. Young Jr., testifying in support of the bill April 14, said that passage of civil rights legislation would be an "empty gesture" for the black poor "unless a massive breakthrough in economic opportunity enables them to consolidate their gains. . . . Negroes today are wary lest they find themselves with a mouthful of civil rights and an empty stomach."

Carl H. Madden, speaking April 14 for the U.S. Chamber of Commerce, opposed the bill. He contended that most of its programs could be implemented at the local level without federal funds.

Five mayors testified April 15 in support of the bill. All pointed to the need of cities for federal assistance in tackling problems of slums, unemployment and inadequate schools. The mayors were Robert F. Wagner of New York, Richard J. Daley of Chicago, Jerome P. Cavanagh of Detroit, William F. Walsh of Syracuse and Raymond R. Tucker of St. Louis.

Business opposition to the bill was expressed at the hearings April 23. The National Association of Manufacturers contended that economic growth was the answer to the unemployment problem. E. Russell Bartley of the Illinois Manufacturers Association called the bill "an impractical, costly, highly dangerous political scheme to force through Congress many old, discredited programs and several new extreme plans for a welfare state."

Gov. Edmund G. Brown of California endorsed the bill April 24 but called it "only a beginning." He requested programs specifically for migratory farm workers and provisions for conducting "a massive assault on illiteracy."

Rep. Peter H. B. Frelinghuysen Jr. (R, N.J.), ranking Republican member of the Education & Labor Committee, introduced April 28 an alternative antipoverty bill (HR11050). The Frelinghuysen proposal would have authorized a program administered by the states under the direction of the Health, Education & Welfare Secretary (it did not provide for the creation of an Office of Economic Opportunity). The bill would have authorized expenditures of $1½ billion over three years; the states would have assumed a third of their projects' costs in the first year and a half in the next two years; 50% of state poverty funds would have been spent on educational programs during the first year, 33⅓% in the next two years.

HR10440 was approved by the House Education & Labor Committee on a party-line vote (19 D. vs. 11 R.) May 26. A new bill (HR11377) incorporating the committee's changes was introduced by Rep. Landrum for reporting to the House. Among changes made in the original bill were the elimination of a program to provide loans to businessmen as an incentive to hire the long-term unemployed. The new bill permitted women as well as men to enlist in the Job Corps and added an adult literacy program. It authorized the poverty program for a three-year period (fiscal 1965–67) but authorized an appropriation ($962.5 million) for only the first year. The bill was reported June 3, with 11 of the 12 Republican committee members signing minority views "strongly" opposing its enactment. The Republicans characterized the bill as "a hastily assembled amalgam of old offerings, having little or no legislative support, interspersed with a varied assortment of discredited past programs and a partial duplication of existing programs." The statement said: the bill "creates a new and unneeded layer of federal authority . . . headed by a poverty czar upon whom is conferred an ill-defined and wide-ranging authority"; it "represents a dangerous assault on the established system of state-federal relationships, as well as upon the orderly administration of programs and policies already entrusted to established agencies of government."

Hearings on the Senate's antipoverty bill (S2642) were held June 17, 18, 23 and 25 by a Select Subcommittee on Poverty of the Senate Labor & Public Welfare Committee. The subcommittee was headed by Sen. Pat McNamara (D,

Mich.). Testimony was taken from many witnesses who had appeared earlier before the House Subcommittee on the Poverty War Program.

The full committee approved the bill July 7 by 13–2 vote with Sens. Barry Goldwater (R, Ariz.) and John G. Tower (R, Tex.) opposed. Minority views were submitted by Goldwater and Tower when the bill was reported July 21.

The Senate committee bill was similar in most respects to the House committee version. It added a provision for federal assistance in the establishment of state job corps camps. The bill's section on the community action program modified a House bill provision to permit the grant of funds to any community agency combating a cause of poverty whether or not a community action plan was being developed. (The Administration bill had limited aid to communities developing an antipoverty plan.) The House provision required the maximum feasible participation of the public agency or private nonprofit organization primarily concerned with the community's poverty problems.

The minority report signed by Goldwater and Tower said that "the bill, whatever its professed purposes, seems designed to achieve the single objective of securing votes; the problems of the truly destitute will not be solved by this legislation." An individual report signed by Sen. Jacob Javits supported the bill but said that "provision must be made ... to encourage and facilitate the full cooperation of the states, and the integration wherever possible of this program with existing state and community public and private agency activities."

Before the antipoverty bill reached the Senate floor, it was taken up as a campaign issue by the Republicans at their national convention. The 1964 Republican platform, adopted July 14 in San Francisco, said: "This Administration has refused to take practical free enterprise measures to help the poor. Under the last Republican Administration, the percentage of poor in the country dropped encouragingly from 28% to 21%. By contrast, the present Administration, despite a massive increase in the federal bureaucracy, has managed a mere 2% reduction. This Administration has proposed a so-called War on Poverty which characteristically overlaps, and often contradicts,

the 42 existing federal poverty programs. It would dangerously centralize federal controls and bypass effective state, local and private programs. It has demonstrated little concern for the acute problems created for the poor by inflation. . . ."

Announcing the party's intention to "rely on the individual's rights and capacities to advance his own economic well-being," the Republican platform pledged: "Enlargement of employment opportunities for urban and rural citizens, with emphasis on training programs to equip them with needed skills ...; Incentives for employers to hire teen-agers, including broadening of temporary exemptions under the minimum-wage law; ... To continue Republican sponsorship of practical federal-state-local programs which will effectively treat the needs of the poor, while resisting direct federal handouts that erode away individual self-reliance and self-respect and perpetuate dependency."

The 1964 Democratic platform, adopted Aug. 25 at the Democratic National Convention in Atlantic City, endorsed the antipoverty program and pledged to "carry the War on Poverty forward as a total war against the causes of human want."

(Barry Goldwater attacked the Administration's War on Poverty Sept. 18 as he campaigned in Charleston, W. Va. as the Republican Presidential nominee. He said: The extent of poverty in the U.S. had been "misrepresented"—the "average income of our 'poor,' by this Administration's standard, represents material well-being beyond the dreams of a vast majority of the people of the world." Goldwater's conception of poverty was challenged Sept. 26 by Sen. Hubert H. Humphrey, the Democratic Vice Presidential nominee, as he toured the economically depressed Appalachia area. Humphrey said poverty "is measured by the standards of a man's own community. . . . If most American children have adequate clothes, shoes and schoolbooks, then the children who don't have these things are poor.")

S2642 was passed by the Senate July 23, after 2 days of debate, by a roll-call vote of 61–34 (51 D. & 10 R. vs. 22 R. & 12 D.). Goldwater voted against passage. The only provisions of the bill cut back substantially were in the rural poverty section. A program to provide grants of aid to farm families for agricultural purposes was replaced with a program that would provide such aid in the form of loans of up to $1,500. This was done in an amendment by minority whip Hubert Humphrey (Minn.). A program to help farm development corporations buy farm land (at market value) for resale to poor farmers in family-size units (at appraised value) was deleted by an amendment offered by Sen. Frank J. Lausche (D., O.) and adopted by a 49–43 vote. The rural poverty program's authorization of $50 million was then reduced by an amount equal to the estimated cost of the farm corporation plan—$15 million. This was the only financial cut made in the Administration's draft bill.

The Senate bill also contained two compromise "states' rights" amendments: one, adopted July 22, was designed to permit governors of states to veto the establishment of Job Corps camps in their states; another, adopted July 23, would permit governors to veto antipoverty projects contracted between the federal government and a private agency. Harsher "states' rights" amendments proposed by Sens. Winston L. Prouty (R., Vt.) and Spessard L. Holland (D., Fla.) were narrowly defeated in debate July 22–23. Sen. Jacob Javits was the only Republican to vote against them.

The bill was passed by the House Aug. 8, 1964 by a roll-call vote of 226–184 (204 D. & 22 R. vs. 144 R. & 40 D.). Amendments added on the floor of the House: (1) required all persons receiving federal funds under the program to sign written disclaimers of belief or membership in any organization seeking to overthrow the government by force; (2) allowed governors to veto all federally financed antipoverty projects in their states within 30 days; (3) barred political parties from receiving grants for antipoverty projects; (4) barred private institutions or organizations not previously engaged in antipoverty projects from receiving federal funds for such purposes.

The Senate approved the House amendments by voice vote Aug. 11 with only 12 Senators present for the final action.

The Economic Opportunity Act of 1964 (Public Law 88-452) was signed by President Johnson Aug. 20. In signing the act, the President said: "Today is the first time in all the history of the human race a great nation is able to make and is willing to make a commitment to eradicate poverty among its people. ... We are not content to accept the endless growth of relief rolls or welfare rolls. We want to offer the forgotten fifth of our people opportunity and not doles. That is what this measure does for our times."

1964 Economic Opportunity Act's provisions. The Economic Opportunity Act (EOA) of 1964 had the declared purpose of eliminating poverty by giving all Americans opportunities for work, for education and training and for the chance to live in "decency and dignity." The antipoverty program, to be supervised by the director of the Office of Economic Opportunity (OEO), was authorized for three years (fiscal years 1965 67), with specific programs authorized for fiscal 1965. Among the provisions of the act:

Title I. (a) Established a Job Corps for men and women aged 16 21. Participants would enroll for two years and would be assigned to residential centers, either rural conservation camps or urban training centers. The OEO director was authorized to arrange for the establishment of centers with federal, state and local public and private nonprofit agencies.

Enrollees would be provided with room and board and living and travel allowances. They would receive an allowance of $50 per month at the end of their participation. Payment of up to $50 per month to an enrollee's family was permitted, with half of the amount to be deducted from the Corpsman's separation pay. Enrollees were required to take an oath swearing allegiance to the U.S. and to sign a disclaimer affidavit swearing that they neither believed in, belonged to, nor supported any organization teaching the overthrow of the government by violence or other illegal means. Discrimination in the selection of Corpsmen because of political beliefs was prohibited. No Job Corps center was to be established in a state unless a plan for such a center had been submitted to the state's governor and had not been disapproved by him within 30 days.

(b) Established a work-training program, which came to be called the Neighborhood Youth Corps (NYC). The program was to provide full- or part-time jobs to youths aged 16–21. The OEO director was authorized to cooperate with state and local organizations (except political parties) in developing NYC programs; when possible, they were to be coordinated with local public education and training programs. The federal government could pay up to 90% of a local program's total cost for the first two years and up to 50% thereafter, unless the OEO director decided that additional financing was necessary. Funds were to be distributed among the states in accordance with ratios of population, unemployment and family income levels, with no more than 12½% of the total program's funds to go to any one state.

(c) Established a Work-Study Program designed for college youth whose parents lacked the financial means to support them through college. Under the program, the OEO was authorized to make grants to institutions of higher learning; the grants could total up to 90% of the program's cost for the first two years and up to 75% thereafter. The student was to work while in college either for the institution itself or for a public or private nonprofit organization.

Title II. (a) Established a Community Action Program (CAP) to combat poverty locally through state or local public and private nonprofit agencies. Such programs were to be "developed, conducted, and administered with the maximum feasible participation of residents of the areas and members of the groups served." The act authorized federal financing of up to 90% of the cost during the first two years of community programs involving health, housing, home management, welfare, job training and educational assistance. The federal government could pay up to 50% of the cost of such programs thereafter, unless determined otherwise by the OEO director. Funds were to be equitably distributed within each stage between urban and rural areas.

(b) Established an Adult Basic Education program, under which state educational agencies would receive grants to conduct educational programs for functionally illiterate adults. The estimated cost for the program's first year was $25 million, with each state to receive a minimum of $50,000. The federal contribution could be up to 90% in the first two years, up to 50% thereafter.

(c) Established a program for preschool children in economically deprived neighborhoods, which came to be called Project Head Start. The program was meant to counteract the disadvantage preschool children from low-income families suffered as they entered school.

(d) Required that no contract or assistance under Titles I and II be given to any public agency or private institution unless the governor of the state involved had been provided with a plan outlining the project and had not disapproved it within 30 days.

Title III. (a) Established a rural loan program. Loans were authorized to low-income rural families for agricultural and/ or nonagricultural enterprises and to local processing or marketing cooperatives. Loans could be made only if credit was not otherwise available; interest rates were to be set by the Treasury Department. Individual loans were to have a maximum maturity of 15 years; loans to cooperatives were to be repaid within 30 years.

(b) Established programs to assist migrant workers; directed the OEO director to assist state and local agencies, institutions, farm associations or individuals in aiding such workers in the areas of housing, sanitation, education and day care of children.

(c) Established a program of indemnity payments to dairy farmers, under which the Agriculture Secretary would make payments to farmers who had been ordered since Jan. 1, 1964 to take their milk off the market because it contained pesticides that had received government approval at the time of their use. The program was to expire Jan. 31, 1965.

Title IV. Established a program of small business loans, to be administered by the Small Business Administration. Loans ranged up to $25,000 and were repayable in 15 years at interest rates to be set by the Treasury Department.

Title V. Established a Work-Experience Program to provide job training for unemployed heads of families. The program was to be administered by the Health, Education & Welfare Department. Participants were to be family heads receiving aid under HEW's Aid to Families with Dependent Children (AFDC) program.

Title VI. (a) Established an Office of Economic Opportunity (OEO) in the Executive Office of the President; the President was permitted after one year to establish the OEO elsewhere in the Executive Branch. A director, deputy director and three assistant directors were to be appointed by the President, subject to confirmation by the Senate. The director was authorized to develop administrative criteria and establish guidelines for the separate programs and to assist the President in coordinating the antipoverty efforts of other federal agencies.

(b) Established Volunteers in Service to America (VISTA), a program under which volunteers would work in cooperation with state and local agencies combatting poverty at the state and local level, helping such groups as Indians, migratory workers and the mentally ill and retarded, and furthering the activities authorized by Titles I and II. Volunteers were to receive living and other allowances and a stipend of up to $50 monthly.

(c) Authorized an Economic Opportunity Council of federal department and agency heads to advise the OEO director and established a National Advisory Council of the director and 14 representatives of the general public to review OEO activities at least once a year.

(d) Required that any individual receiving payment under any part of the act sign the same disclaimer affidavit required of Job Corpsmen.

Title VII. Exempted individuals receiving payments under the antipoverty program from the provisions of the Social Security Act requiring that all sources of income of public assistance recipients be considered in determining need and the amount of public assistance payments.

$800 million appropriated. Appropriations for the War on Poverty were voted by Congress Oct. 3, the last day of the 1964 session, as part of a supplemental appropriations bill. The final bill provided $800 million for the antipoverty program for fiscal 1965; the Administration had requested $947½ million (the full authorization); the initial House bill had called for $750 million, and the Senate had voted $861,550,000. The bill included a House restriction establishing a ceiling of 4,000 on the number of permanent employes to be hired by the program. The Administration had asked for funds to employ a staff of 4,518.

Antipoverty act revised in 1965. The Economic Opportunity Act of 1964 was revised extensively by a bill that cleared

Congress Sept. 24, 1965. President Johnson signed the measure Oct. 9. The 1965 antipoverty bill made these important changes in the 1964 Economic Opportunity Act:

It (a) gave the OEO director the authority to override a gubernatorial veto of a Community Action, Neighborhood Youth Corps or Adult Basic Education program if the veto were deemed inconsistent with the basic purposes of the law; (b) deleted a provision of the original act requiring Job Corps enrollees to sign an affidavit disavowing belief in the violent overthrow of the government but retained a requirement that Corpsmen swear allegiance to the U.S. and extended that requirement to VISTA volunteers; (c) authorized enrollment of Cuban refugees in the Job Corps and the Neighborhood Youth Corps; (d) extended for one year (through Aug. 20, 1967) the authority for 90% federal financing of Neighborhood Youth Corps, Community Action, Work-Study and Adult Basic Education programs; (e) authorized the OEO to make Community Action grants directly to private nonprofit agencies rather than to official "umbrella" agencies if "good cause" could be demonstrated for doing so; (f) authorized $1.785 billion for the program in fiscal 1966.

The Administration's 1965 antipoverty bill had been introduced April 1 in the House (as HR7048) by Rep. Adam Clayton Powell Jr. (D, N.Y.), chairman of both the House Education & Labor Committee and its Ad Hoc Subcommittee on the Poverty War Program. An identical bill (S1749) was introduced Apr. 19 in the Senate by Sen. Pat McNamara (D, Mich.), chairman of the Special Subcommittee on Poverty of the Senate Labor & Public Welfare Committee.

Local programs criticized—House hearings on the bill were held April 12-15 and 29-30, 1965 by Powell's ad hoc subcommittee. The hearings were marked by disputes over the alleged intrusion of politics into the antipoverty program on the local level and over the administration of the New York City program.

Powell, in a statement released April 11 and repeated at the first hearing April 12, charged that the program in many communities had given rise to "giant fiestas of political patronage." Saying his criticism was based on reports from four study groups sent by the subcommittee to 11 cities, he also charged that: (a) blacks had been excluded in the South from planning boards and had "the most minimal per-capita participation in poverty programs"; (b) "there has been an obvious failure to carry out a most important objective—that of involving the poor in the War on Poverty"; (c) salaries for program officials were "excessively high and in some instances unreasonable and wildly unrealistic"; (d) there had been "an over-emphasis on planning and a dismal de-emphasis on action programs."

A contrasting picture of the program, however, was presented by Congressmen who had been members of the study groups and by OEO Director Sargent Shriver, the first witness. They conceded that there were problems but maintained that the program had started well. The problems cited were the feeling of non-participation in the program by the poor in some areas and the lack of community understanding, of qualified personnel and of focus on hard-core poverty areas.

Shriver said: The programs were "prudent, practical, focused and patriotic." If "poverty has become popular politics" in many communities and "if the fight for control reflects the views of the poor themselves or of representative community groups, it responds to the intent of Congress." Five thousand jobs had been authorized for poor persons in poor neighborhoods, and this was to be increased to 20,000–30,000 by July 1. His agency did not have entire control over salaries at the local level; "we want the best people we can get for these jobs, and we have to pay them commensurately with their abilities." (Appearing on the CBS-TV "Face the Nation" program April 18, Shriver said the antipoverty drive was "not a give-away program" but a program to "help people to get themselves out of poverty." He said: The program emphasized participation in policy-making by the poor themselves. "There is nobody smart enough in Washington to sit down and figure out how to defeat poverty in every community in America.")

The New York dispute with Powell involved Mayor Robert F. Wagner and Paul R. Screvane, the city's poverty coordinator, who testified before the subcommittee April 15. Wagner and Screvane insisted on the city's prerogative to administer its antipoverty program, especially in the light of its contribution, more than twice that of the federal government, to the $1 billion worth of projects. Screvane explained the city's plan to set up a private, city-controlled corporation. Powell then threatened to try to cut off federal funds from the city program on the ground that it violated the antipoverty law's Title II requirement that Community Action programs be "developed, conducted and administered with the maximum feasible participation of residents of the areas and members of the groups served." He said a city-controlled corporation for the program would be "a monolithic type of structure that is directly contrary to the present act."

The Rev. Lynward Stevenson, director of the private social-service Woodlawn Organization of Chicago, had testified April 13 that the Chicago antipoverty program, which had excluded his group, was run for the benefit of "the rich" and "politicians." He said the roster of its advisory committee "reads like the fund-raising list of the Democratic Party." Dr. Deton J. Brooks Jr., director of the federally-financed Chicago Committee on Urban Progress, retorted that the Woodlawn group had tried to "blackjack its way" into the Chicago program.

A charge that Cleveland's official antipoverty committee lacked representation of the poor was made April 14 in testimony by the Rev. Paul Younger, director of the Protestant Ministry to Poverty of Cleveland. He said Cleveland politicians were against ending poverty for fear that such a development would "upset the power balance."

Rep. Roman Pucinski (D, Ill.), a subcommittee member, warned after the April 14 hearing that the antipoverty program was in grave danger because of the "fantastic power struggle going on all over America" to control it.

Powell announced May 12 that he would not offer amendments to the bill despite his earlier charges that the program had spawned "giant fiestas of political patronage." Powell said he had held a "summit conference" with federal antipoverty officials and had promised quick action on the bill in return for pledges, in a letter from Shriver, that independent agencies would have access to federal anti-poverty funds and that the poor would be represented on local governing boards. As a result of the meeting, Powell said, he was convinced that the "giant fiesta will simmer down to a little ham sandwich." An OEO spokesman said the Shriver pledges "represent no change in policy" since "we've had this policy all along."

(Shriver, responding to criticism that antipoverty directors' salaries were too high, had released a list of such salaries May 1. Averaging $16,325 annually, they ranged from $25,000 in Los Angeles and Washington to $8,400 in Scranton, Pa.)

Los Angeles Mayor Samuel Yorty said May 29 that "cheap politics and abominable administration" were delaying the establishment of antipoverty programs in his city. He charged that "mayors all over the United States are being harassed by agitation promoted by Sargent Shriver's speeches urging those he calls the 'poor' to insist upon control of local poverty programs.... The Shriver organization can go ahead with programs without the city having any voice in the programs at all, and perhaps that is what is being planned —a real political boondoggle."

U.S. Chamber of Commerce research director Carl H. Madden June 9 criticized the Neighborhood Youth Corps and Job Corps programs as intensifying, instead of ameliorating, the problem of school drop-outs. Dr. Madden said the Neighborhood Youth Corps "is encouraging some youngsters to drop out of school rather than encouraging them to stay in": "Youngsters are drawn to work-training jobs by money considerations, a temptation made all the stronger by an administrative decision to pay such trainees the minimum wage of $1.25 an hour." The criticism was expressed at an antipoverty hearing conducted by a group of House Republicans, led by Peter H. B. Frelinghuysen (N.J.), who considered the regular committee hearings inadequate. A committee spokesman acknowledged that the chamber's statement had been inadvertently omitted from the published record of the hearings.

During Senate Labor & Public Welfare Committee consideration of the legislation, Sen. Ralph W. Yarborough (D, Tex.) charged Aug. 3 that Texas Gov. John B. Connally was trying to "defeat and destroy" the antipoverty program in Texas. He said Connally had approved Neighborhood Youth Corps projects paying $1.00 an hour while delaying or vetoing those paying $1.25 an hour. "This abuse of power must stop," Yarborough said. "We cannot allow an arbitrary governor to impose one-man rule upon entire communities and force thousands of people to adhere to his wishes against their better judgment." Connally replied Aug. 4 that "no governor in any state in this nation has spent as much time as I have on this program trying to assure its success. I have no apologies to make." He explained his April veto of a Neighborhood Youth Corps project sponsored by the State Farmers Union by saying that the union was "quasi-political." The Farmers Union Aug. 5 denied the allegation.

Militancy in Poverty Movement

As the War on Poverty proceeded, the campaign to aid the poor began to assume many of the aspects of a "movement," which became increasingly militant. To a great extent, the inspiration—as well as many leaders and grass-roots followers—for this militancy came directly from the civil rights movement.

Mississippi 'live-in.' About 50 impoverished black Mississippians and black and white civil rights workers invaded the deactivated Greenville Air Force Base at Greenville, Miss. Jan. 31, 1966. After refusing to leave, they were carried out by Air Force police Feb. 1.

The "live-in" had been organized by the Poor People's Conference, a group partly financed by the Delta Ministry of the National Council of Churches; the conference was affiliated with the Mississippi Freedom Democratic Party (MFDP) and with the Mississippi Freedom Labor Union (MFLU). The tactic had been decided on at a three-day meeting Jan. 28–30 at Mount Beulah, a former black school at Edwards, Miss.

In their invasion Jan. 31, the demonstrators broke a lock on one of the base's buildings and moved in mattresses, food and portable stoves. They then issued a statement explaining that "we are at the

Greenville Air Force Base because it is federal property and there are hundreds of empty houses and buildings. We need those houses and the land. We could be trained for jobs in the buildings." The statement charged that surplus food distributed to the poor in Mississippi was "old and full of bugs and weevils." It added: "We want the Office of Economic Opportunity and the U.S. Department of Agriculture to hire poor people we say represent us. We, the poor people, want to distribute the food."

Air policemen from nearby Air Force bases were flown into Greenville during the night of Jan. 31–Feb. 1; Maj. Gen. R. W. Puryear, commanding general of Keesler Air Force Base in Biloxi, arrived to assume command early Feb. 1. (Meanwhile, infiltration into the base had raised the number of demonstrators to about 100.)

Gen. Puryear told the squatters that if they left peacefully he would "see that your demands are presented in an official manner to whomever you designate—even the President of the United States." The demonstrators voted unaminously not to leave, and the air police proceeded to carry the biting, kicking and screaming squatters out of the base.

The squatters then returned to a "tent city" established near Greenville in the summer of 1965 to house tenant farmers belonging to the Mississippi Freedom Labor Union who had been evicted from their homes after striking for higher wages. The "city's" population, which included civil rights workers as well as local Negroes, had grown to about 200.

Washington 'camp-in'—Ninety unemployed black plantation workers from Mississippi, most of whom had been living in the Greenville tent city, went to Washington, D.C. March 31. They set up four tents April 3 in Lafayette Square, opposite the White House, and camped there until April 7 in a protest against delays in their applications for $1,300,000 in anti-poverty funds.

The delegation had arrived in Washington by bus March 31 and had conferred in the House Education & Labor Committee hearing room with Reps. Adam Clayton Powell (D, N.Y.), committee chairman, William F. Ryan (D, N.Y.) and Charles C. Diggs Jr. (D, Mich.). After a five-hour meeting Apr. 1 with OEO

officials (they described the meeting as "very discouraging"), the group had decided on the camping tactic.

The demonstrators represented three local organizations—Neighborhood Developers, Inc., the Delta Opportunities Commission and the Poor People's Corp. The groups had applied Feb. 28, after two months of negotiations for OEO financing of similar projects, to build homes for 300 displaced plantation workers and simultaneously to provide training in construction skills. The delegation was led by Frank Smith, 25, director of Neighborhood Developers.

The Interior Department announced April 4 that no action would be taken against the campers despite their violation of department regulations. The campers slept in the tents in groups of 30, the remainder being housed in local homes and churches. Churches provided food and blankets.

The campers folded their tents April 7 and prepared to return to Mississippi; 60 left Washington April 8, but the remaining 30 stayed behind, at least temporarily, "because we didn't accomplish what we came for, and we are going to stay until we do." At an April 8 news conference, Smith said he planned "to organize bigger and better things" in Mississippi, and Dr. Harvey Cox, a Harvard University divinity professor, announced that 25 theologians had sent OEO Director Sargent Shriver a telegram protesting the delay in granting anti-poverty funds to the Mississippians. The signatories included the Rev. Dr. Martin Luther King Jr., president of the Southern Christian Leadership Conference, and Dr. Eugene Carson Blake, secretary general of the World Council of Churches.

Theodore M. Berry, director of the OEO's Community Action Program, had said at a Jackson, Miss. news conference April 7 that the three organizations had been asked to provide additional information in connection with their anti-poverty applications. He said that Mississippi had "been awarded more than $32 million" so far for anti-poverty projects.

Head Start protests. Forty-eight black five-year-olds from Mississippi, accompanied by 25 teachers, nurses and parents, invaded the hearing room of the U.S. House Education & Labor Committee Feb. 11, 1966 to demand that their application for a Head Start grant be expedited. The children sang and played as the adults conferred with five members of the House of Representatives. The delegation represented the Child Development Group of Mississippi, which had conducted a $1,400,000 Head Start program in the summer of 1965 and had applied in November 1965 for $6,700,000 for a year-round program to benefit 10,000 children and employ 3,500 poor persons. Theodore Berry, director of Community Action Projects for the Office of Economic Opportunity, told the delegation he had just that day received the group's application from the OEO regional office in Atlanta.

The New York City Economic Opportunity Committee was picketed Aug. 18 by persons protesting a $3.4 million cut in the city's Head Start budget. Demonstrators included more than 600 Head Start teachers, children and parents. The city's Head Start budget had been reduced from $10 million to $6.6 million in June to meet a federal ceiling on funds for the current fiscal year. The city had received $6.4 million for a six-month Head Start Program ending June 30, but it had used only $2.4 million of the grant because of the lack of classrooms meeting Board of Health standards. (New York City anti-poverty officials Sept. 9 allocated $875,000 to expand class enrollment in 47 private Head Start centers until the end of 1966.)

N.Y. job sit-in & traffic tieup. Twenty-two blacks had staged a sit-in at the Economic Opportunity Committee's New York office Jan.24, 1966 to demand more jobs for Harlem's unemployed. In a simultaneous demonstration, 25 blacks blocked an intersection in the center of Harlem; police detoured traffic for more than an hour before arresting 15 demonstrators who refused to disperse. The two demonstrations had been organized by Jesse Gray, a rent-strike organizer and the director of Harlem's Community Council on Housing.

Ohio welfare march. A "march for decent welfare," begun in Cleveland June 20, 1966, culminated June 30 as 1,000 placard-carrying demonstrators marched through Columbus to the Ohio state capitol building. Fewer than 40 demonstrators had walked the 155 miles from Cleveland. But they were reinforced in Columbus by 12 bus loads of protesters from adjoining counties.

The march had been organized by the Ohio Steering Committee for Adequate Welfare, whose major demand was an increase in monthly welfare payments from $33 per dependent child to $45. Llewellyn Coles, an executive assistant to Ohio Gov. James A. Rhodes, had addressed the marchers at Otterbein College in Westerville June 28 and had assured them that Rhodes would give their demands "sympathetic consideration."

(A demonstration for increased welfare benefits was also held June 30 in New York City, where 250 men, women and children marched on city hall.)

Jersey City aides protest in N.Y. Jersey City (N.J.) antipoverty workers staged sit-ins at the OEO's New York City regional headquarters Aug. 17 and 23, 1966 in protest against administration of the Community & Neighborhood Development Organization (Can-Do), the Jersey City anti-poverty program. Twenty persons participated in the Aug. 17 sit-in, and police arrested 13 for unlawful trespass. None were arrested Aug. 23 as about 70 participated.

The protesters, members of a group called the Jersey City Ad Hoc Committee of the People for a Better Anti-Poverty Program, were supporting Roy H. Kennix, 26, the program's ousted black director, in his bid for reinstatement. They also demanded that alleged nepotism in the program be eliminated and that elections to neighborhood anti-poverty boards be assured.

Kennix and his supporters announced at a meeting in Jersey City Aug. 24 that they would open a rival anti-poverty center in Jersey City as part of a "black power" movement. Stokely Carmichael, chairman of the Student Nonviolent Coordinating Committee, asserted at the meeting that anti-poverty programs were a "calculated plot" against poor blacks. He urged local blacks "to join the struggle to take over that poverty program."

Poverty march in capital. About 500 blacks, whites and Puerto Ricans participated Sept. 27, 1966 in a Poor People's March on Washington to protest "the current lack of concern for effective anti-poverty legislation." The group was addressed in the Cannon House Office Building by Rep. William F. Ryan (D, N.Y.), Rep. John Conyers (D, Mich.), Sen. Edward M. Kennedy (D, Mass.), Sen Jacob K. Javits (R, N.Y.), and Rep. Adam Clayton Powell (D, N.Y.), whose remarks elicited loud cheers. Powell told the group that the U.S. would not be saved by the war in Vietnam or foreign aid but by effective action to break the grip of poverty and give "poor people ... a little green power...."

The march had been organized by New York City's Community Action Group, led by Frank Espada, Washington's Poverty Rights Action Center, led by George Wiley, and Jersey City's Grass Rooters Interested in Poverty Education of Jersey City, N.J., led by Cornelius Given.

Poverty aides & riots. Following the urban riots of the late 1960s, some critics of the antipoverty program accused OEO (Office of Economic Opportunity) workers of fomenting riots or racial clashes. Officials and supporters of the program defended the OEO aides.

Newark (N.J.) Mayor Hugh J. Addonizio and Public Safety Director Dominick A. Spina became involved in such charges after racial rioting in Newark in July 1967.

At a Senate Labor & Public Welfare subcommittee hearing in Washington July 19, Sen. Winston Prouty (R., Vt.) had said that Spina had telegraphed OEO Director Shriver May 25 to protest the use of antipoverty funds for "fomenting and agitating against the government and agencies of the City of Newark." According to Spina, the antipoverty officials had rented cars "to agitate against the [Newark] Planning Board" and had pressured employes of the UCC (United Community Corp., Newark's antipoverty agency) to picket. Shriver said the cars were used to move chairs.

Addonizio said July 20 that he indorsed Newark antipoverty programs but added that he could not "condone all the activities that have taken place under the name of community organization." "My only wish," he said, "would be that all community action would concentrate as much on jobs and training for poor people as they do in fighting among themselves and accusing public officials of wrongdoing." (The UCC had announced July 15 that it had received federal grants totaling $3,352,386 to finance 7 new or already existing antipoverty projects.)

The OEO's Northeast Regional Office asked the UCC Aug. 1 to suspend Willie Wright, 35, a member of the UCC executive board and president of the United Afro-American Association, pending an investigation of charges that he had made inflammatory statements after the July riot. Wright reportedly said at a Negro rally that it was his "firm conviction that complete chaos will have to prevail in the streets of American cities and blood will have to flow like water before the black man will become an accepted citizen of this society." He was reported to have told Negroes to arm themselves for "the next time the white man walks into the black community." The UCC refused to suspend Wright since he was "not an employe of the UCC but a duly elected board member." The OEO withdrew its demand Aug. 4 pending the Aug. 17 board meeting of the UCC, and the full UCC membership voted unanimously Aug. 17 against suspending Wright.

Defending OEO's aides, Shriver said July 24: "The over-all antipoverty program has turned out to be probably the best anti-riot weapon ever devised. Through all OEO programs we have provided the disadvantaged and previously inarticulate citizens of many communities an opportunity for self-help and for self-expression. We have started to eliminate the basic causes for unrest and impatience. In numerous cases, local antipoverty officials have been particularly helpful in stopping or minimizing violence in situations where tempers had almost reached the breaking point. ... We have stressed the firm policy of the Office of Economic Opportunity not to permit the use of federal funds for any activities that are contrary to law or are partisan in nature. ... There will be absolute insistence that every OEO employee and every employee of an OEO grantee scrupulously avoid and resist participation by OEO-founded resources in any activities which threaten public order. ... I shall insist upon immediate and full penalties for any individuals found guilty of wrong behavior in this connection. Furthermore, I shall insist upon the withholding of OEO funds from any grantee or delegate agency which is shown to be encouraging or tolerating such behavior."

Mayor Harold M. Tollefson of Tacoma, Wash., then president of the National League of Cities, said July 24 that the antipoverty program had helped minimize and in some cases avert violence. He said: "We are disturbed at recent charges" that the antipoverty program "has been responsible for stirring up [racial] unrest [and violence]. The antipoverty program in city after city has been responsible for just the opposite of that. It has attacked some of the most basic social ills in the community which breed impatience and antagonism. It has provided the vehicle for the peaceful expression of this impatience. And in city after city, persons associated with the poverty program have actually made important contributions to preventing or minimizing disturbance which has threatened."

A Labor Department report released July 28 said that young Negroes of the Neighborhood Youth Corps, an antipoverty program, had given invaluable aid during the height of the rioting in Newark and Detroit. According to the report the youths operated phone switchboards and performed other tasks to relieve regular officers for riot duty.

Rep. John R. Dellenback (R, Ore.), a member of the House Education & Labor Committee, told Shriver July 31: "I spent 3 or 4 hours last Friday night on the streets of one of our major cities, walking with some of your people, and I was completely favorably impressed by the manner in which these people. . . were making a real effort to stop trouble and not to create it." Another committee member, Rep. Charles S. Goodell (R., N.Y.), said July 31: "Poverty workers generally have helped defuse riots."

Shriver said on the CBS-TV program "Face the Nation" Aug. 20 that of the 65,000 persons employed in antipoverty programs in 28 cities where disorders occurred during the summer, only 13 were arrested in the disturbances. None of the charges exceeded a misdemeanor, it was reported. Shriver said that the $2.06 billion the Administration had requested for the antipoverty program was insufficient. But, he said, if the Administration had asked for a substantial increase "we might get nothing because many people in the Congress would consider that irresponsible, even though we need may be there."

"Poverty workers are not responsible for riots. It's poverty that is responsible for riots," Shriver told 230 Volunteers in Service to America (VISTA) "summer associates" Aug. 22. Addressing outgoing volunteers who had been working in Washington ghettos, Shriver said that the impact of the recent summer riots had been "harmful" because "lots of people are looking around for a scapegoat and we're a very easy target." He said, however, that even the "model" antipoverty programs in cities such as Detroit and Hartford "are not big enough to get the quantitative results to stop a riot."

Robert Schrank, director of the N.Y. City Neighborhood Youth Corps (NYC) summer program, told 500 delegates at an NYC evaluation conference in New York Sept. 5 that corps members should be credited for easing racial tensions in the slums. "It was a perfect demonstration of what needs to be done in the cities in preventing rioting conditions," he said. "We pumped $16 million into the ghettos, into the hands of people who need it, and in a constructive way."

The OEO announced Sept. 7 that its own investigation of the summer riots showed that antipoverty workers had played a significant role in stopping and preventing racial trouble. The investigation included 32 cities that escaped riots and 11 cities that suffered violence. The OEO report said: "Not one police chief or mayor said OEO heightened tensions. On the contrary, most mayors and police officials felt OEO summer programs had helped to prevent violence in their communities."

Appalachian 'sedition' case. Five antipoverty aides were indicted on sedition charges in Pikeville, Ky. Sept. 11, 1967, but the charges against them were dismissed when the U.S. District Court in Lexington, Ky. Sept. 15 declared Kentucky's sedition law unconstitutional. The case was complicated by charges that the attack on the five stemmed not from the allegation of subversion but from such political considerations as the antipoverty workers' support of grass roots resistance to allegedly destructive strip mining.

The sedition case became public Aug. 11 when three of the poverty workers were arrested in nighttime raids on their homes in Pikeville on the sedition charge. Commonwealth Atty. Thomas Ratliff of Pike County, then GOP candidate for lieutenant governor, said two truckloads of "subversive literature" had been confiscated from the homes of the defendants, Joseph Mulloy, 23, field worker for Appalachian Volunteers, Inc. (AV), and Alan McSurely, 31, and his wife, Margaret, 28, field organizers for the Southern Conference Education Fund. The seized books were said to include *The Essential Works of Lenin*, *The Communist Manifesto*, *The Poems of Chairman Mao* and Joseph Heller's satirical novel *Catch-22*.

Welfare recipients demonstrate. More than 1,000 welfare recipients picketed the Health, Education & Welfare Department building in Washington Aug. 28, 1967 in protest against the welfare restrictions in a House-passed Social Security bill. The mass anti-government protest came at the end of the first convention of the National Organization for Welfare Rights, a coalition of 250 local Welfare Rights organizations in 70 cities.

The demonstrators distributed a resolution denouncing the Social Security bill as "a betrayal of the poor, a declaration of war upon our families, and a fraud on the future of our nation." Dr. George A. Wiley, who had organized the Welfare Rights Movement in 1966 to improve welfare benefits and extend them to persons not yet covered, said at the convention Aug. 26 that the long-term objectives of the movement were to build a national organization of poor people based on the model of organized labor.

None of the 16 Senators the convention invited to meet with them in the caucus room in the old Senate Office Building were present. N.Y. Sens. Jacob K. Javits (R.) and Robert F. Kennedy (D.) sent staff aids who spoke to the convention.

Thousands of welfare recipients had demonstrated in cities and towns across the country June 30 in protest against inadequacies of the welfare system. Most demonstrators carried "basic need forms" prepared by the National Welfare Rights Movement. The forms, which included blank space for listing minimum requirements for food, clothing, rent and furniture, said, in part: "Federal and state laws require that families be provided with welfare benefits adequate to insure a minimum standard of health and decency. Contrary to these laws, I do not get enough money in my welfare grant to meet my family's needs."

Some 45 members of Mothers for Adequate Welfare in Boston marched to Boston Common for a noon rally. They asked that policemen be removed from welfare offices and that welfare recipients be included on boards making decisions about welfare problems.

About 200 persons rallied in front of the County Board of Public Assistance in Philadelphia and demanded "rights and respect" for welfare recipients. They carried signs that read: "Millions for the moon—pennies for us." "Our kids go hungry while you make us wait." "Welfare is a right, not a privilege."

150 persons staged a 5-mile march to Cuyahoga County Welfare Department in protest against inadequate welfare payments.

About 40 welfare recipients picketed branch offices of the Cook County Public Aid Department on the North and West Sides of Chicago.

More than 100 welfare recipients staged a one-mile march from Pershing Square to the County Board of Supervisors' hall in the Civic Center in Los Angeles. They carried signs that read: "Stop welfare brutality." "General relief O.K. for dogs, not for us." "Aid to the dead is like putting sugar on the ocean." "More money now."

Nearly 800 Negroes staged a "poor people's march" from the Negro Masonic Temple in Jackson, Miss. to the state capitol Aug. 14. The marchers were stopped at the doors to the statehouse by state troopers. Charles Evers, NAACP state field director for Mississippi, said the Agriculture Department had "food stores by the millions being eaten by worms, and my people are going hungry." Dr. Aaron Henry, NAACP state president, said the march was a response to an alleged statement of Gov. Paul Johnson's that the only Negroes he had seen were "big, fat, black and greasy."

More than 600 poor people from New York City, most of them Puerto Rican and/or black, rallied in Washington, D.C. Oct. 16 in a campaign for massive increases in federal antipoverty spending. After hearing speeches on the Mall near the Capitol, they marched to the Mount Carmel Baptist Church for a "poor people's Congressional hearing." None of the Congress members invited to the hearing attended. The demonstration was sponsored by the Citywide Community Action Groups, headed by Major R. Owens.

1968 campaign in Washington. A "Poor People's Campaign," first announced by the late Rev. Dr. Martin Luther King Jr. Aug. 15, 1967, brought thousands of poor people and sympathizers to Washington, D.C. in May and June 1968 for lobbying and demonstrations designed to put pressure on Congress and the Administration to act to relieve the poor.

Details of the plan had been worked out in late November 1969 at an SCLC (Southern Christian Leadership Conference) staff meeting in Frogmore, S.C. The plan was then presented publicly in greater detail by King in Atlanta Dec. 4. He said the participants would demand "jobs and income for all."

According to King, 3,000 demonstrators were to be recruited from 10 cities and five rural areas and trained for three months in nonviolent discipline to serve as a nucleus of the campaign.

King said in Atlanta that the "angry and bitter" mood of many poor blacks in the nation's slums could make the campaign "risky" but that Negroes would respond to nonviolence "if it's militant enough, if it's really doing something." "These tactics have done it before," he asserted, "and this is all we have to go on." King said the Washington campaign would be a "last desperate demand" by Negroes, an effort to avoid "the worst chaos, hatred and violence any nation has ever encountered." He said he hoped the non-Negro as well as the Negro poor, Negro militants and anti-war groups would participate in the protests, but he said all participants must pledge to avoid violence in the campaign. The Rev. Bernard Lafayette Jr., 27, a founder of the Student Nonviolent Coordinating Committee (SNCC) and program administrator of the SCLC, was named by King Dec. 13 to direct the Washington project.

Activists gather in Washington—Martin Luther King Jr. was slain April 4, 1968, just before the start of the influx of demonstrators into Washington. Despite his death, his followers decided to continue with the project, almost as a monument to the late King.

The Poor People's Campaign brought nine caravans of poor but trained potential demonstrators to Washington beginning May 11, 1968. Plans were made for the encampment of thousands of participants in a canvas-and-plywood "Resurrection City U.S.A." in the capital and for massive demonstrations. The caravans started from various parts of the country May 2–17. They held rallies and picked up additional participants along the way to Washington.

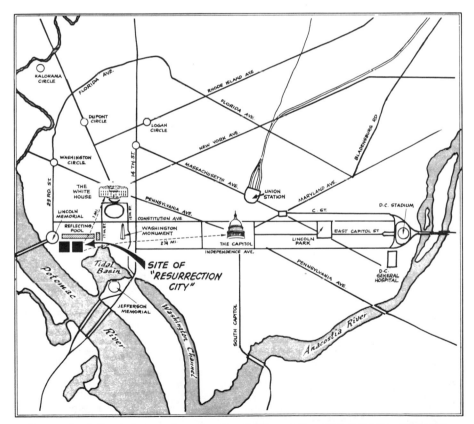

Congressional Quarterly map shows location of "Resurrection City, U.S.A." in Washington. Encampment was set up by Poor People's Campaign for 3,000 people who came from all parts of the U.S. to put pressure on Congress and the Administration to take action against poverty.

An opening phase of the Poor People's Campaign began April 29 when the Rev. Ralph David Abernathy, 41, president of the Southern Christian Leadership Conference (SCLC), led a "delegation of 100" (ranging at times from 130 to 150 persons), representatives of Negroes, Puerto Ricans, Mexican-Americans, American Indians and Appalachian whites, in conferences in Washington with Cabinet members and Congressional leaders and presented a long list of legislative demands. (Abernathy had been elected in Atlanta Apr. 9 to succeed King as SCLC president.)

The delegates Apr. 29 met first with Agriculture Secy. Orville L. Freeman. They described the "incontestable fact" of hunger and malnutrition in the country as a "national disgrace" and then declared in a statement to Atty. Gen. Ramsey Clark: "Justice is not a reality for the black, Mexican-American, Indian and Puerto Rican poor. Discrimination in employment, housing and education not only persists but in many areas is rapidly increasing."

At a meeting with Labor Secy. W. Willard Wirtz, Abernathy said: "We ask you to eliminate programs that try to fit poor people to a system that has systematically excluded them from sharing in America's plenty. We say that the system must change and adjust to the needs of millions who are unemployed or underemployed." The delegation also said in a prepared statement to the Office of Economic Opportunity that the poor "have been sold into bondage to local politicians and hostile governors."

In testimony before the Senate Subcommittee on Manpower, Employment & Poverty Apr. 30, Abernathy called for "an immediate income maintainance program," "thousands of new units of low-income housing" and a minimum of a million jobs in the public and private sector in the coming year plus a 2d million in the next 4 years. He said: "We are tired of training programs that either screen us out by discrimination or meaningless tests, which ask our families to suffer from inadequate support while we are in training." "The most bitter mockery of all," he continued, was to discover that "either there is no job waiting at the end or that we are once again condemned to exchange our manhood for dead-end jobs which pay a boy's wages."

Abernathy conferred Apr. 30 with various Congress members, including Senate majority leader Mike Mansfield (D., Mont.), Senate minority leader Everett M. Dirksen (R., Ill.), House Speaker John W. McCormack (D., Mass.), House majority leader Carl Albert (D., Okla.) and House minority leader Gerald R. Ford (R., Mich.).

The delegates met Apr. 30 with Housing & Urban Development Secy. Robert C. Weaver and Health, Education & Welfare Secy. Wilbur J. Cohen. After meeting with State Secy. Dean Rusk May 1, Abernathy led a procession of 50 delegates through the State Department lobby. Abernathy then told newsmen: "I think this is the most fruitful 3 days ever seen in the history of this city. The leaders here for the first time heard the cries and groans of the poor people speaking in their own language, unpolished— an outpouring from the souls of poor people. The poor are no longer divided. We are not going to let the white man put us down any more. It's not white

power, and I'll give you some news, it's not black power, either. It's poor power and we're going to use it." That afternoon the delegates met briefly with Interior Secy. Stewart L. Udall.

The National Park Service of the Interior Department May 10 issued a 37-day renewable permit to allow the campaign leaders to erect their plywood-and-canvas shantytown for 3,000 participants on a 16-acre West Potomac Park site. The campsite was about 2½ miles from the Capitol and a mile from the White House [see map].

Many Southern members of Congress had reacted adversely to the prospect of the encampment of poor in the capital. But efforts to prevent or limit the campaign were largely abortive. The House Public Works Subcommittee on Public Buildings & Grounds held hearings May 6 on 75 bills designed to limit large-scale demonstrations on federal property, to limit the chances of violence and to set bond requirements to compensate for any possible damage.

In a Senate speech Apr. 26, Sen. John Stennis (D., Miss.) called for the abandonment of the demonstration since "nothing good" would come of it. Sen. Jennings Randolph (D., W. Va.) charged in the Senate May 2 that there were "strong evidences of Communist planning and participation" in the demonstrations. Sen. John L. McClellan (D., Ark.) asked Pres. Johnson May 7 to announce, "promptly and firmly," that "the government of the U.S. in its capital city will not be subjected to intimidation." He cited "sworn" intelligence statements that "militant advocates of violence who will swarm along the marchers' routes" planned to incite rioting and looting.

The Defense Department announced May 11 that "selected troop units" had been alerted to help District of Columbia police in the event of violence. Pres. Johnson, at his news conference May 3, had announced that the government had made "extensive preparations" to meet "the possibilities of serious consequences flowing from the assemblage of large numbers over any protracted period of time in the seat of government, where there's much work to be done and very little time to do it."

The 2d phase of the campaign began May 12 when Mrs. Martin Luther King Jr. led a 12-block Mother's Day march of "welfare mothers" from 20 cities to the Cardozo High School Stadium in the center of Washington's Negro ghetto.

Mrs. King declared at the rally, attended by 5,000 participants, that she would try to enlist the support of "black women, white women, brown women and red women—all the women of this nation—in a campaign of conscience." She stressed the need for nonviolence but admitted that it was "not an easy way, particularly in this day when violence is almost fashionable, and in this society, where violence against poor people and minority groups is routine." But, she continued, "I must remind you that starving a child is violence. Suppressing a culture is violence. Neglecting school children is violence. Punishing a mother and her family is violence. . . . Ignoring medical needs is violence. Contempt for poverty is violence. Even the lack of will power to help humanity is a sick and sinister form of violence."

Mrs. King was accompanied by several white women, including Mrs. Robert F. Kennedy; Mrs. Joseph S. Clark, wife of the Democratic Senator from Pennsylvania; Mrs. Philip A. Hart, wife of the Democratic Senator from Michigan, and Mrs. Harry Belafonte, wife of the singer.

The erection of the prefabricated plywood-and-canvas shelters was started May 13 when Abernathy, dressed in blue denims, drove a ceremonial nail at the dedication of "Resurrection City, U.S.A." At each stroke of the hammer about 500 Negro members of a "construction battalion" cried "Freedom!" Before he started, Abernathy asked Linda Aranayko, 20, a member of the Creek tribe of Oklahoma, for permission to "use this land."

Abernathy said he would conduct a nonviolent protest "to arouse the conscience of the nation." He vowed to "plague the pharaohs of this nation with plague after plague until they agree to give us meaningful jobs and a guaranteed annual income." Abernathy said: "Unlike the previous marches which have been held in Washington, this march will not last a day, or 2 days, or even a week. We will be here until the Congress of the United States decide that they are going to do something about the plight of the poor people by doing away with poverty, unemployment, and underemployment in this country." If necessary, "we will stay until Congress adjourns." "And then we're going to go where Congress goes, because we have decided that there will be no new business until we first take care of old business."

Troubles batter campaign—As demonstrations got under way in Washington May 21 to pressure Congress and the Administration to eliminate poverty in the U.S., the Poor People's Campaign was confronted by mounting crises. The campaign seemed to suffer from lack of organization and from disunity in the staff leadership. The problems of insufficient cooking, bathing and sanitation facilities were compounded by unusually heavy rainstorms, which forced many people out of the campsite. The crisis in organization was dramatized by the appointment of an outsider, Bayard Rustin, to lead a special June 19 Solidarity Day March and his subsequent resignation June 7 following a dispute among campaign leaders over Rustin's role.

The Rev. Andrew J. Young, SCLC executive vice president, arrived in Washington May 18 and said at a news conference that reports of serious managerial and financial crises were incorrect.

The Rev. Ralph David Abernathy, SCLC president, announced May 21 the postponement of the planned massive Memorial Day demonstration to June 19. He said that Bayard Rustin, executive director of the A. Philip Randolph Institute, had been asked to organize the campaign's June 19 National Day of Support. At a May 20 SCLC staff meeting, Rustin had been asked to organize the previously planned May 30 demonstration.

300 demonstrators were barred from the House of Representatives' visitors gallery May 21 by 100 Capitol and city policemen because they did not have proper admission passes. After a 2-mile silent march from Resurrection City, the marchers, led by the Rev. Jesse K. Jackson, supervisor of the shantytown, were stopped at the bottom of Capitol Hill. Jackson negotiated with police, who were willing to let the demonstrators pass in groups of 20 or less. During 10 minutes of negotiations, staff members of 4 sympathetic Democratic Congressmen Reps. John Conyers (Mich.), Phillip Burton (Calif.), Joseph Y. Resnick (N.Y.) and Benjamin S. Rosenthal (N.Y.) distributed 50 gallery passes.

250 welfare mothers, led by George A. Wiley, executive director of the National Welfare Rights Organization, marched to the Longworth House Office Building May 23 to "keep an appointment" with Rep. Wilbur D. Mills (D., Ark.), chairman of the House Ways & Means Committee. 150 persons gained entrance to the lobby of the building while the rest remained singing and chanting outside. The marchers were warned by police to quiet down and were barred from the building. When the demonstrators continued to sing, police began making arrests. About 18 persons were charged with violating a special statute prohibiting "unlawful assemblages" on the Capitol grounds. After receiving a call from Wiley, the Rev. Jesse Jackson rushed to the scene, negotiated with police and persuaded them to make no more arrests. The demonstrators then marched to a rally in a hearing room in the Rayburn Building. Later the demonstrators marched to Mills' home on Connecticut Avenue and arrived just minutes after Mills had left.

Abernathy and 200-300 demonstrators met May 23 with Agriculture Secy. Orville L. Freeman, who promised to enlarge the department's food distribution program to 331 counties beginning July 1. Freeman said 6 new commodities would be added to the list of 16 foodstuffs.

A bipartisan *ad hoc* committee of 30 Senators and Representatives was formed May 23 to help the marchers present their demands to the government. Sen. Edward W. Brooke (R., Mass.), chairman of the group, said: "We are against violence and disruption. We are not opposed to peaceful demonstrations within the confines of the law."

The Rev. James Bevel had announced May 22 that about 200 Negro youths, mostly members of Chicago and Detroit street gangs had been sent home. "They went around and beat up on our white people," Bevel said. "They interfered with the workers and were hostile to the press. We had to get them out."

The U.S. Weather Bureau reported May 28 that during the 2 weeks of the Poor People's Campaign, 3.16 inches of rain had fallen, including 2.05 between 7 a.m. May 27 and 1 p.m. May 28. The campsite had been flooded May 23–24. Residents May 28 accepted offers of temporary quarters elsewhere, and 1,200–1,500 persons were evacuated.

The House Public Works Committee May 29 approved a bill to prohibit the use of federal property in the District of Columbia for overnight campsites. The bill would also prohibit renewal or extension of the camping authorization—dated to expire June 16—extended to the Poor People's Campaign.

Leaders of non-Negro groups participating in the Poor People's Campaign May 25 bitterly denounced the treatment they had received from Negro leaders and members of the march. Spokesmen for the American Indians, the Mexican-Americans and the Appalachian whites said Negro leaders had ignored them for the most part and militant Negroes had abused them. They said that tension had been "building up for weeks" among non-Negro groups but had been "played down for the sake of unity."

Reies Lopez Tijerina, 41, leader of a militant group of Mexican-American claimants to 300-year-old land grants in New Mexico, said that 3 Indian leaders had left Washington after several disagreements with SCLC staff members. Abernathy met with Tijerina May 27 and later told newsmen: "We're going to live together. I'd like to say that there is no division in our ranks whatsoever." Tijerina said the dispute had been "partly settled." The march's 400 Spanish-speaking and 100 Indian participants had not yet moved into Resurrection City; they were quartered temporarily in a private school and a church basement.

150 demonstrators led by Abernathy and Jackson were denied admittance to the Agriculture Department's cafeteria by Asst. Agriculture Secy. Joseph M. Robertson May 28. Robertson demanded that before entering, the marchers pay a $292.66 bill for meals they had eaten May 27. Jackson retorted that the bill was a token of what the country owed the poor.

300–400 demonstrators, including 150 Indians, swarmed onto the Plaza of the Supreme Court building May 30. They banged on the building's closed bronze door; some managed to unlock a window and enter an empty filing and records room; others smashed basement windows with stones after they were refused an audience with the justices of the court. The Indians had intended to present a petition protesting the court's May 27 decision upholding the right of the state of Washington to prohibit net fishing for salmon. The Indians contended that an 1854 treaty took precedence over state game laws. The demonstrators finally accepted the court's offer to allow 21 members of the group to enter the building.

In what was described as a "shifting of gears," the Rev. Andrew J. Young announced May 31 the replacement of Jackson, 26, by the Rev. Hosea Williams as supervisor of Resurrection City. Young said that Jackson, SCLC director of Operation Breadbasket, would start work on organizing "action cadres" in various part of the country. The groups would be called to Washington to replace demonstrators in the event of massive arrests.

Nearly 500 demonstrators May 31 took over an auditorium in the Department of Health, Education & Welfare (HEW) and demanded a meeting with HEW Secy. Wilbur J. Cohen. When they were told Cohen was not available, they said they would stay "until he comes to see us." Cohen appeared at 6 p.m. and made a statement indorsing a proposed uniform federal welfare system.

More than 400 demonstrators, led by a group of Mexican-Americans, staged a 7-hour camp-in on the steps of the Justice Department June 3 in protest against the "unjust arrest and indictment" of 13 Mexican-Americans on charges of conspiring to disturb the peace by leading a walk-out and boycott of 4 predominantly Mexican-American Los Angeles high schools in March. Declining to meet with the entire group, Atty. Gen. Ramsey Clark said he would see a 20-member delegation. His offer was rejected. After 7 p.m. Clark relented and agreed to meet a delegation of 100 persons the next day. A 2-hour conversation between Clark and a small group followed while the crowd outside swelled to more than 700. When Hosea Williams returned and said they had not reached agreement, the group formed a ring around the building to prevent Clark's departure. But Clark slipped out through an unwatched entrance.

Clark met with the campaign delegates (25 Mexican-Americans, 15 Indians, 20 whites and 40 Negroes and Puerto Ricans) June 4. They charged that "there is no justice for the poor in America." Clark gave the delegates a 15-page summary of current Justice Department actions in promoting equal opportunity in the areas of employment, education, housing and legal protection.

Speaking at a news conference in Washington June 3 Bayard Rustin issued a "Call to Americans of Goodwill" for a massive "national mobilization" in the capital June 19 to support the Poor People's Campaign and for enactment of an economic bill of rights.

Rustin urged the federal government to meet the following "immediate demands," which, he said, "are attainable even from this miserable Congress": (1) the creation of a million federally financed "socially useful career jobs in public service"; (2) 6 million new dwellings in the next 10 years; (3) repeal of the "punitive welfare restrictions" in the 1967 amendments to the Social Security Act; (4) extension to farm workers of rights guaranteed in the National Labor Relations Act to organize unions and bargain collectively; (5) restoration of Congressional budget cuts for bilingual education, Head Start, summer jobs, the Economic Opportunity Act and the Elementary & Secondary Education Act. Rustin also called on the President to declare a "national emergency" to meet health and food needs of the poor.

Hosea Williams denounced Rustin June 4 as "out of order" in making this policy statement. Williams said the statement was "unauthorized" and "a bunch of foolishness." He said Rustin's only responsibility was to "do some public relations work."

Rustin announced June 6 that he was suspending his activities as coordinator of the June 19 demonstration pending clarification of his role by the campaign leaders.

Rustin resigned June 7. While Abernathy said the conflict had involved "only minor differences," it was reported that the Rustin appointment had been unacceptable to the entire campaign steering committee. The N.Y. Times June 8 quoted a campaign official as saying: The controversy over Rustin's appointment and his subsequent statement of campaign goals had forced Abernathy to "choose between mere reform with the system, as represented by Rustin, and really revolutionary change, as demanded by his people." "It was really no choice because he can't lay down the law to them."

In response to a question at a press conference Abernathy said: Among the goals that Rustin had not pressed were jobs, a guaranteed income for the unemployed, major housing and welfare reform and a call for an end to the war in Vietnam.

Abernathy announced June 7 that Sterling Tucker, 44, executive director of the Washington Urban League, had been asked to replace Rustin. (Abernathy had designated Tucker May 25 as Washington, D.C. march coordinator.) Tucker June 9 accepted the appointment. Tucker issued a new call for support with a revised list of demands on Congress and the Administration. The demands included "a lessening of war and world violence" and the establishment of "strong federal gun controls."

Abernathy, speaking at a news conference June 10, said the campaign had made "significant gains," but "not enough for us to go back to rat-infested slums where jobs do not exist." Among accomplishments he cited: the Agriculture Department had announced an agreement to "provide food in the neediest counties in this country"; the Senate had approved an amendment removing restrictions on Agriculture Department use of contingency funds; the Senate had approved an amended bill to increase low-income family housing; the Office of Economic Opportunity had decided to free $25 million for expanded programs.

Demands & demonstrations—A revised and more specific list of objectives and proposals was issued by the campaign leaders June 12. The 49 "basic" demands included (1) passage of pending housing and employment bills; (2) repeal of Social Security amendments stiffening criteria for welfare payments; (3) passage of a collective bargaining bill for farm workers; (4) maintenance of current spending for poverty programs, and (5) legislation to strengthen and broaden food distribution programs.

About 250 persons began a vigil outside the Agriculture Department June 12 in support of demands for broader food distribution to the poor. 320 demonstrators marched from Resurrection City to the department the same day and presented the demands to Asst. Agriculture Secy. Joseph M. Robertson, who met them outside the building's locked gates. Robertson gave the demonstrators copies of testimony in which Agriculture Secy. Orville L. Freeman had told the House Agriculture Committee June 11 of the department's past expansion of food services and its intention to expand them further. Abernathy, denouncing Freeman's testimony, read a statement to the demonstrators and a group of sympathetic Congressmen June 13 saying: "The Secretary took some comfort from the fact that he reduced the price of food

stamps to 50¢ a person for people with no income. He didn't tell the committee how a family with no income is supposed to find 50¢ per person for food stamps."

Freeman, testifying before the House Committee again June 12, conceded that he had developed a new awareness of poverty in the U.S. Testifying in support of the Sullivan bill to remove the dollar ceiling from the food stamp authorization program, Freeman said that in the coming year "$100 million more than the present authorization" of $225 million would be needed. As a long-range goal, Freeman said, a food stamp program should be operating in every county and city. He estimated that such a program could cost $1.5 billion annually.

Freeman sent Abernathy a letter June 14 outlining those of the campaign's goals that were under study by the Agriculture Department. These included: (1) A family food assistance program to begin about July 1 in 1,000 of the lowest per-capita income counties; (2) review of the standards for application of the Food Stamp Act; (3) emergency supplementary food assistance programs for about 250 counties cited by the Citizens Board of Inquiry as in need; (4) an improvement in the quality, quantity and variety of surplus foods; (5) pending the appropriation of funds by Congress, increases in free and reduced-price school lunches; (6) a review of Citizens Advisory Civil Rights Committee programs for elimination of discrimination in the department.

Vice President Hubert Humphrey June 15 indorsed some of the campaign's key demands, including an "income maintenance" program and more extensive federal welfare policies, job programs and food distribution. In a 4-page statement Humphrey, however, rejected the idea that the government should serve as the employer of last resort.

House Agriculture Committee Chrmn. W. R. Poage (D., Tex.) issued a 79-page "hunger study" June 16 that indicated there were no verified cases of starvation in the U.S. The report was based on responses of county health officers to queries from Poage.

The health officials generally replied that starvation did not exist. They contended that many instances of malnutrition could be found but that this often was attributable to ignorance or local custom.

A group of welfare protesters clashed with police June 18 as they prepared to march to the home of House Ways and Means Committee Chrmn. Wilbur D. Mills (D., Ark.) to demand repeal of restrictive welfare rules. Nine persons were arrested. 200 demonstrators accompanied by police marched 2 miles along Connecticut Avenue and then boarded buses to Mills' home.

More than 50,000 persons, half of them white, participated in the campaign's Solidarity Day March June 19. The crowd exceeded the 40,000 predicted by march leaders. After a one-mile walk from the Washington Monument to the Lincoln Memorial, the crowd, which briefly included Vice Pres. Hubert Humphrey and Sen. Eugene McCarthy (D., Minn.), heard speeches by Abernathy, NAACP Executive Director Roy Wilkins, United Auto Workers Pres. Walter P. Reuther, Urban League Director Whitney Young, and Mrs. Martin Luther King Jr.

Abernathy declared: "We will stay in Washington and fight nonviolently until the nation rises up and demands real assurance that our need will be met." "I don't care if the Department of the Interior gives us another permit to stay in Resurrection City. . . . I intend to stay here until justice rolls out of the halls of Congress and righteousness falls from the Administration, and the rough places of the government agencies are made plain and the crooked deals of the military-industrial complex become straightforward."

Violence erupted again June 20 when demonstrations were resumed at the Agriculture Department. (The vigil begun June 12 had been suspended June 19 for the Solidarity Day March.) Police arrested 77 persons who blocked the entrances to the building. The demonstrators then moved into the street and sat down, bringing the rush-hour traffic to a standstill. 9 persons were injured in the melee. 300 marchers threw rocks and bottles at police outside Resurrection City in the evening. The police used tear gas to disperse them.

Speaking at a news conference June 21, Abernathy asked President Johnson to explain why poverty existed in the U.S. Abernathy said that one question symbolized all the other questions he was raising: "Why does the U.S. Government pay the Mississippi plantation of a U.S. Senator more than $13,000 a month not to grow food or fiber, and at the same time why does the government pay a starving child in Mississippi only $9 a month, and what are you going to do about it?"

More than 300 persons demonstrated outside the Agriculture Department June 21. 100 Mexican-Americans and Indians marched outside the Justice Department while a delegation met with officials to discuss the restrictions on Indian fishing rights in the state of Washington.

United Auto Workers Pres. Reuther, writing as chairman of the Citizens Crusade Against Poverty, informed Agriculture Secy. Freeman in a letter June 23 that the citizens group had made plans to monitor his department's food programs to insure the enactment of promised reform.

Abernathy said at a news conference June 22 that the campaign would suspend demonstrations for 2 days to begin a "spiritual rededication" to nonviolence. He said that the residents, who had dwindled to 1,500, would remain in Resurrection City in spite of the impending expiration of the Interior Department permit. (Police officials June 22 reported the camp's population totaled 500 persons; the June 24 issue of *Newsweek* magazine reported that at its peak the camp's population had numbered 2,563.)

'Resurrection City' closed—The Poor People's campaign in Washington finally ended in late June.

The campaign achieved little in terms of the dramatic goals asserted by its leaders, but it brought at least a promise of reform in a series of agreements negotiated with federal agencies. These included an expanded food distribution program, changes in welfare guidelines and eligibility requirements, and new provisions for participation of the poor in local operations of several government agencies.

The Interior Department permit for Resurrection City, the Poor People's Campaign encampment erected adjacent to the Lincoln Memorial, expired June 23. 124 residents were arrested after they refused to leave the campsite June 24, while several hundred others were arrested for an illegal demonstration on the grounds of the Capitol.

Abernathy early June 24 had led more than 300 demonstrators from Resurrection City to the Agriculture Department and the Capitol. Abernathy and 260 other demonstrators were arrested at noon for unlawful assembly on the grounds of the Capitol. At the same time, Washington police closed Resurrection City. More than 1,000 police surrounded the site while others moved in and peacefully arrested the 124 remaining residents on charges of demonstrating without a permit. By 4 p.m. Interior Department workers had begun dismantling the camp. The task was completed the following day.

Violence erupted later June 24 when about 150 demonstrators who had not been arrested with the Abernathy group marched to SCLC's Washington headquarters. Gangs of Negro youths gathered and began smashing windows, looting stores and fighting police. The police used tear gas to disperse crowds in a 20-block area. Mayor Walter E. Washington announced at 8 p.m. that 450 District of Columbia National Guardsmen had been called to the city. He declared a state of emergency and imposed an 8 p.m.–5:30 a.m. curfew. As the violence spread, the Guard contingent was increased to 650 and then to 900 men.

Mayor Washington removed the curfew June 25 and placed the Guardsmen on standby status. It was reported that arrests between 4 p.m. June 24 and 4 p.m. June 25 totaled 316, including 106 for curfew violations.

Abernathy was sentenced to 20 days in jail June 25 for leading the unlawful assembly at the foot of Capitol Hill. Those arrested with him were given sentences ranging from 2 to 45 days. From his jail cell, Abernathy released a letter in which he called on the nation's clergy to demonstrate in Washington the next day. The letter said: "I am in jail with the poor and today I ask you the clergy to join us." The letter was distributed nationally but fewer than 25 clergymen answered Abernathy's call.

(The campaign's Mule Train, which had left Marks, Miss. May 13, arrived in Washington June 25. The caravan made a 25-mile tour through the city and then returned to its camping site in Virginia. The government impounded the mules June 26 on charges that they were not being properly cared for.)

Abernathy later announced July 16 that the Washington direct-action phase of the campaign was ended and called on the 300 demonstrators remaining to go home and await assignments for protest "on a national level." (Most of the campaigners had left Washington by the time Abernathy had been released from jail July 13.)

Abernathy said that even though Congress had "failed to move meaningfully against the problem of poverty," the campaign had made major gains. He asserted that poverty would never again be ignored in the U.S. and that national attention had been turned from the question of violence to the deeper issue of "the poverty and exploitation that breed violence."

(Abernathy said Nov. 21 that the campaign had no intention of paying a $71,-795 bill presented in August by the National Park Service for the cost of dismantling Resurrection City, built to house the campaigners, and repairing damage to the park site. Instead, he said, the campaign planned to sue the govermnent for more than $100,000 in damages. Abernathy argued that the group had been given only a few hours notice when ordered to leave the Washington site and had had no time to restore the area.)

Demonstration during GOP convention. The Poor People's Campaign moved to Miami Beach, Fla. Aug. 6 to make its protest visible while the 1968 Republican National Convention was held there. According to the Rev. Ralph D. Abernathy, the demonstration's purpose was to educate the GOP delegates about the campaign against poverty. The demonstrators, he declared, were "representatives of the 51st state—that of poverty."

In addition to leading a number of demonstrations at convention headquarters in the Fountainebleau Hotel, Abernathy led groups of poor people into the spectators' gallery of Convention Hall Aug. 6 and 7. Those who were unable to obtain tickets waited outside with a mule-drawn covered wagon, the symbol of the Poor People's Campaign. (Delegates Norman O. Jarvis of Washington, D.C., Ogden Reid of New York and Clarence Townes, chairman of the convention's Minorities Division, had obtained the guest tickets for Abernathy and his followers.)

At a news conference Aug. 6, Abernathy lauded Gov. Nelson A. Rockefeller of New York, an unsuccessful candidate for the Republican Presidential nomination (Richard M. Nixon won the nomination and, later, the election) as "a man with the intelligence and courage to carry out a platform to end poverty and injustice in America." In a statement all but indorsing the governor, he declared that Rockefeller "was one of the last chances for the Republican Party to really win back the black vote."

Poor People's Campaign workers participated in a day of demonstrations Aug. 7 during which they visited the Miami Beach headquarters of the major candidates. The denim-clad, singing demonstrators were greeted with cheers at the Rockefeller campaign hotel but were met with counter-demonstration by Nixon supporters at Nixon headquarters. They were barred from a news conference given by Gov. Ronald Reagan of California, another unsuccessful candidate for the GOP Presidential nomination.

Administration Action

Jobs & unions. Labor Secretary W. Willard Wirtz announced March 22, 1966 that three-man federal teams would visit the Harlem area of New York City and the Watts area of Los Angeles to identify the hard-core unemployed and to "assist the community to develop meaningful job and training opportunities." The project, ultimately to reach 30 cities, had been recommended by the President's Committee on Manpower. The investigating teams were to include officials of the Labor and Health, Education & Welfare Departments and the Office of Economic Opportunity.

(Wirtz also announced plans to provide transportation to Neighborhood Youth Corps [NYC] participants in Watts. He said that 1,000 NYC jobs in Los Angeles were unfilled, "mainly because of transportation problems" caused by the fact that the job openings were in areas "many miles away from the Watts area.")

Wirtz March 29 ordered an "intensive assault" on unemployment among Mississippi blacks. The drive was to include training programs that would reach 9,325 persons. He said that a study conducted by the Mississippi Employment Security Commission showed a 66% unemployment rate among blacks in Bolivar and Washington Counties in the Mississippi Delta. Sixty-five percent of the sample had 1965 incomes of $500 or less.

A federal grant of $6,790,288 for job-training programs in Newark, N.J. had been jointly announced Feb. 14 by Wirtz and Newark Mayor Hugh J. Addonizio. The grant was to finance 14 training projects under the Manpower Development & Training Act and five NYC projects; 4,463 unemployed or underemployed persons were to benefit from the program.

The Labor Department Aug. 27 announced plans to relocate 5,000 unemployed workers and their families to areas with available jobs in the next nine months. Fourteen hundred workers had been relocated under the program in 1965 at an average cost of $400 per worker.

A project to provide a comprehensive job-placement service for the unemployed in the slums of eight major cities was announced by Wirtz March 15, 1967. The program was to be administered through local community-action groups in cooperation with the Office of Economic Opportunity and the Health-Education-Welfare and Housing & Urban Development Departments. The objective was to supply counseling, health, education and training services to the individual for placement in a job.

The cities: Cleveland, Chicago, Detroit, New York, Boston, St. Louis, Los Angeles and Washington.

A special Labor Department survey leased March 15 showed that unemployment in 10 urban slum areas was about 3 times the national rate of 3.7% and that the rate exceeded 30% if it included those too discouraged to look for work, those involuntarily working part time and those working full time for an income below the poverty level.

Ghetto job plan. President Johnson Oct. 2, 1967 announced a pilot plan to attract big business to expand or to build in ghetto communities and to invest in job training programs for the hard-core unemployed. The program was aimed at reducing the risks of investing capital in the economically less attractive urban ghettos. Commerce Secy. Alexander B. Trowbridge appointed William E. Zisch, vice chairman of the board of the Aerojet General Corp., to head the program.

Under the new program: (a) The Small Business Administration would guarantee leases on property, plant and equipment for businesses building or providing jobs in or near a ghetto or rural poverty area. (b) The Labor Department would declare certain ghettos and poverty areas to be labor surplus areas and thereby enable businesses to bid on certain government contracts. (c) Transportation for workers to ghetto plants would be provided by federal funds available under the urban mass transit program. (d) Ghetto employes would receive health services from the Health, Education & Welfare Department. (e) The Federal Economic Development Administration would provide grants to enable big companies to give technical advice to small companies. (f) The federal government would pay the cost of bonding employes against theft and other loss.

Johnson announced Feb. 24, 1968 that 60 major business executives had enlisted in the JOBS private/public program to find jobs for the hard-core unemployed in the slum areas. The announcement was made after a meeting at the LBJ Ranch in Texas with Ford Motor Co. Chrmn. Henry Ford 2d, Coca-Cola Co. Pres. J. Paul Austin and Ford Vice Pres. Leo C. Beebe. All 3 were active in the National Alliance of Businessmen, a group working to avert racial rioting. Ford was chairman of the alliance, Austin vice chairman and Beebe executive vice chairman.

After meeting with the President, Ford told newsmen: "It is no longer merely a matter of social justice and the principles of democracy" to solve the nation's racial problems. "Our very national unity and domestic peace are at stake." "And it is also plain that bringing these disadvantaged people out of the ghettos and into the mainstream of the American economy is a goal that can be accomplished only if business grabs the heavy end of the load."

Business pledges jobs—The Labor Department and the National Alliance of Businessmen said May 22, 1968 that private industry had pledged to find 106,000 jobs for the "hard-core unemployed." Labor Secy. W. Willard Wirtz said that 603 firms in the country's 50 largest cities had submitted contract proposals to hire and train 61,000 persons. The government was to reimburse the businesses for the extra costs necessitated by the hiring and training of unskilled workers.

1968 summer goal unmet—The National Committee on Employment of Youth July 29, 1968 reported the results of a nationwide survey showing that business and government had failed to generate a large number of summer jobs for ghetto youth. In releasing the report, a spokesman for the group declared: "There is no indication that private industry has generated any new summer jobs this year."

Watts developments. Progress in improving the Watts section of Los Angeles since the 1965 riot was "encouraging but far from satisfying," the McCone Commission said in its final report Aug. 26, 1967.

The report said that although jobs had been found for 17,900 Watts residents and "a substantial infrastructure of job training has been developed by federal, state and local agencies, it is quite apparent that the unemployment rate among Negroes has not been substantially reduced." The report noted that the welfare rolls had increased to 36,000. (The 2½ square miles at Watts proper had a population of 40,000. The area of the 1965 rioting covered 40 square miles with 130,000 residents.)

The commission found: "The actions taken thus far in Los Angeles, and for that matter elsewhere throughout the United States, fail to meet the urgent existing need, and unless and until we in our city and in our state and throughout the United States solve the fundamental problem of raising the level of scholastic achievement of disadvantaged children, we cannot hope to solve all the problems of our disadvantaged minorities."

OEO Director Sargent Shriver dedicated the $2.4 million South Central Multipurpose Health Services Center in Watts Sept. 16. The center, financed by an OEO grant to the University of Southern California School of Medicine, would provide all medical, dental and supportive health services on a 24-hour, 7-day-a-week basis to the residents of Watts. It would treat 500 patients a day. Previously Watts had had no hospitals, and the Los Angeles County General Hospital was 11 miles away. (The taxi fare to the county hospital was $7, public transportation cost to the county hospital at least $1.15 and required almost 2 hours travel time.)

Watts residents would have a share in policy-making in the health center through the Community Health Council—a 25-member council with 19 Watts residents and 6 representatives of local agencies and organizations in the area.

Job Corps aids employment. A study of the employment of former Job Corps members, released Feb. 5, 1968, showed that graduates of the program had a 71% employed rate as compared to a 58% rate among drop-outs from the program. The study was based on a Louis Harris & Associates survey of individuals who had left the Corps in Nov. 1966.

Female veterans of the Corps, including both graduates and drop-outs, were employed less than male veterans by a 46%–65% ratio. The percentage of employed Negro graduates was identical with that of white graduates.

Funds authorized, new requirements. A bill authorizing $1.75 billion for the anti-poverty program in fiscal 1967 was passed by Senate voice vote Oct. 18, 1966 and 170–109 House vote Oct. 20. President Johnson signed it Nov. 8. For the first time Congress earmarked funds for the Job Corps ($211 million), Neighborhood Youth Corps ($410 million) and Community Action programs ($846 million).

The bill also: (a) required that one-third of the members of Community Action boards be representatives of the poor and chosen by the poor; (b) limited the number of Job Corps enrollees to 45,000 and

the per-enrollee expenditure to $7,500 and required that 23% of enrollees be women; (c) barred funds and services to anyone convicted of inciting or participating in a riot or of engaging in activity resulting in damage to property or persons; (d) specified that an antipoverty official earning more than $6,000 a year could not receive in excess of 20% more salary than he had received in his previous job; limited to $15,000 the federal share of an official's salary.

Discrepancy in grants. The New York Times reported Aug. 16, 1966 that, according to OEO sources, anti-poverty grants to the nation's largest cities had ranged from half of their minimal entitlements to nearly five times that minimum during the fiscal year ended June 30. (Entitlements were allocated on the basis of such factors as unemployment rolls, the number of families on relief, etc.) The discrepancy reflected population, need and, particularly, the aggressiveness of some cities in seeking OEO funds and their technical preparedness in implementing the various types of programs available.

Among the 50 largest cities that received less than their minimal entitlement in fiscal 1965: Birmingham received 34%, Buffalo 50%, Fort Worth 49%, Memphis 60%, Mobile 60%, Portland, Ore. 80%, San Diego 90%, Tulsa 90%. By contrast, Atlanta received 470%, the District of Columbia 430%, El Paso 440% and Pittsburgh 490%. (Above-entitlement money could be obtained through such channels as funds for research-demonstration-and-training projects or aid to migrants.)

Percentages of other cities that received more than their minimal entitlement included: Boston 270, Chicago 220. Cincinnati 200, Denver 210, Detroit 280, Honolulu 270, Houston 220, Los Angeles 220, Louisville 340, Miami 280, Newark 240, Oklahoma City 210, Phoenix 210, San Francisco 200, St. Paul 240, Toledo 200.

Sen. Paul H. Douglas (D, Ill.) had announced April 1 that the OEO had awarded an $11,900,000 grant to the Chicago Committee on Urban Opportunity. This was the largest single grant for a community action program awarded since the inception of the War on Poverty; it was to finance 34 individual projects, which would employ about 2,300 workers recruited from among the poor.

HUD enters poverty war. Housing & Urban Development Secretary Robert C. Weaver announced May 4, 1966 his department's approval of four grants to build community centers and other neighborhood facilities to be used in the War on Poverty's Community Action Program. The grants amounted to $395,711 for Louisville, Ky., $319,660 for Chattanooga, Tenn., $286,307 for Uvalde, Tex. and $237,837 for Marin City, Calif. (to be supplemented with $118,918 in local funds from Marin County.)

A fiscal 1967 appropriation bill was passed by the House Aug. 18 and Senate Aug. 24 and was signed by President Johnson Sept. 6. The bill included $20 million in contract authority and $2 million for rent payments for HUD's rent-supplement program. In a statement that followed the signing of the bill, the President said the rent program was "the single most important breakthrough in the history of public housing." "This means," he declared, that "53,000 families can now give their children a rain-free roof and a rat-proof bedroom. It means that more than 50,000 city children can come off the streets at night, because they have a decent home to come to."

A fiscal 1968 appropriation bill was passed Oct. 26, 1967 by Senate voice vote and 297–88 House vote and was signed by Johnson Nov. 3. The bill provided funds, although sharply reduced from Administration requests, for rent supplements and the model cities program. The final appropriation for rent supplements was $10 million (the Administration had requested $40 million). The model cities appropriation was $312 million (the Administration had requested $662 million).

Originally, the House had deleted funds for the rent supplements program and had approved only $237 million for model cities. But the Senate Sept. 21 restored the $40 million request for rent supplements and approved $537 million for the cities program. The House-Senate conference committee did not resolve the differences in these programs, and each chamber Oct. 24 rejected the other's versions—the Senate by voice vote and the House by 241–156 vote (159 R. & 82 D. vs. 141 D. & 15 R.) on model cities and 251–151 vote (163 R. & 88 D. vs. 136 D. & 15 R.) on supplements.

A second joint conference committee agreed Oct. 25 on the $10 million and $312 million figures for the programs. A move by House Republicans to have the rent supplements funds eliminated was rejected Oct. 26 by 198–184 vote (163 D. & 35 R. vs. 139 R. & 45 D.).

In signing the bill Nov. 3, Mr. Johnson deplored the fund cuts in these programs and cited the vote by "93% of House Republicans" to kill rent supplements and by "80%" to kill model cities. Enactment of the programs, he said, could be called "a legislative miracle—the opposition was that strong." But, he said, "it was no victory for the 200 American cities which have already submitted model-city applications" and "no victory for the 30,000 poor families who will be denied . . . decent housing . . . because the rent supplement program was cut." "The familiar old voice of reaction and *status quo* prevailed" in the House-Senate conference, he said.

New 'strategy' urged. In a special message to Congress March 14, 1967, President Johnson submitted plans for continuing the anti-poverty program. He referred to the plans as the "strategy against poverty," a phrase that was said to reflect a reevaluation of the "war on poverty" concept.

Mr. Johnson proposed that the Economic Opportunity Act be amended to (a) help local community-action groups "define their purpose more precisely," (b) "give public officials and other interested groups in the community a voice in forming policy," (c) "strengthen the role of the states, especially in rural areas," (d) promote more participation by private enterprises, (e) "encourage welfare recipients to become self-sufficient," (f) provide "momentum to the programs in rural areas" and (g) improve coordination among federal programs.

Authorization for 1968. A two-year authorization bill for the War on Poverty was passed by the Senate Dec. 8, 1967 and House Dec. 11 and was signed by President Johnson Dec. 23. The bill authorized $1.98 billion for 1968—$80 million less than the Administration's request—

and $2.18 billion for fiscal 1969.

The bill altered the administration of Community Action Programs (CAPs) to give control to local public officials. Heretofore the CAPs generally were administered by private, nonprofit organizations. The new provision specified that community action boards would be composed ⅓ of public officials, ⅓ of poverty-area representatives and ⅓ of representatives of business, labor, civic and charitable groups.

The local-control provision, sponsored by Rep. Edith Green (D., Ore.), was called the "bosses and boll weevil" amendment because of its appeal to Southern Democrats and big-city Democrats. Added to the bill by the House Education & Labor Committee, the Green amendment in large measure was held responsible for keeping the Southern Democratic vote from backing Republican proposals to transfer most of the individual OEO (Office of Economic Opportunity) programs to other federal agencies. None of the GOP proposals, which, in effect, would have eliminated the OEO, were accepted.

Alabama aid threatened. Alabama was threatened Jan. 12–13, 1967 with the loss of federal aid to its welfare and mental health programs because of its refusal to comply with Title VI of the Civil Rights Act of 1964.

Health, Education & Welfare Secy. John W. Gardner announced in Washington Jan. 12 that federal support for Alabama welfare programs (estimated at $95.8 million for the fiscal year ending June 30) would be ended Feb. 28 unless the state complied with Title VI and administered programs without racial discrimination. This was the first time welfare funds had been threatened because of racial discrimination.

Federal welfare aid to Alabama represented about ¾ of its general public assistance and more than ½ of its child welfare programs. HEW (Health, Education & Welfare) Department efforts to achieve compliance by Alabama had begun Aug. 17, 1965 when U.S. Welfare Commissioner Ellen Winston notified the state that it was not in compliance. After a hearing, a hearing examiner recommended Apr. 6, 1966 that federal aid

be terminated. Miss Winston accepted the examiner's recommendation after further hearings, and she referred the case to Gardner Nov. 16, 1966.

Alabama, the only state that did not comply with the civil rights regulations, filed suit in U.S. District Court in Birmingham, Ala. Jan 13 to enjoin the HEW Department from withholding federal aid because of the alleged racial discrimination. The suit charged that Gardner's action violated his powers under Title VI.

The federal court in Birmingham Feb. 1 barred the withholding of the HEW aid pending further court review.

Birth control. OEO Director Shriver June 29, 1966 denied rumors that his agency was unwilling to provide money for birth control. Shriver said in an interoffice memo: "There is absolutely no hesitation on my part or, as far as I know, on anyone's part in [OEO headquarters in] Washington to approve family planning grants. As far as I know I have signed every such grant which has come to my desk. I shall continue to do so." The OEO so far had approved $1,700,000 for 35 local family planning projects and was processing additional grants. Shriver said in his memo that "it was OEO which first created these [family planning] programs."

The OEO Feb. 3, 1967 notified community action agencies of these new guidelines and safeguards for dispensing birth control assistance to the poor:

(1) "Local agencies operating family planning programs may not discriminate . . . on the grounds of race, color, national origin or religion. They may, however, establish other criteria for eligibility for information, medical assistance and supplies."

(2) "Where a family planning program serves an area or neighborhood in which poverty is concentrated, all residents of the 'target area' will normally be considered to meet this test; in other cases, the following 'poverty line index' of income eligibility shall apply": an annual income for one person of below $1,500 (nonfarm) or $1,050 (farm) and for a couple $2,000 (nonfarm) or $1,400 (farm); the test line rose by $500 (nonfarm) or $350 (farm) for each additional member of the household.

(3) Information, medical supervision or supplies would be provided to individuals who found such aid consistent with their "moral, philosophical, or religious beliefs" and who voluntarily requested the aid.

Printed statements were to inform applicants: "No one is allowed to force you in any way to participate in a family planning program. No one can tell you, 'Unless you take part in the family planning program, you won't be allowed to receive welfare or get job training, or put your child in the Head Start class.'"

Lawyers back neighborhood offices. The board of governors of the 25,000-member American Trial Lawyers Association July 24, 1966 reversed its previous opposition to "neighborhood law office" projects under the anti-poverty program and voted to cooperate "in the implementation of local programs."

The resolution, adopted by 49–1 vote, said the association would choose a representative to the OEO's national advisory council on legal services programs. The vote represented a defeat for the association's president and vice president, Joseph Kelner and Al J. Cone, respectively, who had unsuccessfully backed a resolution scoring the legal services program as "wasteful" and "inferior"; they had sponsored a critical resolution at a February meeting of the board of governors. (The OEO reported July 22 that there were 159 legal services programs in operation.)

Head Start disputes. Samuel F. Yette, OEO special assistant for civil rights, announced Aug. 25, 1966 that sponsors of 25 Head Start programs in seven Southern states had been refused federal funds. The 25 programs were charged with the following civil rights violations: failure to use white schools in areas having substantial numbers of eligible white children; selection of all-black staffs; unequal recruitment efforts favoring black children. Yette emphasized that the violations resulted from the stand taken by school and other local officials opposed to racial integration of the programs. Black participants had not opposed white participation in the programs.

The OEO Oct. 2–11 announced major changes in the allocation of federal funds for Mississippi's Head Start programs. The revisions prompted charges that the OEO had yielded to segregationist pressures.

The controversy became public Oct. 3 with the OEO's announcement of the cancellation of federal funds previously allotted to the Child Development Group of Mississippi (CDGM) because of alleged mismanagement. The CDGM operated in 28 counties and had spent at least $5-1/2

million in federal funds. An internal OEO report the preceding week had charged that $654,000 had been inadequately or irregularly accounted for. The report alleged nepotism, payroll padding, excessive salaries and improper diversion of federal funds. OEO Director Shriver asserted Oct. 17 that the money had been used to "pay salaries of CORE [Congress of Racial Equality] and SNCC [Student Nonviolent Coordinating Committee] organizers who had nothing whatever to do with Head Start classes." He had criticized the CDGM Oct. 10 for "racially segregated programs."

The charges and the announcement of the fund cut-off were mailed to CDGM officials Oct. 2 after they had refused to meet Oct. 1 with OEO officials in Mississippi. Shriver's pending action and the CDGM's replacement by a 12-member board of white and black leaders had been announced Sept. 30 by Sen. John C. Stennis (D, Miss.). (Stennis had charged that the CDGM had used some of its money to pay the bail of jailed civil rights leaders.)

About 3,000 Negroes held a mass meeting in Jackson Oct. 8 in protest against the OEO's "political deal" with white Mississippi Democrats. The Rev. James F. McRee, CDGM chairman, pledged to fight until the CDGM funds were restored. McRee, who had received a telegram of support from the Rev. Dr. Martin Luther King Jr., was joined by the Rev. Charles Leber Jr. of the United Presbyterian Church and Richard W. Boone, head of the Citizens' Crusade Against Poverty, a private group sponsored by Walter Reuther of the United Auto Workers and the Ford Foundation. Mrs. Fannie Lou Hamer of the Mississippi Freedom Democratic Party said at the protest meeting: "We aren't ready to be sold out by a few middle-class bourgeoisie and some of them Uncle Toms who couldn't care less."

Reuther met in Washington Oct. 10 with members of the Citizens' Crusade Against Poverty in an effort to persuade the OEO to refinance the CDGM. The Reuther group said its 10-member committee of inquiry had found no evidence to support the OEO charges against the CDGM.

Seventy churchmen, urban specialists of the Episcopal Church, the United Presbyterian Church and the United Church of Christ, picketed OEO headquarters in Washington Oct. 15. They charged the

OEO with "throwing road-blocks in the way of maximum feasible participation of the poor in anti-poverty programs," and they threatened to halt cooperation of their denominations with the War on Poverty. Shriver met with the church officials Oct. 17 and denied charges of political pressures. He added that he was prepared to confer with the CDGM's board of directors to discuss the possible continuation of the group's program.

Shriver met with CDGM officials in Atlanta Oct. 24. He conferred briefly with the Rev. Dr. Martin Luther King, who defended the Mississippi program as "one of the finest in the country—a paragon of what a community action program should be." After the meeting Shriver said the OEO funds to the CDGM would not be resumed without "comprehensive reorganization."

CDGM Director John Mudd announced Oct. 31 that since Oct. 1 more than 50 of the group's centers had reopened on a voluntary basis without federal funds.

Programs aid Indians. OEO Director Sargent Shriver announced Oct. 12, 1966 that nearly $32 million in federal funds had been spent in the year ended June 30 to aid American Indians on federal reservations. (The Washington Post reported Oct. 13 an estimated 315,000 [of approximately 600,000 American Indians] living on federal reservations in 23 states.)

In aiding Indians: $19,874,680 was spent on community action programs including Head Start projects, remedial education, community betterment projects, credit unions and health and home improvements; OEO demonstration, research, training and technical assistance grants totaled $4,598,239; the Labor Department granted $3.4 million for Neighborhood Youth Corps; the Health, Education & Welfare Department gave over $2.8 million for work experience projects and $154,986 for adult education; the Small Business Administration made 12 loans totaling $96,000.

Citizens Corps for VISTA. OEO Director Shriver said March 1, 1967 that Volunteers in Service to America (VISTA) would enlist an estimated 8,000 volunteers in a Citizens Corps for tutorial, cultural enrichment,

consumer education and other projects. He said 6 pilot projects would be conducted by the United Planning Organization, the Washington Community Action Agency and the St. Thomas Episcopal Church, all in Washington, D.C.; the Ohio University Institute for Regional Development in Athens; the Hole in the Wall, a community center in the Hough area of Cleveland; New Opportunities for Waterbury, Conn.; Operation Citizenship, a University of Oregon student organization.

Aid to needy children. A special message proposing $650 million of aid to poor children was submitted to Congress by President Johnson Feb. 8, 1967. "Our goal must be clear," he said, "—to give every child the chance to fulfill his promise."

A major part of the program would be an expansion of the Head Start program from preschool training to "follow-through" training in the first 3 elementary grades. The program would also be extended to reach backwards to 3-year-olds and, experimentally, to some 2-year-olds. A pilot lunch program was also recommended for "pre-school children who now lack proper nourishment."

Another proposed program, to be supervised by a cabinet-level council headed by Vice President Hubert Humphrey, would feature a "Share a Summer" campaign "to encourage more fortunate families" to take in disadvantaged children for part of the summer. $20 million was requested to help private groups or clubs sponsor summer tent-camps in federal parks.

The President also proposed: (a) to provide poverty areas with child and parent centers for such services as prenatal counseling, infant care, supervision of children for working mothers; (b) to help the states train specialists in child care; (c) to increase Social Security benefits by an average of 15% for 3 million children whose parents were retired, disabled or dead; (d) to strengthen the child welfare programs by requiring states to provide payments up "to the level the state itself sets as the minimum for subsistence" and by permitting beneficiary families to earn up to $150 a month without a reduction in welfare payments; (e) to intensify programs for the early diagnosis and treatment of handicaps and for fighting mental retardation; (f) to institute a pilot program of dental care for first-grade children; (g) to improve juvenile courts and provide half-way houses and other treatment facilities for juvenile delinquents.

Welfare minimum urged. A 12-man Advisory Committee on Public Welfare, authorized by Congress to conduct a two-year study of the nation's public welfare system, presented its report June 29, 1966 to Health, Education & Welfare Secretary John W. Gardner. The report called the current welfare system "a major source of the poverty on which the government has declared unconditional war" because the income of families receiving welfare in about half of the states fell below the national poverty standard.

The committee recommended that the federal government establish a nationwide minimum for welfare payments, with each state's contributions to be based on its ability to pay and with the federal government to contribute the remainder. The current system of matching federal and state contributions, according to the report, resulted in welfare standards ranging from $8.71 monthly per dependent child in Mississippi to $52.28 in Minnesota.

The establishment of the nationwide welfare minimum proposed by the committee would increase the federal cost of the program from $4 billion to an estimated $9 billion yearly.

The advisory committee was headed by Dr. Fedele Fauri, dean of the University of Michigan School of Social Work.

Guaranteed income. In a May 27, 1968 statement, more than 1,000 economists from 125 colleges and universities endorsed "a national system of income guarantees and supplements." The statement, released in Washington and Cambridge, Mass., had been circulated for signatures by Prof. Paul A. Samuelson of MIT, John Kenneth Galbraith of Harvard, James Tobin of Yale and Harold Watts and Robert Lampman of the University of Wisconsin.

The statement did not support any of the detailed plans for a guaranteed income but urged that the system be based solely on need related to family size and that it provide for incentives to allow for added income through employment.

Guaranteed annual income plans and their variations had been under discussion for several years but most of their supporters acknowledged that there was little public support for any one of the plans or even for the idea itself.

A Gallup Poll published June 16 showed that 58% of those polled opposed a guaranteed income of $3,200 annually for a family of 4 while 36% supported the plan and 6% had no opinion. In the same poll 78% of those asked had favored a plan to guarantee "enough work each week" for the head of a family to earn "a wage of about $60 a week or $3,200 a year."

CRC urges war on slums. The U.S. Civil Rights Commission, in a report Nov. 22, 1967, called for an attack on slum problems as the nation's "first priority." The commission reported a general deterioration in the conditions of Negroes living in big-city slums.

Unlike other commission studies, the 133-page report, "A Time to Listen . . . A Time to Act," contained testimony of ghetto residents to "provide insights into what slum residents think and feel about the conditions in which they live." The 88 pages of direct testimony from slum residents was taken during commission and state advisory board hearings throughout the U.S. during 1967.

The report held that the summer riots and the growing Negro militancy should be viewed in the context of the "great frustrations, of laws and programs which promise but do not deliver, of continued deprivation, discrimination and prejudice" in an increasingly prosperous society.

The commission said the Federal Housing Administration and the Office of Federal Contract Compliance of the Department of Labor had failed to help the poor by not enforcing anti-discrimination policies in federal housing and job projects.

Health plan for urban poor. President Johnson said Jan. 20, 1968 that a new federal-private program would be launched in Washington to provide health and housing facilities for the poor, particularly the elderly poor. The program was sponsored by the National Medical Association (NMA), 97% of whose members were Negro, in cooperation with the federal government, the District of Columbia and Howard University.

Dr. Lionel F. Swan, NMA president, said that the project would be started with a $60,550 planning grant from the Health, Education & Welfare Department. The plans were to use a 335-acre site near Howard University to build facilities for group medical practice, a nursing home, a medical office building, housing for the elderly, social care facilities, a neighborhood service center for the elderly and a job-training center in health posts.

Plans were to be developed for similar projects in other urban areas.

Welfare probes to be cut. The Health, Education & Welfare Department Nov. 19, 1968 published a new regulation that would virtually end investigations of welfare applicants before they received relief. The proposed rule, published in the *Federal Register* Nov. 20, would require that eligibility for federally-assisted welfare be determined on the basis of a statement of need by applicants. The regulation, which would substitute spot checks for universal case-by-case investigations, was to take effect July 1, 1969 unless vetoed by the incoming Nixon Administration.

HEW officials estimated that under the new system, spot checks would be held on about 10% of applicants. The change was decided on after experiments in N.Y. City and other areas showed infractions to number about the same under both systems. States already using statements of need included California and Maine. The new regulation would be obligatory for all states.

Federal officials said the new system would free many welfare workers for field work. They estimated that 70%–90% of the average welfare worker's time was spent in case-by-case investigations to determine eligibility. The statement-of-need approach was one of the key demands of the Poor People's Campaign during its Washington encampment in the spring of 1968.

Regulations revised—The Health, Education & Welfare Department Jan. 18, 1969 announced tighter controls against relief cheating and a test elimination of routine welfare investigations. State welfare agencies were to begin, on a trial basis, accepting recipients' statements of need without further checking. The "declaration method," renamed the "simplified method," was to be put in use by the states by July 1, but it was not to apply to the program of Aid to Families with Dependent Children until results of the trial program were analyzed by incoming HEW Secretary Robert Finch.

Hunger & Food Stamps

Even in the U.S., the poor are often hungry. The U.S. has tried several ways of aiding the hungry poor. Welfare payments, federal donations of "surplus food" (the major food-aid program of the 1960s) and food stamps are the most important.

The food-stamp program enables poor people to buy coupons redeemable in food worth much more than the coupons cost. The current food-stamp program was started as a pilot project in 1961, and even after the passage of food-stamp legislation in 1964, food stamps were available in only 110 counties of the U.S. in 1965. (The program grew rapidly, however, during the following years. The average number of Americans using food stamps was one in 439 during 1965, one in 157 in 1967, one in 47 in 1970 and one in 17 by 1973. The recession and accompanying unemployment that then gripped the U.S. brought participation up to a peak of 19.5 million persons by April 1975, but the figure declined thereafter to about 18.5 million in early 1976.)

1967 food aid controversy. Thousands of blacks in seven Southern states were said to be facing starvation in 1967 as some of the nation's poorest counties ended programs of free distribution of government surplus food to the poor and turned to the sale of federal food stamps. Many of those receiving food assistance were unemployed and unable to pay for food stamps.

According to the Agriculture Department, 208,000 persons in 28 counties in Mississippi had been receiving direct food aid in Apr. 1966. With the conversion to the food stamp program, only 128,000 persons received aid. In Washington County (Greenville), Miss., 20,218 persons received direct food aid in Apr. 1966; in Apr. 1967 the number receiving aid through the food stamp plan was 10,160. In Jones County, Miss. 17,500 persons received free food in 1967; only 4,700 of them bought food stamps when the county switched programs in 1966.

The free distribution of surplus farm commodities had begun in many Mississippi counties in 1954, and a 3-year, $375 million food stamp program was enacted in 1964. A two-year, $425 million extension of the program was adopted by both houses of Congress Sept. 19, 1967 and signed by President Johnson Sept. 27 (as Public Law 90-91). State food-stamp programs, set up only when states requested them, replaced the state's existing program of free distribution of federally owned food.

Agriculture Secy. Orville L. Freeman told the House Agriculture Committee Mar. 15 that the food-stamp program had enabled families to buy 50% more food than they previously received. He said: On the average a family paid about 64% of the total value of the coupons it received monthly; the value of coupons averaged about $6 a month per person; 51,900 retail food stores were authorized to accept coupons; in 1964 some 351,000 persons had participated in 43 pilot programs in 22 states; in Jan. 1967 there were 1.4 million participants in 589 programs in 21 states and the District of Columbia; spending rose from $35.1 million in fiscal 1965 to $70.3 million in fiscal 1966 and to $140 million in fiscal 1967. (The Agriculture Department reported Sept. 8 that more than 1.8 million poor persons in 838 areas in 41 states and the District of Columbia had participated in the food-stamp program in fiscal 1967.)

Negroes in Jackson, Miss. had denounced the stamp plan Feb. 17 at a hearing on welfare problems conducted by the Mississippi State Advisory Committee to the U.S. Commission on Civil Rights. Anzie Moore, a Negro from Cleveland, Miss. and spokesman for a Bolivar County antipoverty group, said: "Now they're going to sell us stamps. . . . That means starve or go to Chicago. We don't want the stamps unless it's a free stamp program." Mrs. Beulah Mae Miller of Itta Bena, the mother of 6 children, told the committee that except for an occasional cheap flavored drink, her family consumed nothing but surplus commodities (rice, flour, cornmeal, powdered milk and canned meat) "ever since they been giving it."

Kenneth Dean, director of the Mississippi Council on Human Relations, told the Senate Labor & Public Welfare Subcommittee on Employment, Manpower & Poverty Apr. 25: In 7 Mississippi counties his agency had found "poverty that could, at any given moment, turn into acute hunger or a slow starvation if federal programs are not upgraded."

His agency's report mentioned a family "too poor to participate in a poverty program" and said that adults in such families fluctuated between the "human and subhuman level." "It is not accurate to describe these victims of poverty as starving. A large number of people do not have a balanced diet or adequate food for normal development." His spot checks in Hinds, Bolivar, Washington, Yalobusha, Grenada, Lafayette and Madison Counties showed "poverty situations that are of such extreme nature that the people involved do not have adequate food, housing, clothing or health care." It was "misleading" to conclude that the problems of poverty resulted from farm mechanization and the minimum wage law.

The subcommittee, in a letter delivered to the White House Apr. 28 (made public Apr. 29), asked Pres. Johnson to invoke emergency measures to fight hunger in Mississippi and wherever else it existed. The letter said: The food-stamp program was inadequate; many families had no cash income and therefore could not buy stamps. Subcommittee members had "heard testimony and observed . . . conditions of malnutrition and widespread hunger in the delta counties of Mississippi that can only be described as shocking and which we believe constitute an emergency." A family with 13 children "told us that they had had grits and molasses for breakfast, no lunch, and would have beans for supper. Some of the children could not go to school because they had no shoes, and had distended stomachs, chronic sores of the upper lip, and were extremely lethargic—all of which are the tragic evidence of serious malnutrition." The subcommittee recommended: "First, the Office of Economic Opportunity should utilize its emergency family loan authority to subsidize the purchase of food, whether through the food stamp mechanism or otherwise. 2d, the Department of Health, Education & Welfare should consider invoking its authority to extend supplementary welfare assistance on a demonstration basis, seeking the required matching funds from private, nonprofit sources. 3d, consideration should be given to invoking such other emergency authority as may be vested by law in the executive branch."

The Office of Economic Opportunity

(OEO), at the President's request, issued a news release expressing its "hearty concurrence" with the subcommittee letter. It said, however, that similar "crises" existed in the states of the Senators who signed the letter. The OEO release said: "We should at this point in the fiscal year realize that every additional dollar devoted to Mississippi would divert money from other areas desperately in need"; 18 months previously Administration officials had described the critical nature of the situation and had "literally begged that the minimum requests submitted to Congress to finance these programs be granted"; the Agriculture Department could not lawfully issue free food stamps, and it could not authorize emergency action under the Food Stamp Act.

OEO Director Sargent Shriver May 3 announced a $1 million emergency grant for a 4-month Food Stamp Loan Program in 20 poor counties in Alabama, Arkansas, Georgia, Louisiana, Mississippi, South Carolina and Tennessee. Theodore M. Berry, director of Community Action Programs (CAP), said that CAP would make small cash loans ($2 to $12 a month depending on the size of the family) to "a head of family or individual who had been certified as eligible [by the local welfare department] to purchase federal food stamps and has shown that he is unable to purchase the food stamps without . . . such a loan." Berry also said poor people would be hired as county loan aides to find all eligible households and inform them of the program.

A team of doctors studied the situation under a Field Foundation subsidy and told the Senate subcommittee June 16 that nutritional and medical conditions in Mississippi were "shocking." The doctors urged the government to permit the rural poor to obtain food stamps free. " 'Malnutrition' is not quite what we found," the doctors said. "The boys and girls we saw were hungry—weak, in pain, sick; their lives are being shortened. . . . They are suffering from hunger and disease and directly or indirectly they are dying from them—which is exactly what 'starvation' means." The doctors gave their testimony after a 4-day inspection of conditions in Humphreys, Leflore,

Clarke, Wayne, Neshoba and Greene Counties, Miss.

The doctors composing the team were: Dr. Robert Coles, a child psychiatrist with the Harvard University Health Service; Dr. Raymond Wheeler, an internist from Charlotte, N.C. and executive committee chairman of the Southern Regional Council; Dr. Alan Mermann, a pediatrician and assistant clinical professor at Yale Medical School; Dr. Joseph Brenner of the MIT medical department. Wheeler said he had found an "absence of compassion and concern" among health and welfare workers. Brenner, who had spent a year in East Africa, said that health conditions in the South were as bad as or worse than those among the primitive tribal Africans in Kenya or Aden. The doctors said the families they saw were totally isolated and outside the "American money economy." They described families who struggled to live on $15 a week which had been earned for working 55 hours.

Gov. Paul B. Johnson Jr. of Mississippi announced Aug. 4 that a team of prominent Mississippi doctors had found no evidence of starvation in the state. The 5 doctors, selected by the governor from a list of specialists at the University of Mississippi Medical Center and the Mississippi State Medical Association, had inspected Washington, Bolivar, Humphreys and Leflore counties. Johnson said the physicians reported that "in none of the counties could any condition approaching starvation be found to support the charges of death by starvation." He asserted that the recent allegations were "unfair and exaggerated," although it was true that "in many localities sanitary conditions are below the acceptable minimum and there are varying degrees of undernutrition, malnutrition and anemia as there are in other parts of the nation."

"As Mississippi makes the transition from an agrarian to an industrial society," the Mississippi doctors reported, "it is inevitable that major social problems will arise." They attributed the inadequate housing, clothing, medical and dental care and diet to low income, ignorance of budgeting, meal planning and personal hygiene and overloaded health and welfare staffs. The report was filed with the Senate subcommittee Aug. 25.

These changes in the food-stamp program went into effect July 1: (1) a reduction of more than $\frac{1}{2}$ in the cost of food stamps; (2) a reduction in the minimum monthly purchase by families from $2 a person to 50¢ a person (for $12 a family of 6 had received food stamps worth $70); (3) a proposal to get county boards of supervisors to underwrite the cost of minimum stamp purchases for families without income; (4) an increase in trained federal workers to recruit, hire and train new "program aides" to work with the poor on nutrition, food buying and food preparation.

Hunger Widespread in U.S. "Millions of Americans are being deprived of the food they need," the Citizens' Board of Inquiry into Hunger & Malnutrition in the United States said April 22, 1968 in a 100-page report titled "Hunger and Malnutrition in the U.S.A." The board, organized on the recommendation of the Citizens Crusade Against Poverty, headed by United Auto Workers Pres. Walter P. Reuther, scored the Agriculture Department's commodity distribution and food stamp program as a "failure" and "nightmare for the hungry."

The board recommended a long-range free food-stamp program under which eligible recipients would file federal income tax returns and receive vouchers for food stamps. It said money that should have been used to feed the hungry had been turned back to the Treasury by the Agriculture Department because, according to Leslie W. Dunbar, co-chairman of the board and executive director of the Field Foundation, the department was interested chiefly in making crop producers richer and had "little interest in feeding people." The board recommended that the Agriculture Department's responsibilities for feeding the poor be transferred to the Office of Economic Opportunity (OEO) or to the Health, Education & Welfare Department (HEW).

The board said that the authority, money and staff were available for viable commodity distribution and food-stamp programs but that the adoption of such programs had been inhibited by influential Congress members and because of "the mode of administration adopted, the discretionary decisions made, and the failure to use the full statutory power available to fulfill the purpose of these programs."

The 9-month private study concluded that "victims of hunger exist in all parts of the nation," although principally in the South and Southwest. The report said: Only 5.4 million (about 18½%) of more than 29 million poor persons in the country participated in government food programs, and many of them were not the poorest. While malnutrition had increased during the last 6 years, the number of participants in federal food programs had decreased by 1.4 million. 10–14½ million Americans were underfed, and the situation was "worsening." 256 counties in 20 states were so "distressed as to warrant a Presidential declaration naming them as hunger areas" in immediate

need of emergency food programs. The "terribly insufficient" diets caused high infant mortality rates, "organic brain damage, retarded growth and learning rates, increased vulnerability to disease, withdrawal, apathy, alienation, frustration and violence."

Agriculture Secy. Orville L. Freeman said in a prepared statement Apr. 23 that the report had some "validity" and that its conclusions "parallel findings of Department of Agriculture studies and my own personal observations on field trips to hunger areas." "The feelings of board members at the disgraceful paradox of hunger amidst plenty are my feelings, also," he said. He criticized the report, however, for not recording progress made since he became Agriculture Secretary in 1961. At that time, he said, only 1,200 of the U.S.' 3,091 counties had food programs and only 3½ million persons benefited from them. Currently, he said, there were 2,200 counties with food programs aiding 5.8 million persons. The distribution program in 1961 consisted of 5 surplus commodities worth about $2.20 per person a month; the current distribution program had 16 different foods worth 4 times the 1961 amount. Money was returned to the Treasury ($200 million in the current year) instead of being used to aid the hungry because county officials sometimes blocked department programs and because Congress members applied "budgetary pressures," the department declared.

In testimony before the House Labor & Education Committee May 22, Freeman said that public indifference and complacency as well as a lack of cooperation on the part of public officials were the reasons for the failure of the efforts to feed the poor. "Time and time again when the poor cried for a full loaf of bread they were forced to settle for half because the public support to fund antihunger campaigns was weak or nonexistent," he asserted.

Freeman announced May 23 that distribution of surplus food to 331 counties not covered by food stamp programs would begin July 1. He said that a total of $60 million worth of food commodities would be added to the current distribution program.

Freeman said at a news conference May 27 that a May 21 CBS-TV documentary "Hunger in America" was a "biased, one-sided and dishonest presentation." Freeman released a letter to CBS Pres. Dr. Frank Stanton in which he demanded "equal network time to refute" the program's "errors of fact,

. . . misinterpretations and . . . misinformation . . .
and to assure the hungry of this nation that the . . .
[Agriculture Department] does care—that it is doing
what it can for them—and that it wants to do a great
deal more."

The Agriculture Department announced Apr. 1
that it was beginning the direct distribution of food
to the needy in Elmore County, Ala. because local
officials had failed to establish and administer a food
program.

The department notified officials of 34 additional
Southern counties May 21 that it would open its own
food distribution centers in any of the counties that
failed to adopt food aid programs by May 29.

The department announced June 3 that it was beginning direct federal food distribution programs in
42 counties that had refused to administer federal
food relief programs.

A $10 million program to provide emergency food
and medical aid to the poor had been announced by
the Agriculture Department, the OEO and HEW
Mar. 23. The OEO would administer $5 million of
aid in 256 priority counties in 21 states. (The OEO
Feb. 13 had extended to June 30, 1968 the Emergency Food Stamp Loan program authorized in May
1967 to provide poor families in 18 counties in 6
Southern states with funds to buy food. The extension cost $685,000.)

U.S. District Court Judge George L. Hart Jr. in
Washington Mar. 25 rejected a motion filed by 32
heads of Alabama households to issue an injunction
ordering Agriculture Secy. Freeman to distribute
free food stamps to "starving" Alabama families
with little or no income. He reprimanded 2 lawyers
"for traipsing" 130 poor Alabamans to Washington
"for what I suspect to be purely political purposes
rather than to seek quick justice." The lawyers,
Donald A. Jelinek, director of the Southern Rural
Research Project, and Edgar Cahn of Washington,
had charged that the Agriculture Department was
charging too much for food stamps. They contended
that Freeman had authority to declare an emergency
in some counties to force food stamp and surplus
commodity programs in counties having only one or
neither. The lawyers appealed to the U.S. Court of
Appeals in Washington Mar. 28. The appeal was
denied Apr. 16.

Suits for food aid—Suits were filed
in 26 states Nov. 19 in an attempt to force
the Agriculture Department to start
either food-stamp programs or free commodity distribution in 500 counties that
had neither.

The suits, coordinated by the Center
on Social Welfare Policy & Law at
Columbia University, were filed by lawyers representing some 1,000 poor persons. A spokesman for the group said
that it hoped to establish a new legal doc-
trine that "hunger in the United States is
illegal."

The suits, based on the 5th and 14th
Amendments to the Constitution, contended that federal programs provided in
some areas had to be extended to all
under the "due-process" and "equal-
protection" doctrines.

FBI quizzes protesters. The Washington Post reported Dec. 8, 1968 that
FBI agents on loan to the Agriculture
Subcommittee of the House Appropriations Committee had interrogated individuals involved in protests and reports
about the existence of hunger among the
poor. People and organizations involved
in preparing the TV documentary "Hunger in America" (shown on CBS May 21)
and various reports by private organizations had been questioned by the agents,
the *Post* said.

Subcommittee Chrmn. Jamie L. Whitten (D., Miss.) acknowledged that FBI
agents had been used to investigate
charges of hunger, but he denied any
impropriety. "If what's said is true,"
Whitten said, "we need to correct it. If
not, we need to stop folks from making
wild charges." Whitten said he considered
such complaints, at least in Mississippi,
"completely misleading."

Several people questioned by the agents
were reported to have charged that from
the line of questioning used by the agents
the investigation was an attempt to dis-
credit reports of widespread hunger.

Food-stamp program improved—Agriculture Secy. Orville L. Freeman announced Dec. 11 that the food-stamp
program would be liberalized to give the
poorest families at least $10 more in food
stamps for the same amount of money.

Freeman estimated that the revised
program, scheduled to begin in Feb. 1969,
would cost an additional $14 million in
fiscal 1969 and $25 million in fiscal 1970.
The current program was funded at $230
million although Freeman held that
about $1 billion was needed to assure the
poor of "fair minimum" diets.

The revisions would benefit 500,000
of the 2.7 million people receiving food
stamps. The revised program increased
the value of stamps sold to families with
an income of less than $70 a month. The
average food-stamp user could buy $10
worth of stamps for $6.

The Agriculture Department had announced Nov. 18 that it had added 235
more counties and cities to the list of
those with food-stamp programs. The department announced Dec. 19 that an additional 388 areas would be added to the
program by June 30, 1969. This would

mean that more than 3.6 million persons would be receiving stamps.

Poor pay more for food. The House Government Operations Committee reported Aug. 10, 1968 that supermarkets in New York, St. Louis and Washington charged higher prices for inferior food in ghetto neighborhoods. The report indicated that its investigations, although confined to only 3 cities, found evidence that the same practices probably existed in other major cities.

The report was signed by a majority of the 35-member committee, but 11 of the 15 committee Republicans disputed the majority findings. Their minority report contended that high-income and low-income areas appeared to be treated equally by the grocery chains.

The majority charged that the supermarkets sold "to low-income consumers . . . food items of lower quality than are available in [their] outlets located in middle and upper-income areas" and that "evidence . . . that shoppers pay higher prices at food chain stores in poverty areas, though not conclusive, is sufficient . . . to warrant immediate attention by the responsible federal agency."

The majority report said: Federal agencies had paid too little heed to "recurring reports of consumer injustices and grievances in America's low-income areas." The FTC should "scrutinize food retail operators in low-income areas" and take legal action against chains that falsely advertise uniform prices and quality. "There is considerable evidence to support the case" that ghetto stores raise their prices on days when welfare checks are delivered.

Rep. Fletcher Thompson (R., Ga.) warned in his minority report that "by improperly asserting that discrimination exists, this report may very well offer justification to some for additional riots, burning, looting and destruction in the ghetto areas, and those guilty may try to cite this report as an excuse for such action."

Sources close to the committee told newsmen that the supermarket industry had lobbied to have the report suppressed or modified.

The Agriculture Department June 17 had released a study of food prices in 6 cities; it reported "no identifiable pattern of differences between sample stores of the same chain operating in high and low-income areas."

(The FTC reported July 8 that low-income buyers in the District of Columbia were "frequently confused and deceived" by the deceptive practices of some ghetto merchants. "Bait-and-switch" advertising, advertising low-priced products as "bait" with the intention of selling more expensive goods, was found to be the most frequent deceptive practice; it accounted for 41% of the complaints investigated.)

U.S. diet study. The Agriculture Department reported Feb. 26, 1968 that members of 20% of U.S. households had nutritionally "poor" diets. The last previous survey of this kind, in 1955, found 15% of Americans in the "poor" diet category. The report indicated that "poor" diet was not equated with hunger or malnutrition.

The data was gathered from 7,500 households in the spring of 1965. A diet was described as "good" if the members of the household received enough total food and enough of these 7 nutrients: protein, calcium, iron, Vitamin A, thiamine, riboflavin and ascorbic acid (Vitamin C). A diet was considered "poor" if it contained less than ⅔ of these allowances of the 7 nutrients.

The report said that 9% of high-income families had nutritionally "poor" diets, 63% of the high-income families "good" diets. Of households with incomes under $3,000 a year, 37% had "good" diets, 27% "fair" diets and 36% "poor" diets.

The survey also noted regional differences in diet patterns: "Southern households spent less for food than households in other regions, but they had a greater nutritional return for each dollar spent."

Agriculture Secy. Orville L. Freeman said of the report: "From this, we must conclude that many Americans are making a poor choice—nutritionally—of our food abundance, and that to a large extent income does not determine nutrition."

City Programs in Trouble

The urban antipoverty programs were reported to be in difficulties throughout the U.S. New York City, with the biggest poverty burden, was perhaps the prime example of a city with such programs in trouble.

N.Y. spending cutback. James R. Dumpson, chairman of the New York City Council Against Poverty, announced June 29, 1966 that his agency had accepted an Office of Economic Opportunity ceiling of $36 million to cover city antipoverty programs for fiscal 1967. Dumpson said his agency had cut its original request for over $52 million, submitted to the OEO June 2 in defiance of the ceiling.

The cutback announcement drew angry reactions from some groups affected. Manuel Diaz Jr., executive director of the Puerto Rican Community Development Project, the city's largest antipoverty group affecting Puerto Ricans, charged June 21 that a resulting cut to $826,690 in his organization's $2 million request for fiscal 1967 was "keeping us behind other ethnic groups in the war against poverty." One hundred fifty members of a coalition of antipoverty organizations called Citywide Community Action Groups, which had staged a May 27 demonstration protesting the OEO ceiling, picketed the New York City office of Gov. Nelson A. Rockefeller June 24; they sought an interview with the governor to urge him to persuade the state Legislature to allocate $25 million for antipoverty programs; 34 demonstrators were arrested when they sat down on the sidewalk after being told Rockefeller was too busy to see them.

OEO Regional Director Robert J. Mangum announced on June 30 that future grants to HARYOU-ACT, the controversial antipoverty agency serving the New York City section known as Harlem, were being made contingent on reforms in its operation. Mangum said the OEO had approved grants of $600,000 for a HARYOU-ACT summer program and of about $2½ million for year-round programs but would require a report showing compliance with new regulations. The reforms involved organizational changes to lessen the authority of HARYOU-ACT

Director Livingston L. Wingate and improvements in fiscal practices.

Mayor John V. Lindsay reorganized New York City's anti-poverty program Aug. 15 by merging the Welfare Department and Youth Board into a new Human Resources Administration and establishing within the administration a Department of Manpower & Career Development and a Community Development Department. He named Mitchell Sviridoff, 47, director of Community Progress, Inc., the New Haven, Conn. antipoverty set-up, to head the city's antipoverty administration. Sviridoff had recommended the reforms following a Ford Foundation-financed study he had conducted at Lindsay's behest.

Welfare becomes N.Y.'s top cost. New York City Controller Mario A. Procacino reported Oct. 31, 1968 that welfare had become the city's biggest expense item in the fiscal year ended June 30. The city spent $1.4 billion on welfare programs such as aid to dependent children, the aged and handicapped persons, and the welfare share of total city expenditures rose from 20.7% to 26.6%. (The federal government paid about ½ of the city's welfare bill; the rest was split between the city and state.) City welfare figures released Oct. 16 covering expenditures through August showed the number of welfare recipients rising by a rate of more than 20,000 a month. (The total on relief in the city in August: 916,116.)

(According to estimates released by the city Social Services Department Dec. 9, nearly $1 million in welfare checks were stolen and fraudulently cashed in the city each month.)

The city received federal and state approval for a "simplified payments system" under which relief recipients would get $100 a year for clothing and household furnishing items instead of applying for special grants to cover these needs. A state official said Aug. 26 that the purpose of the new system was to help people on relief to plan for their needs better, to make aid more equitable by not favoring those most insistent and to simplify the relief procedure by eliminating the investigations required by special grants. The program was put into effect Aug. 27. The state Nov. 13 announced its approval of a plan under which, beginning Jan. 1, 1969, the city would be able to start an applicant on relief with merely the applicant's statement that he was eligible; detailed investigation of every case would be replaced by a random audit of 10% of the applications for welfare; (A federal study released Oct. 16 showed that 18% of assistance payments in N.Y. State were "overpayments," 15.1% were "underpayments." The national averages were 10.4% for "overpayments" and 11.2% for "underpayments.")

Welfare recipients, mostly Negro women organized by the Citywide Coordinating Committee of Welfare Groups, began a systematic attack on the city's new "simplified payments system." Complaining that they received less money under the new system, they demonstrated Aug. 27-28 at City Hall Park and clashed with police. Police arrested Mrs. Beulah Sanders, 33, chairman of the committee, and 32 other demonstrators. The demonstrators next focused on individual welfare centers around the city, seizing some centers and destroying records and furniture. 100 welfare policemen picketed city offices Sept. 30 to demand increased on-the-job protection. The committee employed other tactics, including a "rent revolt," announced Oct. 25, whereby welfare recipients would spend rent allocations on food, clothing and furniture, and a demonstration Nov. 21 in a Brooklyn discount department store to demand credit for the purchase of winter clothing.

Hulbert James, 27, director of the coordinating committee, had explained July 14 that a "campaign of further disruption" would be conducted by welfare recipients in a program aimed at replacing the welfare system with a guaranteed annual income. Such an income should be "close to $6,000 a year" for a family of 4 in New York, he said. James warned Oct. 16 that a newly announced plan for a federal review of New York welfare might be an effort "to cut costs by forcing people to go to work, thus enforcing the punitive welfare laws passed by Congress last year."

N.Y. Gov. Nelson A. Rockefeller announced Oct. 29 that an $11 million city work incentive program designed to comply with provisions of the 1967 Federal Social Security Act amendments had received state and federal government approval. The program was to provide jobs or job training for some 8,400 employable welfare recipients. State Social Services Commissioner George K. Wyman in Albany Oct. 31 denied charges that the program would "force people to accept employment."

To comply with the federal mandate for "maximum feasible participation" of the poor in federally-financed antipoverty programs, the city established a new employment standard for Human Resources Administration clerical jobs. Under the new standard, reported Nov. 12, poor applicants would be granted up to 12 extra points on civil service tests.

Youths had participated in a rock-and-bottle-throwing demonstration outside City Hall July 10 in protest against cutbacks in the summer job program. Youth Corps Director Willie J. Smith, 29, was suspended July 11 for organizing the demonstration. (He was reinstated July 17 on the understanding that he would resign or be dismissed if he took future "public action" against city policy.) Mayor Lindsay said July 11 that the city would add up to $5 million to the job program. He emphasized that the decision had been made before the demonstration.

Charges of fraud in the Youth Corps and embezzlement by a city fiscal administrator led to major investigations of the Human Resources Administration (HRA) by city and federal authorities during 1968. The investigations resulted in several arrests and threats that federal funds would be withheld from the HRA, which directed the city's $1½ billion welfare and antipoverty program.

HRA Administrator Mitchell I. Ginsberg Sept. 13 announced the arrest of 4 Youth Corps officials, 3 of whom had been found Aug. 26 with $4,067.10 worth of agency checks made out to fictitious persons. An investigator said Oct. 1 that the amount of money that had disappeared from the corps over the past 2 summers was "definitely in the millions."

Mrs. Helynn R. Lewis, ex-HRA fiscal director, was arrested in Los Angeles Oct. 3 on charges that she had embezzled $22,912.69 in agency funds. She had been dismissed from her $19,000-a-year job Sept. 19 for refusing to answer questions asked by the City Department of Investigation.

Los Angeles reorganization. The OEO announced April 7, 1966 a decentralization of the administration of community action programs in Los Angeles County, Calif. The county's "umbrella" agency, the Economic & Youth Opportunity Agency (EYOA), was relieved of responsibility for operating programs; any municipality or contiguous area within the country with a population of at least 100,000 was permitted to establish an independent community action agency. The EYOA was to operate as a coordinating and planning agency. The OEO said that the plan was intended to adapt the community action program to the "unusual geographic characteristic" of Los Angeles County.

In antipoverty elections held in Los Angeles March 1, less than 1% (2,659 out of 400,000) of those eligible had voted. Fifty-six candidates ran for 7 seats on the 23-member EYOA board. Local officials speculated that eligible voters might have been reluctant to attest that their income did not exceed $4,000 yearly, a requirement for voting; they also pointed out that the election had inadvertently been scheduled for the day county welfare checks were due. Mayor Samuel W. Yorty called the election a "costly farce."

Detroit youth fund abuses. The Government Accounting Office (GAO) told Congress Jan. 2, 1969 that it had found serious spending abuses in 16 Detroit Neighborhood Youth Corps projects in fiscal 1966 and 1967. The programs involved $15.7 million in federal funds.

The GAO said that hundreds of high school graduates and some college students had been paid by Detroit projects designed to provide jobs and training for high school dropouts and that some youths whose families did not meet federal low-income criteria had received federal aid. The GAO reported that a local sponsor had paid only half of the required 10% contribution and had used other federal grants to pay part of its share.

According to the GAO, the discrepancies had gone undetected because federal authorities "were performing very little monitoring of . . . activities in Detroit."

(In a letter to the GAO, Labor Secretary W. Willard Wirtz said that his department had "stepped up monitoring activities" over the Detroit Youth Corps programs and that the irregularities cited were being eliminated.)

Gardner on Urban Aid. Urban Coalition Chrmn. John Gardner asserted at the annual National Governors' Conference in Cincinnati July 22, 1967 that "a great deal more" federal spending would be needed to cure the problems of the cities. He called on the governors to lead the country "out of our trance" and to reject "the rhetoric of public men who offer big ideas with small price tags. . .or no price tags at all."

Many of the governors disputed Gardner. In remarks following his address, some insisted that urban problems stemmed from lack of initiative among the poor and encouragement of migration from rural to urban areas. Gov. Charles L. Terry Jr. (D., Del.) told Gardner that "the unrest in my state stems from the hard-core unemployed who won't work." Gov. Lester Maddox (D., Ga.) said the country should "stop talking about spending all this money and start instilling in these people the spirit that made this country great." Gov. Warren Hearnes (D., Mo.) said: "We have jobs in my state, but you have people who won't get on a bus and go 5 miles to work, and they are the ones who are hollering the loudest for welfare." Gov. Spiro T. Agnew (R., Md.), who had not yet been named to the Vice Presidency, said the government should standardize welfare benefits nationally and "stop giving more and more incentives for the rural poor to move to urban areas."

Neighborhood service centers. The approval of $24 million in antipoverty grants for neighborhood service centers in 11 cities was announced Jan. 8, 1968 by Office of Economic Opportunity Director Sargent Shriver and Secretaries W. Willard Wirtz of the Labor Department, Robert C. Weaver of the Department of Housing and Urban Development, and John W. Gardner of the

Department of Health, Education & Welfare. Pres. Johnson had pledged "the establishment—in every ghetto in America—of a neighborhood center to service the people who live there." The experimental project would attempt to coordinate federal, state and local services in the ghettos.

The cities selected were Boston, Chattanooga, Chicago, Cincinnati, Dallas, Detroit, Louisville, Minneapolis, Philadelphia, St. Louis and Washington.

Aid disparity caused migration? The Citizens Budget Commission, a New York research organization, asserted Oct. 13, 1968 that about 10% of U.S. welfare cases had moved since 1959 from rural Southern states with low welfare levels to Northern cities where more relief was available. The commission urged the federal government to set and enforce national welfare standards that would make allowances for local variations in the cost of living. The shift of the poor from the rural South was "a major cause of the urban crisis," the commission said.

Urban data & trends. A special U.S. Census study asserted Feb. 28, 1969 that although most "indicators of well-being" pointed to progress in the cities since 1960, the rate of progress and the impact of such declines as were discovered could lead "to differing interpretations." The study, entitled "Trends in Social & Economic Conditions in Metropolitan Areas," reported on developments in the 212 major U.S. metropolitan areas since 1960. The 67-page study, prepared by Arno I. Winard, of the bureau's Poverty Statistics Section, Population Division, compared data generally derived from a March 1968 survey with data from the 1960 census.

The report said that the number of people living in the major metropolitan areas rose 14% from 1960 to a 128 million total in 1968. Population increased 1% in central city areas and 28% in the suburbs. There was a 5% decline in the number of whites in central cities and a 25% increase in the number of Negroes. In the suburbs Negroes remained at 5% of the population.

In the metropolitan areas of New York, Chicago and Los Angeles, where overall poverty either declined or remained unchanged, the number of poor nonwhite families rose substantially. The median income of blacks living in central cities rose 28% and began to approach that of white residents, but the median earnings of central-city Negro men with year-round jobs had not risen in relation to that of whites in the period 1959–67. The earnings of central-city Negro women with year-round jobs had grown from 59% of white women's earnings in 1959 to 73% in 1967. Median earnings (based on dollars of equivalent purchasing power) of central city residents in 1967 were reported as $5,623 for Negro families (up from $4,397 in 1959), $8,294 for white families (from $7,160), $5,179 for black men and $3,020 for black women. Although unemployment dropped from 5.8% in 1960 to 4.3% in 1968 for central-city residents 16 years old and older, unemployment for youths 16 to 19 years old increased from 11.8% to 16.1%.

The number of central-city Negro families with women as their heads increased from 23% in 1960 to 30% in 1968. The number of white families headed by women rose from 10% to 12% in the same period.

The data on median Negro family income showed that the Northeast was the only area in the U.S. in which Negro family income had declined as a percentage of white income in central cities: It dropped from 69% of white in 1959 to 68% in 1967 (but rose in dollar figures from $4,790 to $5,385). Elsewhere in the country, the median income for Negro families in central cities had grown to a greater percentage of the figure for white families over the same period: It rose in the North Central region from 68% to 75% (from $5,117 to $6,501), in the South from 52% to 62% (from $3,454 to $5,015) and in the West from 65% to 84% (from $5,037 to $7,203).

Labor economist Nicholas Kisburg said March 1 that the relative income improvement in the South, as compared with the Northeast, was already breaking the trend of South-to-North migration of black families. He said the North's welfare policies were "encouraging the Negro to drop out of society" and that there was a tendency in the North to revolt against the "family-centered, work-oriented ethic" accepted by both blacks and whites in the South.

LBJ for private homes. President Johnson said Dec. 14, 1968 that the key to the urban crisis was in low-cost, private home ownership. Speaking at Austin, Tex. ceremonies on the completion of an experimental low-cost home project, the President said that "because we've failed" to develop low-cost housing "we have all of the trouble and disorder in the cities."

(Ex-Sen. Paul H. Douglas [D., Ill.] had predicted in Washington Nov. 10 that the nation would "run into great difficulties" and more riots unless the public lost its hostility to government-subsidized housing for the poor. Speaking as chairman of the National Commission on Urban Problems, Douglas released a commission research report calling for the elimination of much of the red tape required of non-profit sponsors of low-income housing.)

Housing not riot cause?—Inadequate housing could not be blamed for recent urban unrest and riots, the National Commission on Urban Problems concluded in a study issued Dec. 5. The report, written by Dr. Frank S. Kristof of the N.Y. City Housing & Development Administration, asserted that the U.S. had made "steady and unremitting progress" in housing since the Federal Housing Act of 1949 was passed.

Factors Kristof listed among the causes of the urban disorders: (a) the movement of Negroes "from a scattered and inarticulate rural status to a crowded, increasing political and socially conscious force"; (b) the difference in status between Negroes (and other minority-group members) and the great majority of Americans in an affluent society.

Kristof said great improvements were needed in the environment of poor neighborhoods. The improvements included better streets, lighting, draining, play areas, schools, garbage collection and transportation.

Mortgage money promised—Several large banks and life insurance companies announced plans during 1968 to make loans and mortgage funds available for housing and redevelopment projects in minority group neighborhoods and urban slums. The life insurance companies acted in partial fulfillment of a pledge made Sept. 13, 1967 by the nation's major insurance companies to President Johnson that they would invest $1 billion in ghetto real estate. Among the loan and mortgage developments during 1968:

■The Prudential Insurance Co. of America announced Jan. 17 that it was lending $1,874,000 to finance housing for low-income families in Atlantic City, N.J. Some 150 units were to be built under the project, which was to be operated under the federal rent supplement program.

■Franklin Thomas, executive director of the Bedford-Stuyvesant Restoration Corp., announced Apr. 1 that a $100 million pool of mortgage money had been pledged to renovate and rebuild homes in the blighted Brooklyn, N.Y. neighborhood. Among those contributing money to the pool were commercial banks such as Chase Manhattan and First National City, life insurance companies such as Prudential and the Equitable Life Assurance Society, and savings and loan associations such as the N.Y. State Savings Bank Association.

■Boston Mayor Kevin H. White announced May 13 that Boston banks and loan companies had committed themselves to a $50 million loan fund to finance housing rehabilitation and new construction for low-income families.

■Gary, Ind. Mayor Richard G. Hatcher announced May 29 that Equitable Life had pledged to make $1.3 million in loans available to slum residents to rehabilitate ghetto housing.

■The Bank of America announced July 9 that it intended to allocate up to $100 million in mortgage and loan funds to aid construction and rehabilitation efforts in minority group communities in California. Rudolph A. Peterson, president of the world's largest bank, said that the funds would be made available to "areas classified by the Federal Housing Administration as riot prone and blighted."

Ford Foundation funds. The Ford Foundation said Sept. 28, 1968 that it would invest an estimated $10 million portion in ventures aiding the poor and land conservation rather than in investments offering a higher financial return.

Announcing the plan, Ford Foundation President McGeorge Bundy said priority would go to black business development, integrated housing projects and the purchase of land for aesthetic and recreational purposes.

The Ford Foundation announced Dec. 16 the formation of the Center for Community Change to provide assistance to community organizations in low-income areas. The organization, which received a $35 million grant from the foundation, was essentially a merger of 3 existing organizations: The Citizens' Crusade Against Poverty, the Citizens' Advocate Center, and the Social Development Corp. Jack Conway, a former OEO deputy director, was named president of the new group.

Rural Poverty

Johnson's message. In a special message to Congress Jan. 25, 1966, President Johnson proposed a regional planning program to attack "poverty's grip on rural America." The President noted that almost half of the country's poor lived in rural areas. He said that "too few rural communities are able to marshall sufficient physical, human and financial resources to achieve a satisfactory level of social and economic development."

Johnson called for the creation of community development districts comprising adjacent counties and towns and responsible for developing a cooperative program of economic and social development. He said: "Our purpose is to demonstrate how a common effort can provide the needed district vocational school in one county, the hospital in another, the police training in a third, industry or an adequate library in a fourth—and how it can avoid the waste of duplication, or worse still, the total lack of any such facilities or services in a wide area because of a failure to pool common resources."

In his message the President also announced his intention to appoint a commission on rural poverty to submit recommendations "on the most efficient and promising means of sharing America's abundance with those who have too often been her forgotten people."

Commission's report. The President's National Advisory Commission on Rural Poverty asserted in a report released by the White House Dec. 9, 1967 that "rural poverty is so widespread, and so acute, as to be a national disgrace, and its consequences have swept into our cities violently."

The 160-page report, accompanied by a letter of recommendation from Agriculture Secy. Orville Freeman, had been submitted to the White House in September by the 24-member commission, headed by Kentucky Gov. Edward T. Breathitt (D.). The findings were based on a year's study that included public hearings in which 105 witnesses testified. In a "statement of beliefs" prefaced to the report, the commission said its basic assumption was: "The United States today has the economic and technical means to guarantee adequate food, clothing, shelter, health services and education to every citizen of the nation."

The report said that the nearly 14 million persons numbered among the rural poor were victims of widespread hunger, inadequate housing and education (the average level of 9th grade was rarely achieved by poor adults) and unemployment (one of every 5 persons affected was unemployed). "Contrary to a common misconception," the report said, "whites outnumber nonwhites among the rural poor by a wide margin." It reported that "a high proportion of the people crowded into city slums today came there from rural slums. This fact alone makes clear how large a stake the people of this nation have in an attack on rural poverty."

The commission criticized existing rural aid programs. It said: "In general, the rural poor have received far less than their fair share of antipoverty funds." "Rural areas contain 40% of the nation's poor people . . . yet receive less than $\frac{1}{3}$ of OEO funds." The existing programs were simply "relics of an earlier era"; they helped "to create wealthy landlords while largely bypassing the poor," and they "provide fresh incentive for the rural poor to migrate to the central cities. The only solution is a coordinated attack on both urban and rural poverty."

The commission recommended first that the government immediately institute a national policy aimed at giving the rural poor "equality of opportunity with all other citizens" in jobs, medical care, housing, education, welfare and other public services. Secondly, the commission recommended, "as a matter of urgency," full employment for the rural poor. If private enterprise could not provide jobs for all those willing and able to work, the report said, "the commission believes it is the obligation of government to provide it." The commission said that nearly $5 billion would be needed to close the income gap for the rural poor. (It estimated that in 1964 it would have cost $12½ billion [about 2.6% of the personal income of all Americans] to raise all of the nation's poor above the poverty level.)

Among other commission recommendations: (a) A nationwide food stamp program providing free stamps to the "poorest of the poor." (b) Family planning programs. (c) Major reform of the rural education system. (d) Better medical care programs. (e) Better rural housing programs and "special emphasis on a program providing rent supplements for the rural poor." (f) The reform of public assistance programs in order to assure "enough income to provide a decent living." (g) The reorganization of political subdivisions to create multicounty districts.

Problems & Proposals

Welfare profiteering charged. A Massachusetts legislative committee charged Nov. 19, 1968 that Massachusetts doctors, dentists, furniture stores, taxi companies and others were profiteering from the state's welfare system. The 4-month investigation by the Joint Legislative Committee on Public Welfare reportedly found that one dentist grossed $164,000 during 7 months for treating welfare clients and billing the state. One doctor reportedly billed the state $17 for prescribing a deodorant for a client.

The study blamed the situation on "chaotic and irresponsible management" by the State Welfare Department. The state had assumed responsibility for the welfare system from local municipalities July 1, 1967. The report noted that medical assistance payments in Massachusetts had risen from $74,849,290 in all of 1963 to $129,341,214 in Jan.–July 1968.

'Man-in-the-house' rule invalidated. Alabama's "man-in-the-house" rule, withholding federal aid from dependent children whose mothers lived with men to whom they were not married, was voided by the Supreme Court June 17, 1968. Chief Justice Earl Warren, author of the court's decision, wrote that "it is simply inconceivable ... that Alabama is free to discourage immorality and illegitimacy by the device of absolute disqualification of needy children." The court held that the rule should be based on whether or not the man actually supported the children.

The decision was on a case brought by Mrs. Sylvester Smith of Selma, Ala., who had been denied aid for her 4 children on grounds that a man lived in her home on weekends. The man lived permanently with his own wife and 9 children and had assumed no responsibility for the support of Mrs. Smith's children.

The Health, Education & Welfare Department acted June 26 to prevent states from denying welfare payments to children under the "man-in-the-house" rule.

Under the regulation, published in the *Federal Register*, payments could not be cut off from children receiving Aid to Families with Dependent Children (AFDC) payments because their mother was living with a man (a theoretical substitute parent) other than their father. The regulation required that states notify all families rejected or cut off from aid under the abandoned rule during the past 2 years that they might again be eligible for aid.

18 states and the District of Columbia had "man-in-the-house" rules. The states affected by the change were Alabama, Arkansas, Arizona, Florida, Georgia, Indiana, Kentucky, Louisiana, Michigan, Mississippi, Missouri, New Hampshire, New Mexico, North Carolina, Oklahoma, South Carolina, Tennessee, Texas and Virginia.

Agnew on cities & poverty. Spiro T. Agnew, then Vice President-elect, pledged in New Orleans Dec. 9, 1968, before the 45th annual Congress of Cities, that the incoming Nixon Administration would cooperate with the troubled cities.

Discussing the federal government's antipoverty activities, Agnew hinted that more responsibility would be shifted "to state and local governments." He said that participation by the poor themselves in such activities through community-action projects had led to results ranging "from protracted delay at best to extravagant boondoggling at worst." Turning over federal money to the non-governmental community-action groups was "an open invitation to disaster," he warned.

Many of the mayors at the conference indicated a belief that Agnew had given notice that community participation in the poverty program would be ended. Milwaukee Mayor Henry Maier said that "if I had any stock in the Office of Economic Opportunity, I'd sell it." Mayor John H. Burton of Ypsilanti, Mich. said Dec. 10 that he and other Negro delegates felt "discouragement and dismay" at Agnew's "announced plan to limit the influence and control of the poor over programs affecting them." Mayor Jerome P. Cavanagh of Detroit said Dec. 10 that it was arrogant "to assume that the citizen has no ideas to offer the so-called professions."

During the election campaign, Agnew had said before a crowd of Republicans in Jacksonville, Fla. Oct. 7 that a Republican administration would end "waste and boon-doggling" in the antipoverty program. He said the Republicans would cut out entirely the community action programs, which, he charged, had subsidized radicals and revolutionaries, had been used "to build political organizations" and had provided opportunities for embezzlement.

In Indianapolis Oct. 15, Agnew said that the poor and the dissident youths could tell of their symptoms, but "we will make the diagnosis and we, the Establishment, for which I make no apologies for being a part of, will implement the cure." He said that youths and the poor could not take the lead in solving their problems.

Asked in a Pittsburgh news conference Oct. 16 how he could understand the problems of the urban poor without going into the slums, Agnew replied that "you don't learn from people suffering from poverty but from experts who have studied the problem."

In Detroit Oct. 18, Agnew told TV newsmen that he had been to many racial ghettos and, "to some extent, if you've seen one city slum you've seen them all." In Memphis Oct. 23, Agnew acknowledged that he had "some adverse reaction" to his statement about going into slums; he insisted, however, that he was not oblivious to the plight of the poor. In a speech before a Republican audience in St. Joseph, Mo. Nov. 1, Agnew described the proposal of a guaranteed annual wage as "the socialistic dreaming of a few people in high places in this country."

Aid for higher education. The Carnegie Commission on Higher Education, headed by Dr. Clark Kerr, urged Dec. 12, 1968 a federal Civilian Bill of Educational Rights to guarantee higher education to any qualified student regardless of his ability to pay. The proposal emphasized direct scholarships to students (although each college that accepted a federally aided student would receive a "cost-of-education" allowance).

Objecting to the Carnegie proposal, Executive Director Russell I. Thackery of the National Association of State Universities & Land Grant Colleges declared Dec. 13 that the aid should go "directly to the schools which could then pass the benefits on to the students."

Redistributing income. In its final report for the Johnson Administration, the Council of Economic Advisers Jan. 16, 1969 seemed to favor at least a minor redistribution of income as a way of reducing or eliminating poverty.

In what appeared to be an argument for some form of minimum income plan, the council asserted that poverty in the U.S. could be eliminated within six to eight years, without any substantial sacrifice, if "only a relatively small redistribution" of income growth were undertaken. The CEA said: "If the increase in real income for nonpoor [85% of the households receiving 95% of the total income] is lowered merely from 3% to 2½% a year and if that differential of about $2.8 billion annually is effectively transferred to those in poverty, then family incomes for those now poor can grow about 12% annually" and the $9.7 billion poverty gap could be eliminated in less than four years. Practically speaking, the council said that six to eight years was a more realistic goal. The redistribution would not be unfair, the council said, because proportionately "higher taxes are paid by households in the lower income classes than by those with incomes between $6,000 and $15,-

000." The council's report discussed several specific methods of redistributing income—including the negative income tax proposal—and concluded that "a number of good alternatives are available."

The council noted that while minimum wage laws generally protected the lowest-paid employes, "excessively rapid and general increases in the minimum can hurt these workers by curtailing their employment opportunities." The report suggested that Congress seek other ways of helping low-wage workers.

Other conclusions of the CEA report:
■Tax incentives to bring business into the ghettoes would not substantially contribute to the elimination of poverty, since the incentives would not help the small, indigenous ghetto businesses that have small profits.
■Prosperity, rather than government antipoverty programs, had played the main role in bringing 12.5 million persons above the poverty line in the last five years.
■Only 18% of those persons trained under one major federal manpower program had "critical skills" necessary for their employment. Vocational schools were derelict in stressing agriculture and in not stressing health and technical fields that were short of labor.

Programs Evaluated

As the Johnson Administration prepared to leave office and the incoming administration of Richard M. Nixon readied itself to take control, officials involved in the War on Poverty tried to assess its successes and/or failures.

LBJ claims progress. What "matters is not the ultimate judgment that historians will pass" on his Administration, President Johnson said Jan. 13, 1969, "but whether there was a change for the better in the way our people live. I think there was." Mr. Johnson made the remarks at a testimonial dinner in his honor in New York.

Mr. Johnson said: "Black citizens" were "finding their voice in the voting booth." "The old in their illness know the dignity of independence. Young minds have been enriched, and young horizons expanded, because of America's new concern for its schools. By the millions, families who were poor—and men who were idle—have begun to know the dignity of decent incomes and jobs. A larger share of American earth—of its shores and forests—was set aside for all the American people."

GAO findings. The General Accounting Office (GAO) reported March 18, 1969 that it had found in a Congressionally ordered study of the poverty program mismanagement, misdirection, and underachievement but also some degree of success. It recommended continuation of the Office of Economic Opportunity (OEO).

The report recommended continued OEO administration of demonstration and community action programs and "certain other closely related programs." But it proposed that the planning and coordination authority of the OEO over all federal antipoverty efforts be shifted to a new office to be established in the White House. Currently, ten agencies administered antipoverty programs financed by $20 billion in federal funds.

The report, highly critical of the Job Corps, asked whether the corps was "sufficiently achieving the purposes for which it was created to justify its retention at present levels." It said that corps trainees achieved little more than poor youths who had not had corps training. About $1 billion had been spent on the corps.

The report held that the community action program goal of providing a voice for the poor had been achieved "in lesser measure than was reasonable to expect in relation" to the money spent on it.

The report pointed out the limited affect of many antipoverty programs in their target areas: only 1% of the target population was being served by community action centers for families with children under three years of age; migrant day-care programs served about 2% of the children of seasonal farm workers; Upward Bound helped only 4% of needy youth with college potential; the Neighborhood Youth Corps reached only 6% of its target area and Head Start 29% of its pre-school target.

In comments attached to the GAO report, the OEO claimed a share of credit for a decline in the number of people in poverty from 34 million in 1964 to 22 million in 1968. The OEO noted that Job Corps participants "have been for much of their lives 100% dropouts," so "the score of 70% placed in jobs, school or military service would certainly seem a sufficient achievement."

Fewer in poverty. The Social Security Administration said May 21, 1968 that the number of persons living in poverty had fallen from 38,900,000 in 1959 to 29,700,-000 in 1966. According to the agency's index, an average non-farm family of 4 was living in poverty if its annual income was about $3,380 or less. The agency also reported that in 1966 a greater percentage of the poor were persons whose "earning capacity was limited by age, family responsibilities, race discrimination or other factors."

Census Bureau computations indicated that an estimated 26 million individuals were still at the poverty level at the end of 1967.

According to OEO statistics disclosed Aug. 4 the rate at which non-whites were escaping from poverty had almost caught up with the white rate. Between 1959 and 1964 non-whites left poverty at the rate of 3.6% annually while whites left poverty at a 15.2% yearly rate.

By 1967, non-whites were leaving the poverty group at an annual rate of 20.8%, or just short of the white rate of 21.7%.

Acting Director Bertrand M. Harding of the Office of Economic Opportunity reported Aug. 6 that three million Ameri-cans had escaped from poverty during 1967. Harding said that in the three-year period since the passage of the Economic Opportunity Act (Dec. 1964–Dec. 1967), seven million Americans had left poverty status.

Arthur M. Okun, chairman of the President's Council of Economic Advisers, reported to President Johnson Aug. 8, 1968 that half of all U.S. families had annual incomes of more than $8,000 during 1967. The $8,000 figure represented a 6.5% increase from 1966, and a 4% rise allowing for higher prices. Family purchasing power reportedly had grown 3.5 to 4% during each year of the period 1964–7.

* The median income for Negro families, however, was only $4,900. In the South, the Negro's median income was 54% of the white median while in the Northeast, North Central states and the Far West it was 73% of the white median.

Okun said that 600,000 families had shifted out of the poverty category during 1967. (The official definition of poverty varied according to geographic area and size of family. For a Northern family of 4, for example, the poverty line was set at $3,300.) 5.3 million of the country's 49.8 million families remained in the poverty classification. Of the estimated 25.9 million poor people in 1967, Okun reported that one-third were nonwhite and two-fifths were children.

HEW Secretary Wilbur Cohen said Dec. 5 that "we now have shown that the United States can eliminate poverty in the coming decade and ... assure adequate incomes for the overwhelming majority of Americans."

The OEO said in a Jan. 6, 1969 report that about "four million Americans climbed above the poverty line in 1968."

Nixon Administration Starts

Early Plans & Views

Richard M. Nixon took office as President of the United States Jan. 20, 1969. His Administration professed understanding of and sympathy for the plight of the poor, but it held that antipoverty programs should be run much more efficiently than they had been under the Johnson Administration.

Nixon's poverty message. President Nixon told Congress in a special message on poverty Feb. 19, 1969 that the existence of the Office of Economic Opportunity (OEO) should be extended beyond June 30, the statutory date for its authorization and appropriations to expire. But he proposed shifting its Head Start and Job Corps projects to Cabinet departments.

In the transfer of the two projects, to be effected July 1 under current executive authority, the Head Start program, providing pre-school instruction to children from poor families, would be transferred to the Health, Education & Welfare (HEW) Department. The Job Corps program, providing away-from-home training for school dropouts, would be shifted to the Labor Department. Neither program was to be decreased.

Funds for both programs would continue to go through the OEO.

Two smaller OEO programs—the Foster Grandparents Program and Comprehensive Health Centers—also were to be transferred from the OEO to HEW.

Discussing Head Start, the President spoke of "a national commitment to providing all American children an opportunity for healthful and stimulating development during the first five years of life." "The long-term effect of Head Start appears to be extremely weak," he said, and efforts must be focused "much more than heretofore on those few years which may determine how far, throughout his later life, the child can reach." The purpose of the Job Corps transfer was to achieve a more "integrated and coordinated" manpower effort.

For the OEO itself, Mr. Nixon requested a one-year extension (to June 30, 1971). He said: "OEO's greatest value is as an initiating agency—devising new programs to help the poor, and serving as an 'incubator' for these programs during their initial, experimental phases." "One of my aims is to free OEO itself to perform these functions more effectively, by providing for a greater concentration of its energies on its innovative role."

The President said: "We must frankly recognize" the experimental nature of many antipoverty programs "and frankly acknowledge whatever shortcomings they develop. To do so is not to belittle the experiment, but to advance its essential purpose: that of finding new ways, better ways, of making progress in areas still inadequately understood."

Mr. Nixon stressed the value of "the experience of OEO." "We have learned the value of having in the federal government an agency whose special concern is the poor," he said. "We have learned the need for flexibility, responsiveness, . . . continuing innovation . . . [and] management effectiveness."

Reorganization steps—Plans to consolidate some federal operations were announced by President Nixon March 13 and 27.

The first plan was a move to reorganize manpower programs of the Labor Department. A new office—the U.S. Training & Employment Service—was to be established for manpower programs, and regional administrators in eight geographic regions and the District of Columbia were to be given authority to approve and initiate job activities. The new office also would handle job recruitment and placement activities of the U.S. Employment Service, which was to be eliminated.

Under the reorganization plan of March 27, the President consolidated regional operations of these five federal agencies: the Departments of Labor, Health, Education & Welfare and Housing & Urban Development, the Office of Economic Opportunity and the Small Business Administration. They were to adopt uniform regional boundaries and headquarters locations. The latter would be in Boston, New York, Philadelphia, Atlanta, Chicago, Dallas-Fort Worth, Denver and San Francisco. After a 12–18 month consolidation period, regional councils were to be established in each of the eight areas. The various agencies would be represented on the councils to facilitate cooperation "in defining problems, devising strategies to meet them, eliminating friction and duplications and evaluating results."

A major cutback in the Job Corps program was announced by the Administration April 11. It called for the closing of 59 of the 113 existing camps and the opening of 30 new "inner-city" and "near-city" centers. Labor Secretary George P. Shultz said the revision would reduce the corps'

training capacity from 35,000 needy youths at a time to 22,000. The reorganization, which involved a shift of the Job Corps from the OEO to the Labor Department, entailed a $100 million reduction in the fiscal 1970 budget. The cost of training an enrollee was expected to be cut from the current $8,000 to $5,250. The camps to be closed by July 1 were two (Parks in California and Camp Kilmer in New Jersey) of the six men's centers, seven of 18 women's centers and 50 of 82 rural conservation centers.

The Labor Department report to President Nixon on the revision, circulated the weekend of April 12–13, recommended minimizing "the identity of the Job Corps as a distinct, separate program. Instead, it should be thought of as part of a comprehensive manpower system and identified as residential manpower centers."

Of the new centers proposed, 10 were to be "near-city" residential centers, where corps members would be permitted to commute home on weekends. Twenty would be "inner-city" ones to train local youths for local jobs. Five of the latter would provide training and residential support, the remainder only residential support for "those who need it" and those taking other area manpower-training programs.

The plans came under immediate attack by Congress members and many antipoverty-program officials. A telegram of protest was sent to the White House April 10 (details of the move were known in advance of the announcement) from 15 senators and 11 representatives. Among the signers were Chairman Carl D. Perkins (D, Ky.) of the House Education & Labor Committee, and Chairman Ralph W. Yarborough (D, Tex.) of the Senate Labor & Public Welfare Committee. Their committees handled antipoverty legislation.

The wire stressed the hope that the decision on closing Job Corps camps would be delayed until Congress had an opportunity to cooperate with the Administration "in improving these programs in the light of the experience of the past four years."

Other signers were Sens. Edward M. Kennedy (D, Mass.), Edmund S. Muskie (D, Me.), Fred R. Harris (D, Okla.) and

Edward W. Brooke (R, Mass.). The latter was one of three Republican signers. The other two: Reps. Alvin E. O'Konski (Wis.) and Hastings Keith (Mass.).

Welfare minimum. Support for a national minimum standard for welfare payments was expressed Feb. 2, 1969 by HEW Secretary Robert H. Finch. Interviewed on the NBC-TV "Meet the Press" program, Finch said: "I think you are going to come down the road to a federal floor of some kind [for welfare payments]." "We have to relate to the enormous disparity between the states; something like an $8 contribution in Mississippi and $80 in New York. This has an enormous effect, obviously, on the flow of people, what motivates them to go from one place to another, and it is up to the federal government to rationalize these differences." He was "not sure" that a guaranteed minimum income would be the solution.

Pilot slum project. The Administration Feb. 26, 1969 unveiled an improvement project for the Watts section of Los Angeles. It indicated a hope that the idea would be used in other blighted urban areas. The project featured (a) self-help —a group of Negro and white businessmen forming an Economic Resources Corp. in Watts and buying 45 acres of junkyard land for an industrial park; (b) initiative and help from the private sector—the Lockheed Aircraft Co. leased a $2 million plant for manufacturing aircraft parts in the park; (c) federal assistance—the Economic Development Administration provided $3.8 million in loans and grants for the project, and the Office of Economic Opportunity provided $3.8 million in grants.

There also were plans for other federal assistance in Watts—Small Business Administration loans to businessmen, Labor Department training programs and a Housing & Urban Development model-cities project.

The Lockheed plant was expected to employ 300 persons by 1972. The entire industrial park was designed to provide jobs for 2,400 poverty-area residents.

In announcing the project as "a new approach" to urban development, Commerce Secretary Maurice H. Stans said that President Nixon and he had "a deep enthusiasm for this project and for the concept it represents." "I hope other communities will take a hard look at this formula," he said. "It is not the federal assistance programs that we feel assure the success of this project, so much as it is the initiative and the faith of the private sector in the ultimate benefit of this undertaking."

The project had been initiated during the Johnson Administration.

Private effort. President Nixon lauded the National Alliance of Businessmen March 15, 1969 for its work in finding jobs for the hard-core unemployed. In a brief talk at the second annual meeting of the alliance, a non-partisan group organized during the Johnson Administration, Mr. Nixon told the group that its program had "the complete, unqualified support of this Administration." He suggested that the alliance focus especially on the problem of finding jobs for youths and, if possible, that it extend its program to smaller towns and cities.

The alliance's outgoing chairman, Henry Ford 2d, chairman of the Ford Motor Co., reported that 145,000 persons had been hired under the alliance program and that 87,850 of them were still on the job. Of the latter, 73% were black, 17% white, 8% "Spanish-surnamed," 1% Indian and 1% Oriental. The alliance was working toward an expanded goal of 614,000 job placements in 125 major metropolitan areas by June 30, 1971. Its original goal had been to find 500,000 jobs in 50 cities by that date.

Mr. Nixon agreed that welfare was necessary for the helpless, but he held that when welfare continues and escalates, it "tends to destroy those who receive it and corrupt those who dispense it." He contrasted this with the "dignity" that "comes" from employment.

Vice President Spiro T. Agnew stressed March 21 that businessmen must provide more than money to help black, Mexican-American and other minority businessmen get on a sound business footing. He said corporation leaders must provide "collateral assistance," such as help in public relations, advertising and promotion. Agnew made the appeal in a speech in Washington March 21 before Plans for Progress, a seven-year-old business organization promoting equal employment opportunities.

The importance of the antipoverty effort from the private sector of the economy also was emphasized by Agnew and other cabinet members and officials in a closed-circuit telecast March 26 to an audience of about 20,000 businessmen in 27 cities. Daniel Patrick Moynihan, head of the President's Urban Affairs Council, said there was a growing feeling that "national government is not very good at delivering services" and that the private organizations could do the job better.

The Olin Mathieson Chemical Corp. announced April 8 that it would make large deposits in Negro-controlled banks for use as poverty-area business loans. The deposits would be from payroll withholding tax payments, about $600,000, for a few days' use each month, and from working capital, $400,000, in one-year time deposits. The latter would be paid lower interest rates than obtainable elsewhere.

In similar projects in 1968, the Chrysler Corp. had agreed with the Southern Christian Leadership Conference to put $100,000 of excise taxes each month in an Atlanta bank, and the Episcopal Church agreed to invest $1 million of reserve funds in slum banks, savings and loan associations and small business investment companies.

Labor Secretary George P. Shultz announced July 17 that more than 3,000 of the nation's hard core unemployed would be trained in construction and building skills under the Job Opportunities in the Business Sector (JOBS) program. The program was initiated in May 1968 by the Department of Labor and the National Alliance of Businessmen to find employment for the hard-core jobless in the nation's 125 largest cities.

The plan announced by Shultz was the result of agreements between the Labor Department and 325 building and construction contractors in 26 cities. The government had alloted about $10 million to enable the jobless to learn any of 18 separate construction trades.

Tax proposals. President Nixon April 21, 1969 sent Congress a message proposing a variety of tax changes. A major reform would excempt "persons or families in poverty" from paying the federal income tax.

Nixon said that "the gradual increase in federal revenues resulting" from other proposals and "the growth of the economy will ... facilitate a start during fiscal 1971 in funding ... tax credits to encourage investment in poverty areas and hiring and training of the hard-core unemployed."

Mr. Nixon's "low-income allowance" proposal was expected to apply to more than two million families. The poverty line, below which income would not be taxable, would be $1,700 for a single person, $2,300 for a married couple with no children and $3,500 for a family of four.

Housing plan. Housing & Urban Development Secretary George Romney May 8, 1969 announced a new plan to build low-cost housing for the poor by mass-production methods. Romney said that at the current rate of construction, "we will fall more than 10 million units short of our housing needs."

Romney's plan—Operation Breakthrough— was: (a) to blend the public (federal, state and local) and private (management and labor) effort to identify and focus on a massive market within a community area; (b) to achieve volume production by using more prefabrication of components and less on-site construction.

The plan would be initiated with an inventory of sites and sponsors. The sponsors would then commit themselves to projects using common specifications, materials, methods and building codes. Prototypes would be built in about eight regions. These would be evaluated and a prototype selected for mass production. Romney anticipated volume production under his plan within two years.

Seeking to promote the vital cooperation of all sectors in his plan, Romney met May 7 with nine trade-union presidents, May 8 with 14 governors and 17 mayors and May 9 with building industry leaders.

One of Romney's ideas in the labor area was "some form of sweat equity," permitting a homeowner to make part payment by contributing his own labor.

Health care crisis seen. President Nixon warned July 10, 1969 that the nation faced a "massive crisis" in health care. At a White House news conference called to present a Health, Education and Welfare Department health program, the President gave his "unqualified support" to a series of HEW measures designed to prevent what Mr. Nixon warned would become a breakdown in health care services.

HEW Secretary Robert H. Finch and Roger O. Egeberg, assistant secretary-designate, presented an eight-page report outlining a series of steps planned or already instituted by the department to curb inflated medical costs and to distribute resources more effectively in the nation's medical system.

The report sharply criticized the federal-state Medicaid program covering health costs for the poor as "badly conceived and organized" and warned that a four-fold increase in the program's cost could be expected by 1975. It announced a new Task Force on Medicaid to be headed by HEW Undersecretary John G. Veneman and Blue Cross Associations President Walter J. McNerney. The task force was to plan measures to halt spiraling costs and develop long-range goals for Medicaid.

Hunger & Food Aid

Hunger probed, food stamps given free. Disclosures of chronic poverty, hunger and disease in the U.S. spurred the Administration to begin March 2, 1969 a pilot program of free distribution of food stamps. The disclosures had been made in hearings of the Senate Select Committee on Nutrition and Human Needs Jan. 8–Feb. 20.

The pilot program, the first free distribution of food stamps, was aimed at families with incomes of less than $30 a month in Beaufort and Jasper Counties in South Carolina. Agriculture Secretary Clifford M. Hardin announced the program Feb. 21 after a meeting Feb. 20 with the Senate Nutrition Committee

chairman, George McGovern (D, S.D.), and South Carolina Sen. Ernest F. Hollings (D). Hollings had testified Feb. 18 to the existence of "substantial hunger" in poverty areas of his state he had visited on a recent tour.

Hardin based the free distribution of stamps on a 1969 appropriation bill provision authorizing expenditures of up to $45 million of agricultural customs receipts for "child feeding programs" and for "additional direct distribution or other programs . . . to provide . . . an adequate diet to other needy children and low-income persons determined by the secretary of agriculture to be suffering . . . from general and continued hunger resulting from insufficient food."

The Food Stamp Act itself required that families be charged an amount "equivalent to their normal expenditures for food."

The pilot program, endorsed by South Carolina Gov. Robert E. McNair (D) Feb. 20, was marred by sparse participation at its launching March 2 when a welfare rights group boycotted it on the ground too few people were qualified, because of the unusually low income limitation, to receive the free stamps. Under the existing program, the poorest families had to pay 50¢ per person per month, up to a maximum payment of $3, for stamps redeemable at a food store (for $58 worth of food for a family of four).

McGovern said March 4 that the pilot program was "far from adequate"—that only 203 families in the specified areas were eligible while more than 1,700 families with incomes of less than $100 a month still had to pay 30% to 50% of their income for stamps. He urged free food-stamp distribution to all seven million Americans with annual incomes under $1,000, extension of the emergency pilot program to other needy areas and reduction of the cost of food stamps so no one paid more than the average American's expenditure for food—17% of family income.

Among highlights of the testimony before the McGovern committee:

Jan. 8—Then-Agriculture Secretary Orville L. Freeman recommended extension of the food-stamp program to all areas of the country. To eliminate hunger in the U.S., he said, it would be necessary for Congress to provide funds ($1 billion more than the $1.1 billion currently being spent) and for local governments to cooperate in the effort.

Jan. 9—Three officials of the Office of Economic Opportunity—Dr. Thomas E. Bryant, Dr. Gary D. London and Gerald Sparer—testified that emergency federal food programs were not sufficiently effective because of inadequate staffing of local welfare offices, inaccessible food distribution centers and insufficient income for the purchase of food stamps.

Jan. 10—Wilbur J. Cohen, then secretary of health, education and welfare (HEW), urged formulation of a national policy on nutrition, coordination of "fragmented" federal efforts and the transfer of food programs for the poor from the Agriculture Department to HEW.

Jan. 22—Dr. Arnold E. Schaefer of the Public Health Service reported the initial findings of a National Nutrition Survey authorized in 1967. These findings were based on examination of 12,000 persons in low-income areas of Texas, Louisiana, Kentucky and New York (80% of those covered had annual incomes under $5,000; 50% had incomes under $3,000).

Schaefer reported an "alarming prevalence" of diseases commonly associated with undernourishment, among them endemic goiter and rickets (18 cases) although these diseases were thought to have been eradicated in the U.S. 30 years ago. Marasmus (caloric deficiency) and Kwashiorkor (severe protein and multiple nutrient deficiency) were discovered (7 cases) although, Schaefer said, "we did not expect to find such cases in the United States. . . . In many of the developing countries . . . these severe cases of malnutrition only rarely are found; they either are hospitalized or have died."

Some of the other findings: One-third of the children under six years of age had anemia (15% of the entire grouping studied were anemic); 13% of the group were in a "high risk" category of vitamin A deficiency; vitamin C intake was "less than acceptable" in 12% to 16% of the group; $3\frac{1}{2}$% of the children one to three years old had retarded bone growth, and sufficient evidence was indicated to suggest such a condition was accompanied by retardation of brain growth; 18% of those 10 years of age and over reported it was "difficult and painful" to bite or chew food, 96% of the group averaged 10 teeth either decayed, filled or missing; the nutritional level of those examined was as low as found in similar surveys in Central America.

Among other data of the initial survey: 55% of those in the grouping were Negro; 25% were Spanish-Americans; 50% of the males had not worked full time in the month and year preceding their exam.

McGovern said he was "shocked" at the findings. "Serious malnutrition is inexcusable in a country as rich as the United States," he said.

Jan. 23—Dr. Walter G. Unglaub of Tulane University reported that 3,000 Louisiana children in a Head Start project had been found to show signs of serious malnutrition. 40% were anemic and many had evidence of "hidden hunger" —"irritability, apathy and loss of physical and mental efficiency."

Jan. 28—Nutrition experts—Prof. D. Mark Hegsted of Harvard University, Dr. Charles U. Lowe of the National Institute of Child Health & Human Development and Dr. David B. Coursin of St. Joseph Hospital Research Institute, Lancaster, Pa.—testified that malnutrition of pregnant women resulted in a high mortality rate for their children and retarded brain growth for those infants who survived.

Feb. 18—Sen. Hollings reported that on a recent tour of South Carolina slums and rural poverty areas he had discovered "substantial hunger" and "bottlenecks" in the federal food-aid programs. He said that free food stamps should be distributed where necessary and a national goal established to eliminate hunger.

Hollings conceded that "the quickest way to kill me off [politically] is to ask me to come to Washington and make a dramatic statement like this." While he had until now supported "the public policy of covering up the problem of hunger" in the interest of attracting new industry to South Carolina, he said "what I am talking about here to this committee is downright hunger. The people I saw couldn't possibly work."

Feb. 19—Nutrition experts Drs. E. John Lease and Felix H. Lauter of the

University of South Carolina reported finding that 98 of 177 children examined in Beaufort County were infested with intestinal worms which could grow to a foot in length, and had showed signs of severe malnutrition.

Dr. James P. Carter of Vanderbilt University said that more than 40% of the children he had examined in a personal survey were "seriously malnourished." He said the solution to the problem required "more than just food supplementation" but provision of adequate housing, water, sanitary systems, job training and community and regional health projects.

Feb. 20—Testimony was heard from South Carolina witnesses that a "significant number" of people eligible for food stamps were unaware of their eligibility, that many eligible persons could not afford the stamps and that only 15% of the eligible in Beaufort County were actually participating in the food-stamp program.

Second food program—After the pilot free food-stamp program was started in Beaufort and Jasper Counties, S.C., a delegation of about 40 poor people from Beaufort County traveled to Washington March 6 to protest that it was only a "token effort" and not reaching enough of the needy. A "food-by-prescription" program, sponsored by the Agriculture Department and the U.S. Children's Bureau and supported by state officials, was begun March 10 in the two counties. Under it, federal commodities with high nutrient content were to be distributed free to needy expectant mothers, new mothers and children found to be in need of supplemental food. Certificates to obtain the food—good for three-month intervals—could be obtained at county health clinics.

More food to needy urged. Sen. George S. McGovern March 22, 1969 urged a fourfold increase in the nationwide food-stamp program to a $1½ billion annual level. He said "the poorest of the poor" should be given free food stamps. McGovern contrasted the expenditures with the Administration's proposal for beginning an anti-missile defense system. "Our President wants to lavish $7 bil-

lion to protect two missile systems with dubious military hardware," he said. "We can purchase with half that an end to hunger in America."

An expansion of federal programs to eliminate hunger and malnutrition in the U.S. was urged by John A. Schnittker, former agriculture undersecretary in the Johnson Administration, in testimony March 27 before McGovern's Select Senate Committee on Nutrition & Human Needs. Schnittker suggested federal outlays of $3 billion for the food-aid programs; $1½ billion of the total would go into the food-stamp program and the remainder into the school breakfast and lunch programs, surplus food distribution and similar activities. He also suggested transferring the federal food-distribution programs from the Agriculture Department to the Health, Education & Welfare (HEW) Department.

Schnittker's overall formula: "We should replace commodities with food stamps, adjust the family contribution in buying food stamps to the real ability of the family head to pay, including free food stamps where appropriate, provide enough purchasing power to all income groups to assure a good diet and remove the local and state government veto on the food-stamp program." "Integrated administration of food and welfare programs may help speed the time when this country takes the next step—beyond food programs—to adequate welfare programs geared to minimum national standards of living, and consistent with what this country could afford many years ago from a budget standpoint."

Proposals of free food stamps had been opposed by Sen. Spessard L. Holland (D, Fla.) March 24 as "a general welfare program" although the original purpose of food stamps was disposal of surplus farm products.

Holland stated his opposition after McGovern reported on his committee's tour March 10-11 of poverty areas in Florida's Collier and Lee Counties, where, McGovern said, there were 22,-000 migrant workers and 4,000–5,000 destitute families. Holland disputed the figure. Only 30,000 people lived in Collier County, he said, and at least half of them lived in Naples, Fla. and were not destitute. As for migrants, the state and federal employment services put the total at no more than 2,000 during the height of the harvest season, he said.

At the time of the McGovern tour, none of Florida's counties participated in the food-stamp program; some did participate in the Agriculture Department's commodities or "surplus" food program under which free packages of basic food items were provided for the counties to distribute. County officials had opposed free food distribution on grounds that: (a) it was too expensive; (b) it might tempt migrants to remain permanently, and (c) the poor might refuse to work if they were fed free.

During the tour, McGovern described conditions of hunger and poverty as "simply shocking" and local administration of programs to help the poor as intolerable. Sickness due to malnutrition was found to be prevalent. McGovern was accompanied on the tour by Sens. Jacob K. Javits (R, N.Y.), Allen J. Ellender (D, La.) and Marlow W. Cook (R, Ky.). McGovern said March 11 that "We have seen dirt and living conditions these past two days that one might expect to see in Asia, not America. Most of the cattle and hogs in America are better fed and sheltered than the families we have visited."

McGovern defended his hunger probe March 16 against a charge March 15 by Herbert G. Klein, President Nixon's communications director, that the problem of hunger would not be solved "by traipsing around the country with television cameras." "Hunger knows no politics," McGovern said. "Mr. Klein seems to be aligning himself with those few of Florida's state and local officials who refuse to face up to the problem of hunger and who react defensively to the fact that our committee has turned the public spotlight on an outrageous situation—the existence of hunger in the world's richest nation."

McGovern's committee continued its hunger inquiry with hearings in Washington, D.C. April 15–16 and in California May 8–9. In Washington, committee members visited a slum area in which they were told of rats, hunger and despair about 15 blocks from the White House. In East Los Angeles May 8, they were told that Mexican-American children were sent to school without breakfast and lunch because of lack of money. In San Francisco May 9 they were told that the U.S. Agriculture Department had refused to comply with a federal court order to initiate a commodity distribution program in 16 counties where extreme hunger existed. Since the court order in December 1968, all but three of the counties had adopted food programs voluntarily. But Jesse M. Unruh, Democratic leader and former speaker of the State Assembly, testified that he had "not seen any activity by the federal government bureaucracy in this area."

McGovern had introduced in the Senate April 29 a bill calling for a food-stamp program at an annual level of $1.8 billion, or more than five times the size of the current program. The bill was supported by 31 co-sponsors, including two Republicans—Sens. Theodore F. Stevens (Alaska) and Mark O. Hatfield (Ore.). While he was encouraged by the President's expressed commitment to domestic priorities, McGovern said, he felt that the Administration's budget revisions gave "only the barest nod to the hungry."

Other probes. Among developments in other hunger, malnutrition and health inquiries:

■The House Education & Labor Committee April 14 heard testimony that two million American schoolchildren who needed free or less expensive lunches were not getting them. The testimony was presented by Luther Elliott Jr. of the Social Development Corp. of Washington, which had just completed an inquiry into the Office of Economic Opportunity's emergency food and medical programs in 385 counties throughout the country.

■Dr. Arnold B. Schaefer of the Public Health Service told a House Agriculture Committee April 25 that the poor especially were victimized by food industry reductions in the past 10–20 years in the enrichment of flour, milk and salt. Although the cost of adding certain essential nutrients to these products was negligible, he said, food dealers in some parts of the country charged "several pennies more" for enriched products, and the poor therefore bought the non-enriched version instead. Shaefer said that a malnutrition study he was conducting had found that, as a result of this discontinuance of enrichment, there had been a comeback in poor neighborhoods of various deficiency diseases (rickets in children due to lack of Vitamin D in milk, goiter due to lack of iodine in salt) that "we thought . . . had been eradicated" decades ago.

■The chairman of the Senate Labor & Public Welfare Committee, Sen. Ralph W. Yarborough (D, Tex.), called in a speech in New York May 8 for "a national commitment for improved health care." He said that hunger in the U.S. could be ended within a year at an additional food-aid cost of $2 billion annually but that malnutrition was a more difficult problem. Among his remarks: "The average Mexican-American lives 10 years shorter than the average Anglo-American. And that's not genetic. It's the lack of food." "One doctor testified before our committee that more money was spent conserving migratory birds than is spent on health care of migratory workers."

Nixon program. President Nixon proposed in a message to Congress May 6, 1969 an expanded drive against "hunger and malnutrition . . . in America." The President suggested increasing the federal food relief program by $270 million in fiscal 1970 and eventually by $1 billion a year to a $2½ billion annual level. He called for a major expansion of the food-stamp program. The fiscal 1970 addition in food-aid funds was to come from a "reprograming" of the budget and was not proposed as an increase in overall federal expenditures. (The $1½ billion budget proposal before Congress included $340 million for food stamps.)

Mr. Nixon proposed that everyone participating in the food-stamp program be allotted enough stamps to provide a nutritionally adequate diet and that no one participating spend more than 30% of his income to buy the stamps. "Those in the very lowest income brackets" would receive free stamps. The stamp program was to be incorporated eventually into a revised welfare system to be outlined in a later message.

The President asked Congress to au-

thorize a special program of vouchers for infant formulas and other "highly nutritious special foods" to prevent "serious malnutrition during pregnancy and infancy."

A White House Conference on Food & Nutrition also was to be convened to seek improvements in the private market and federal programs. Participants would be executives from food-processing and distribution companies and trade union officials.

The Administration also was considering the establishment of a new agency—a Food & Nutrition Service—to administer the many separate federal food programs.

In discussing the President's proposals before the Senate Select Committee on Nutrition & Human Needs, Administration officials May 7 disclosed that a principal feature of the welfare reforms would be "cash assistance." Health, Education & Welfare Secretary Robert H. Finch told the Senators that cash income "best preserves the dignity and freedom of choice of the individual to meet his own needs through the workings of the private market." He said that an "income-maintenance" system should eventually replace the food-stamp and other welfare programs.

Agriculture Secretary Clifford M. Hardin testified that the welfare proposals also included a minimum national standard for welfare payments (a probable level of $30 a month a person was projected) and an improved work incentive program.

Committee chairman George S. McGovern (D, S.D.) praised the President's food-aid proposals but said he considered the proposed outlays "probably less than a third of what is needed." Committee member Walter F. Mondale (D, Minn.) said Congress "keeps authorizing dreams and appropriating peanuts."

Hunger needs estimated. A report Aug. 7, 1969 by the Senate Select Committee on Nutrition and Human Needs estimated that an additional $4 billion a year would be needed to close the nation's "hunger gap." Sen. George S. McGovern (D, S.D.), chairman of the committee, said: "We have a long, long way to go before we succeed in eliminating hunger in America." Federal funding of food assistance programs was $671.9 million in fiscal 1968, and $1.3 billion had been budgeted for fiscal 1969. But the committee report, based on six months of investigation, warned that $5.2 billion a year would be needed to eliminate hunger.

The committee estimated that about $10 billion a year would be needed to meet all the basic necessities of the nation's estimated 25 million poor. However, the report contended that since there was little prospect in the near future of allocating enough to close the poverty gap, "we must instead . . . establish a first line of defense against poverty-related hunger by filling the immediate food needs of the poor."

Hunger emergency call urged. The White House Conference on Food, Nutrition & Health voted by acclamation Dec. 4, 1969 to ask the government to declare a national hunger emergency. Some 3,000 delegates recommended four other priority measures at the end of the three-day conference including establishment of an annual guaranteed income of at least $5,500 for a family of four.

On the opening day of the conference Dec. 2, President Nixon said the event "sets the seal of urgency on our national commitment to put an end to hunger and malnutrition due to poverty in America." But although the President said "I claim the responsibility" for putting an end to hunger in the nation, many conference delegates demanded that the Administration take immediate, specific actions to alleviate the hunger problem.

Mr. Nixon promised to follow up the hunger conference, and any future White House conference, with a second meeting a year later to re-examine conference findings and to measure what had been done to implement recommendations. The President also asked support for Administration proposals for a family assistance program, reform and expansion of the food stamp program and the establishment of a Commission on Population Growth & the American Future. Nixon said that "these three measures would virtually eliminate the problem of poverty as a cause of malnutrition."

Dr. Jean Mayer, organizer of the conference, defended the President against critics who contended that the Presidential speech was vague and lacked substance. "If [Mr. Nixon] had announced specific things today," Mayer said, "he would have been criticized for setting up the conference as a cut-and-dried, set-up forum."

Emergency measures on hunger and a guaranteed annual income of $5,500 were urged jointly by a number of groups at the meeting including La Raza (a caucus of Spanish speaking delegates), the Southern Christian Leadership Conference and the National Welfare Rights Organization. A "crisis" approach to the hunger problem was also reflected in several reports of eight special committees established to review conference draft proposals prepared by 26 study panels.

Mayer, who backed the demand for emergency action against hunger, reportedly urged the President to announce some dramatic action on the hunger problem before the conference ended. Through Mayer, Mr. Nixon announced Dec. 4 that within six months food stamp programs would be put into the 307 counties in the U.S. that had no federal food programs. The President also pledged that previously announced steps would be speeded up to grant $106 a month in food stamps to families of four in the program.

Other priority measures urged by the conference included enlargement of the existing federal food-stamp program, free lunches and breakfasts for all school children and operation of food programs by local organizations under federal supervision.

Conference delegates who met with President Nixon Dec. 5 said Mr. Nixon promised to take urgent executive action to alleviate hunger but would not declare a national emergency. The President said at a Dec. 8 news conference: "I unfortunately cannot give really sympathetic consideration" to the proposal for a $5,500 guaranteed income. He claimed that the proposal would cost "approximately $70 to $80 billion in taxes" or in "increased prices. I do not say that to discredit the conference." When asked about the conference's food stamp and free lunch proposals, the President said: "I favor the approach that our Administration had put before the Congress as being the more responsible approach on both scores."

Hunger reforms. Agriculture Secretary Clifford Hardin announced two major reforms in the food stamp program Dec. 18, 1969. Hardin said the changes would guarantee that a family of four would receive $106 worth of food stamps a month, enough to pay for what the Agriculture Department determined to be a minimum "economy diet." Hardin also said the department was reducing the amount a poor family would have to pay for stamps to no more than 25% of the family's monthly income in most cases.

Dr. Jean Mayer, President Nixon's special consultant on hunger problems, announced Dec. 24 a Nixon Administration plan to provide hot school lunches to 6.6 million needy children by the end of 1970. Under the plan, the Agriculture Department would revise requirements that prevented schools from hiring private food management companies to provide free lunches and would allow schools to employ the same companies that supplied food in colleges, airliners and factories.

'Widespread malnutrition.' Dr. Arnold Shaefer, director of the National Nutrition Survey, told the Senate Committee on Nutrition and Human Needs April 27, 1970 that a federal survey conducted in Texas and Louisiana had found "widespread malnutrition." In testimony updating preliminary findings reported to the committee in January 1969, Shaefer said: "There is no longer any doubt that the incidence of malnutrition is related to poverty income levels."

Shaefer said data on 13,373 persons examined in the two states confirmed preliminary findings of serious malnutrition and also showed evidence of widespread growth retardation, anemia and dental decay. He reported finding two or more nutritional deficiencies in 48.5% of children aged one to nine; 39.5% aged 10 to 12; and 54.5% aged 13 to 16.

School lunch measure passed. Congress completed action May 4, 1970 on a bill to provide free or reduced-price school lunches to an estimated eight million needy school children. President Nixon May 14 signed the bill, which had been approved by a Senate-House conference committee April 27.

The legislation made it mandatory for schools to provide free or reduced-rate lunches for all children whose families fell under the poverty level, currently $3,600 a year for a family of four. Although a school lunch program operated under previous legislation, no more than four million children received subsidized lunches. The conference report, passed by the Senate April 30 and by the House May 4, adopted the House provision of subsidized lunches for children whose families fell under the poverty level rather than the Senate version, which set the standard at $4,000 or less a year.

The report accepted the Senate provision for $25 million to be spent on a pilot school breakfast program in fiscal 1971 but eliminated authorizations for the program in fiscal '72 and '73. The bill, in its final form, retained the Senate's 20-cent limit for the maximum price of a reduced-rate meal and a House provision requiring states to use tax revenues for their share of funds to match federal contributions. The bill also established a National Advisory Council on Child Nutrition.

Food stamp plan extended. The Senate Dec. 31, 1970 passed a compromise bill continuing the food stamp program for three years but barring such assistance to any family in which an able-bodied adult refused to work.

A $1.75 billion expenditure for fiscal 1971 was authorized. The bill with its work requirement was approved by the House Dec. 16 by a 290-68 vote in contrast to a more liberal version approved in 1969 by the Senate. A deadlock developed in the Senate-House conference, but a compromise was worked out to retain the "must work" provision but free the states from sharing the cost of the program. The House approved the compromise bill Dec. 30, the Senate Dec. 31. Sen. George S. McGovern (D, S.D.) threatened to filibuster the bill with its must-work provision but dropped his opposition in the interest of getting the food-stamp program renewed before it expired in January 1971.

President Nixon signed the measure Jan. 11, 1971.

Revisions Planned

Welfare overhaul urged. President Nixon Aug. 8, 1969 urged a full overhaul of the nation's welfare system that would set a federal minimum standard of aid for every family with children. The President, addressing a nationwide television audience, described his welfare program as "a new federalism in which power, funds and responsiblity will flow from Washington to the states and to the people." The new program, which would guarantee a federal payment of $1,600 a year to each family of four on welfare rolls, also provided for revamping job training programs and for sharing of federal taxes to ease the financial burden of the states and cities.

The President proposed that his new welfare plan begin in fiscal 1971 at a starting cost of $4 billion a year. Federal revenue sharing would begin midway through fiscal 1971 and would cost $1 billion annually. Administration officials said the plan could increase the number of persons on welfare rolls from 10 million to 22.4 million.

Mr. Nixon asked for a new "family assistance system" to replace the present welfare program's system of aid to families with dependent children. He said the present system "has to be judged a colossal failure" and provided "grossly unequal" benefits, with aid for a family of four ranging from an average of $263 a month (New Jersey) to $39 a month (Mississippi). (Under the new plan, the $1,600 annual federal payment to a family of four could be supplemented by the states.)   •

Mr. Nixon declared: "Our states and cities find themselves sinking in a welfare quagmire, as caseloads increase, as costs escalate, and as the welfare system stagnates enterprise and perpetuates dependency. What began on a small scale in the depression 'thirties has become a monster in the prosperous 'sixties. The tragedy is not only that it is bring-

ing states and cities to the brink of financial disaster, but also that it is failing to meet the elementary human, social and financial needs of the poor. It breaks up homes. It often penalizes work. It robs recipients of dignity. And it grows."

Mr. Nixon argued that the old system created "an incentive for desertion" by denying payments in many states to families where a father was present. He said the effect of the old system was to "draw people off payrolls and onto welfare rolls" since it was often possible for a man to receive more money on welfare than in a low-paying job. Under the new system, a worker could keep the first $60 of outside earnings without reduction in benefits. Mr. Nixon insisted his plan was not a "guaranteed income" since a father, or mother with school-aged children, would have to accept work or job training to receive benefits unless disabled. He said mothers of pre-school children could also accept jobs under the new system because the proposal included a major expansion of day-care centers for children.

He asserted: "This national floor under incomes for working or dependent families is not a 'guaranteed income.' Under the guaranteed income proposal, everyone would be assured a minimum income, regardless of how much he was capable of earning, regardless of what his need was, regardless of whether or not he was willing to work.

"During the Presidential campaign last year I opposed such a plan. I oppose it now, and will continue to oppose it. A guaranteed income would undermine the incentive to work; the family assistance plan increases the incentive to work. A guaranteed income establishes a right without responsibilities; family assistance recognizes a need and establishes a responsibility. It provides help to those in need, and in turn requires that those who receive help work to the extent of their capabilities. There is no reason why one person should be taxed so that another can choose to live idly."

The President said aid to the aged, blind and disabled would be continued, but he called for national minimums. He said the food stamp program, to be discontinued for those in the new family assistance system, would be retained to aid needy persons without children. Mr. Nixon proposed that the Social Security Administration administer directly the family assistance program. He said the plan would reduce state and local welfare costs by 10% to 50%. No family's present level of aid would be lowered, he asserted.

The President presented details of the family assistance proposal to Congress Aug. 11.

As part of his plan for a "new federalism," the President asked that much of the authority for administering federal job training programs be transferred to state and local governments. He also called for a computerized job bank to match job seekers with vacancies, for persons on welfare to be offered a $30-a-month incentive to enter training programs and for 150,000 new training openings to be made available to heads of families on welfare. "In the final analysis," he said "we cannot talk our way out of poverty; we cannot legislate our way out of poverty; but this nation can work its way out of poverty. What America needs now is not more welfare but more 'workfare.' "

In his message to Congress on job training Aug. 12, the President proposed a new manpower training act under which persons seeking job training would apply at local state employment agencies rather than directly to a federal training program such as the Job Corps or the Neighborhood Youth Corps.

The President's tax revenue sharing plan called for a portion of federal revenues to be "remitted directly to the states—with a minimum of federal restrictions . . . and with a requirement that a percentage of them be channeled through for the use of local governments." Although the amount sought for the second half of fiscal 1971 would be only a half billion dollars, Mr. Nixon said the plan was "a gesture of faith in America's states and local governments, and in the principle of democratic self-government."

The President sent details of the plan to Congress Aug. 13.

Mr. Nixon also proposed revamping the Office of Economic Opportunity (OEO) Aug. 8. He asked that OEO be continued as a "laboratory agency where new ideas for helping people are tried on a pilot basis." He said that successful programs could then be transferred to "operating departments," leaving OEO free "to concentrate on breaking even newer ground."

Plan questioned—Congress members asked whether Mr. Nixon's welfare plan would do enough for Northern states. Sen. Abraham A. Ribicoff (D, Conn.) said Aug. 8: "It sounds great for Mississippi, but what does it do for Hartford?" Sen. Charles E. Goodell (R, N.Y.) expressed "deep concern" over a plan that would "give the least aid to states like New York that are now providing the most generous welfare benefits." New York Mayor John V. Lindsay Aug. 9 and New York Gov. Nelson A. Rockefeller Aug. 10 expressed similar objections.

Other leaders praised the plan in principle but argued that the amounts of funding involved were inadequate. George Wiley of the National Welfare Rights Organization said Aug. 8 that the President's income subsidy proposal was "a victory for welfare rights" but added that the subsidy "is totally inadequate" and "will not satisfy the poor." Dr. James M. Whittico Jr., a spokesman for the predominantly Negro National Medical Association, which was meeting in San Francisco for its 74th annual convention, said Aug. 11 that the association considered the welfare plan "only a first step" towards alleviating domestic problems. A statement issued Aug. 14 in New York by the Action Council of the Urban Coalition suggested several ways to improve the welfare plan, including abandoning the requirement that welfare mothers of children in school register for work or job training.

AFL-CIO President George Meany charged Aug. 14 that the President's plan would "subsidize employers who pay less than a living wage with public money raised through taxes." Meany approved of Mr. Nixon's attempt at comprehensive welfare reform, but he said the Administration would aid the working poor more by supporting a higher minimum wage.

Food stamp debate—Dr. Jean Mayer President Nixon's special consultant on food, nutrition and health, said Aug. 19 that the President's welfare reform plan would not deny federal food stamps to needy families. He said widespread reports that welfare families would lose food stamps if Mr. Nixon's welfare proposals were passed were the result of "confusion due to people jumping to conclusions."

Although initial reactions to the President's welfare proposals generally were favorable, several congressmen and organization leaders expressed fears that families would lose benefits if food stamps were cut off. Mr. Nixon had proposed a major expansion of the food-stamp program May 6. Later, however, Administration spokesmen who briefed newsmen on the new welfare plan Aug. 8 had said that families aided under the "family assistance system" would no longer receive stamps.

The alleged denial of food stamps to needy families had been assailed by Sens. George S. McGovern (D, S.D.) and Walter F. Mondale (D, Minn.), both members of a special Senate Select Committee on Nutrition & Human Needs. McGovern, chairman of the committee, said Aug. 8 that the denial of stamps would be "a misleading response to the problems of our hungry poor people." Mondale said it would be "outrageous" to scrap the stamp program. John R. Kramer, who had succeeded Mayer as executive director of the National Council on Hunger & Malnutrition, charged Aug. 11 that cutting off food stamps would reduce the purchasing power of poor people in 44 states. Kramer said the Administration pledge to eliminate hunger had become "a casualty of the war against inflation, with deflated pocketbooks and bellies the inevitable consequence." White House Press Secretary Ronald L. Ziegler said Aug. 14 that the May 6 Administration proposal for increases in the food-stamp program would be maintained as an interim measure until the family assistance system could be put into operation.

Mayer, in his Aug. 19 statement, indicated that there had been confusion within the Administration on the future of the food-stamp program. He said that at the time Presidential aides briefed reporters on the President's plan Aug. 8, "perhaps all the figures were not worked out." Mayer said he had been assured, after "a lot of exchanges back

and forth" with Administration officials, that both the welfare reform plan and the expanded food-stamp program, if approved by Congress, would "continue together for some time." The White House confirmed Aug. 19 that food stamp assistance for a family of four would be continued until the family's income reached a level of $4,000 a year.

Administration analysis. HEW Secretary Elliot L. Richardson told the Senate Finance Committee July 21, 1970 that the Administration's welfare reform proposals were based on an analysis of the welfare system that had begun before President Nixon took office and had continued through the following year. Among findings of the analysis:

"The first conclusion compelled by the Administration's analysis of the current [welfare] system was that it is not a system at all, but a confused clutter of many systems. From this has flowed disparity, inequity, and inefficiency.

"... The 'Aid to Families with Dependent Children Program' is in reality 54 different programs in 54 different jurisdictions. It provides no national standards for benefits or eligibility ceilings. AFDC payments vary from an average of $46 per month for a family of four in Mississippi to $265 for such a family in New Jersey. The disparity in payment levels is aggravated by complicated state-by-state variations in criteria for eligibility and methods of administration....

"... [T]his galaxy of welfare systems has uncontrolled access to federal resources and their allocation. Each state establishes its own benefit levels, and the federal government has an open-ended obligation to provide whatever funds are necessary to match them....

"... The most striking defect of AFDC, however, ... is its artificial restriction of eligibility. Since 1935, AFDC eligibility has been confirmed by the uncritically-accepted notion that families headed by a full-time male worker do not need assistance. AFDC was accordingly designed for families headed by women and shaped by the belief female heads of households could not and should not be required to work.

"The unfortunate truth, of course, is that the assumption on which AFDC rests—

that the income of full-time workers is by definition adequate—is simply not valid for large numbers of families. In 1968, 39% of the poor families with children in this country were headed by full-time workers. Their poverty is seldom the result of a defect of character or a failure to try. It is rather the result of the inescapable fact that large numbers of jobs, for a variety of economic reasons, just do not pay an adequate wage—especially for persons with large families.

"...[I]n no state is any federally-assisted welfare available to families headed by full-time working men who earn poverty wages—the working poor. While these families may be in equal financial need with families who are helped, they are not entitled to receive federal public assistance under current law.

"This is the heart of the problem of the working poor. AFDC eligibility involves exclusions which cannot be morally or rationally sustained. We have produced a system which reaches only 34% of the poor children in the country. We have backed ourselves into a situation in which we will help men who don't work (under the AFDC-Unemployed Fathers program), but we cannot help those who do work.

"Under current law, it is easily possible for a man on welfare who does not work at all to be economically better off than a man who works full-time.... Under present law...AFDC-UF contains a work requirement. If a man complies with this requirement, however, he very often will be economically worse off than if he manages to evade the law. Thus we are telling him to penalize himself financially by taking full-time work....

"...The exclusion of the working poor from federally-aided assistance has yet another perverse effect—encouragement for families to dissolve, or for couples never to marry. In situations in which a full-time working man is not making as much as his wife or the mother of his illegitimate children could receive in welfare benefits, the couple is better off financially if the man leaves the home.

"...[O]ver 70% of the fathers of families currently on AFDC are absent from the home, and...the present welfare system provides a prima facie incentive for break-up. Our current welfare law clearly discriminates against those intact, poor families who are making substantial efforts to work themselves out of poverty..."

Welfare rights convention. The National Welfare Rights Organization's second biennial convention opened Aug. 21, 1969 at Wayne State University in Detroit with a keynote address by Rep. John Conyers (D, Mich.). About 600 delegates representing the group's 35,000 members in 186 cities and 46 states attended the five-day convention. Conyers discussed what was to emerge as a major concern of the convention—President Nixon's new welfare proposals.

Conyers charged that the President's proposed $1,600 annual minimum family assistance figure was a "step backward" and called for a $3,200 minimum and the "elimination of forced-work requirements." Dr. George A. Wiley, executive director of the organization, seconded Conyers' objections to forced work in an address Aug. 23. Wiley said: "Only the stupidest person would put emphasis on work when there are no decent jobs paying a decent wage" and "when the overwhelming number of persons on welfare are the aged, the blind, the disabled, children, and mothers of children. The welfare program must protect the right of a mother to be with her children until she herself decides that the time has come to leave them for a job." (Under the President's plan, a welfare mother of school-aged children would be required to accept job training or jobs to be eligible for aid.)

Mr. Nixon's welfare program received cautious praise from some convention speakers. Mrs. Johnnie Tillmon, 42, national chairman of the organization, said Aug. 23 that at least the President "did have the initiative to get started." Urban League Executive Director Whitney M. Young Jr. urged the delegates Aug. 22 to "recognize what is good" in the President's "inadequate" program and avoid supporting reactionary critics of welfare reform.

The delegates Aug. 25 approved a series of militant tactics proposed by the organization's leaders. The group resolved to begin using welfare rent allocations for other basic needs considered to be inadequately covered by welfare allowances. The delegates also approved a plan whereby a welfare recipient would pay only that part of his household utility bill that was covered by his welfare check's monthly utility allotment.

Governors urge federal funding of all welfare. The nation's governors, at their annual National Governors Conference in Colorado Springs, Colo., called on the federal government Sept. 2, 1969 to finance all welfare costs. The resolution was drafted by a committee headed by Gov. Nelson A. Rockefeller (R, N.Y.), who commented after its adoption that the governors had "moved ahead of the Washington scene in their perception of the needs and the problems we face as a nation." The welfare resolution, urging federal absorption of all costs within five years, was passed with only Gov. Lester G. Maddox (D, Ga.) dissenting.

The plan was endorsed by Vice President Agnew Sept. 2. But Agnew said that while he approved the plan for full federal funding of the welfare system as a "final objective" and "as funds become available," such funds were not currently available. He urged the governors to support the Administration's welfare program.

Commission for federal financing—The Advisory Commission on Intergovernmental Relations urged that the federal government take "full financial responsibility" for all public assistance programs. In a report prepared in April and released Dec. 2, the panel, authorized by Congress in 1959, also recommended that states assume "substantially all fiscal responsibility for financing local schools."

At a Washington, D.C. news conference Dec. 2, William G. Colman, executive director of the commission, said that the panel recommended federal welfare funding because "state and local governments have no real control over the root causes of poverty and little to say about how welfare is administered; nevertheless, they pay about half the total cost." The commission said that administration of welfare programs should continue at the local level. The panel's recommendation conflicted with President Nixon's "new federalism" plan of cost-sharing included in the President's welfare proposals. An official of the commission estimated that the proposal would cost the U.S. Treasury an additional $10 billion to $12 billion a year.

Panel urges income plan. The President's Commission on Income Maintenance Programs, in a report released Nov. 12, 1969, urged adoption of an "overall system of economic security" that would include a "universal income supplement program . . . making payments based on income needs to all members of the population." Although the findings of the commission, based on a 22-month study, agreed with President Nixon's welfare proposal of an income subsidy for the poor, the panel rejected the concept inherent in Mr. Nixon's plan that able recipients would have to accept work to receive benefits.

The 21-member panel, drawn from business, education and former government leaders, was appointed by President Johnson and was headed by Ben W. Heineman, a Chicago railroad executive. The commission recommended that an income supplement be initiated that would provide a family of four with a base income of $2,400. The report said that figure was chosen not because it would "meet the full income needs of families with no other income," but because "it is a practical program that can be implemented in the near future."

The program, according to the report, would provide an estimated $6 billion in additional income to 10 million households in 1971. To set payments at the poverty level immediately, the panel said, would cost an estimated $27 billion to be supplied to 24 million households. "We believe that a program of that potential magnitude must be adopted in steps," the commission added. The panel also recommended that the working poor should not lose their right to some supplemental income.

The commission argued that income supplements should be provided according to need because the nation's "economic and social structure virtually guarantees poverty for millions of Americans. . . . The simple fact is that most of the poor remain poor because access to income through work is currently beyond their reach." In support of its contention the panel cited the following statistics: "over one-third of the poor live in families in which the family head works throughout the year"; "fully 70% of the nonaged heads of poor families worked for part of the year in 1966"; and "most of those who did not work at all were ill or disabled or were women with absent husbands and small children."

JOBS plan expanded. Secretary of Labor George P. Shultz and Paul Kayser, president of the National Alliance of Businessmen, announced Nov. 13, 1969 that the JOBS Program (Job Opportunities in the Business Sector) would be expanded. The program, operating in 125 major cities, subsidized employers to hire and train the hard-core unemployed.

Shultz and Kayser said the program would be expanded to operate nationwide. They also said the process of subsidy payment would be simplified and speeded up and said the program would emphasize programs offered by employers to provide "upgrade" training to workers hired under earlier JOBS contracts. Since the program began in May 1968, 269,000 disadvantaged persons had been hired.

Poverty income index up. The Labor Department, in new guidelines announced Nov. 30, 1969 and effective immediately, raised the official government definitions of poverty levels to determine eligibility for federal assistance in various manpower programs. According to the guidelines, used by the Labor Department and the Office of Economic Opportunity, the annual poverty index for an urban family of four was raised from $3,300 to $3,600 and for a similar rural family from $2,300 to $3,000.

The department said it defined a disadvantaged person as one who is poor, without suitable employment and included in one or more of the following categories: a school dropout, member of a minority group, under 22 or over 45 years of age, or handicapped.

Antipoverty program extended. A bill extending the antipoverty program through fiscal 1971 and authorizing appropriations for it was passed Dec. 20, 1969 by 243–94

House vote and 54–21 Senate vote and was signed by President Nixon Dec. 31.

The authorization totaled $2,195,500,-000 for fiscal 1970 and $2,831,900,000 for fiscal 1971; $328.9 million was reserved in each fiscal year for community action programs.

OEO cuts off summer youth funds. The Office of Economic Opportunity issued guidelines, effective March 6, 1970, requiring that funds previously spent on summer recreational programs for urban youth be directed into year-round youth development programs. The agency said that evaluations of summer projects, sponsored since 1966, indicated that "youth programs which are geared to meeting summer crisis periods, and which emphasize leisure time activities only, are not relevant to either the immediate or long-term needs of poor youth."

Under the guidelines, OEO would no longer fund programs "devoted exclusively to recreation, camping, cultural enrichment and other leisure time activities." The agency planned to use the $35 million annually spent on summer projects for 12-month programs that help poor youth "deal with problems affecting their lives, . . . bring about positive changes in their values, aspirations and behavior . . . [and] prepare youth to deal more effectively with the institutions designed to serve them."

The agency had begun revising its guidelines to transfer funds from summer to 12-month programs in 1968 and in 1969 had required projects to be year-round. However an OEO official said the '69 guidelines were largely ineffective.

Poverty data reported. More than one million Americans rose above the official government poverty line in 1969, according to Census Bureau statistics July 15, 1970. The bureau said that 24.3 million persons were classified as poor in 1969, compared to 25.4 million persons in 1968 and 39.5 million in 1959.

The poverty line, as defined by the government, was based on such factors as the number of persons in a family and the average price of necessities. In 1969, the poverty line was $3,743 in annual income for a non-farm family of four.

The bureau reported that the number of Negroes on poverty rolls decreased from 7.6 million in 1968 to 7.2 million in 1969; the number of poor whites decreased from 17.4 million to 16.7 million; and the number of poor of other races remained constant at about 400,000. The median family income of Americans in 1969 was $9,400, a rise of 9% from 1968. But the gain in real purchasing power was only 4% due to cost of living increases. The median family income of Negroes in 1969 was $6,000, compared to $9,800 for whites.

Parents gain power in Head Start. According to new guidelines issued by the Office of Child Development and reported Dec. 23, 1970, parents of children in Head Start projects were granted governing authority over the program, including veto power over the hiring and firing of local staff members. The program, operated under the Health, Education and Welfare Department, provided educational, medical and social services for 263,000 preschool children.

The new guidelines set up as a national policy veto authority that parents had exercised in scattered projects. An official said the guidelines were a clarification of the original 1967 rules governing Head Start, which were described as "very vague." Parents would participate in the program through local policy panels where they would have at least 50% representation. The guidelines said Head Start staff members "must learn to ask parents for their ideas and listen with attention, patience and understanding."

About 700 Head Start parents had demonstrated in Washington Nov. 23 to demand more authority over the programs and to protest budget cuts. The parents had announced the formation of the National Head Start Committee Nov. 24, a board to advise the government on the administration of Head Start programs.

In a related development reported Nov. 28, HEW announced that aged, blind and disabled persons receiving federally aided state welfare services must have a voice in administering the programs by April 1, 1971. The statement said: "In order to involve poor people directly in these programs, welfare recipients as well as representatives of community groups will be asked to serve on advisory committees for service programs directed by state welfare agencies."

OEO nominee assures VISTA funds. In testimony before the Senate Committee on Labor and Welfare Dec. 30, 1970, Frank C. Carlucci, named director of the Office of Economic Opportunity (OEO), denied reports that the Nixon Administration would eliminate all funds for VISTA. Carlucci said no final budget determinations had been made but that "I'm confident there will be an adequate level of funding for VISTA."

VISTA (Volunteers in Service to America), which cost about $39 million during the current year, supported the work of about 5,100 volunteers to help urban and rural poor people in the U.S. It had been reported that funds for the program would be eliminated as part of a 23% OEO budget reduction.

Medical aid for poor areas. The Emergency Health Personnel Act was signed into law by President Nixon Dec. 31, 1970. The legislation, passed by the 91st Congress—by the House Dec. 18, 1970 and the Senate three days later—authorized the assignment of personnel, including doctors, to areas with critical medical manpower shortages. The bill was sponsored by Sens. Warren G. Magnuson (D, Wash.) and Henry M. Jackson (D, Wash.).

The assignment of personnel would be made by the Public Health Service, and the salaries of the personnel would be paid by the federal government, which also had the options of setting no fees for the services performed or of setting fees and having them paid directly to the federal treasury or paid through Medicare or Medicaid programs.

Other Criticism

Misuse of educational funds charged. The NAACP Legal Defense and Educational Fund Inc. and the Washington Research Project of the Southern Center for Studies in Public Policy charged Nov. 8, 1969 that federal education funds earmarked for disadvantaged children had been "wasted, diverted or otherwise misused by state and local authorities." The two organizations based their charge on a six-month study into the use of $4.3 billion in funds appropriated under Title I of the Elementary and Secondary Education Act since it had been passed in 1965.

The 137-page report said that the U.S. Office of Education, the Health, Education and Welfare Department (HEW) agency which administered the act, had been "reluctant and timid" in using its authority to demand proper use of the funds. The act was intended to supply special aid to schools with a high concentration of children from low-income families. The report said that parents of poor children saw the program as "only another promise unfulfilled" because of "flagrant" daily abuses in administration "without fear of reprisal." Referring to challenges from some educators who questioned the effectiveness of programs aimed at poor children, the report said: "Ultimately, it is educationally deprived children who will be held accountable for the federal investment. All the tests and evaluations to determine the effectiveness of Title I will be administered to poor children, not to school administrators or to state and federal officials."

The report contended that funds had been diverted from poor children to be used for salaries, buildings and equipment for programs that served all the children in a school district or for projects outside the scope of the act. The authors concluded that Title I "is caught in a political thicket" in which local officials, allowed wide latitude under the act, defied federal standards for the use of funds.

Insufficient credit for poor. The National Urban Coalition Nov. 20, 1969 released a study citing lack of accessible and reasonably priced credit as one of the most pressing problems for the urban poor. Although the U.S. had a credit economy, the report said, "in many inner city neighborhoods there is little or no access to legitimate, reasonably priced sources of credit, such as banks, retail establishments or credit unions."

The Urban Coalition, a national organization of civic, industry and union leaders, said its study indicated that "the poor can and do pay their obligations."

Senate study scores Medicare wastes. A staff study released by the Senate Finance Committee Feb. 9, 1970 scored the fiscal administration of the Medicare and Medicaid programs and recommended legislation to set limits on fees paid to doctors.

The study said carriers under the Medicare program—private insurance groups such as Blue Shield that served as intermediaries between the federal government and doctors receiving payments—often paid more for Medicare patients than they ordinarily paid for their own subscribers. In allowing these payments, the study said, the Social Security Administration abandoned the provisions of the Medicare statute and "the clear Congressional intent" of the law and contributed to "enormous inflation" of doctors' costs under the program. (Medicare costs had doubled since the law went into effect in 1967 and Medicaid costs had quadrupled. In the fiscal year ending June 30, Medicare costs were predicted at about $8 billion and Medicaid costs at $5 billion.)

The report also contained statistics on thousands of doctors and groups of doctors who had received $25,000 a year or more in Medicare and Medicaid payments in 1968. To curb spiraling Medicare costs, the study group recommended that regional advisory groups be empowered to establish maximum fees for services covered under the program. The group also suggested that Medicaid fee schedules be established and that a new Medicaid fraud and abuse unit be set up to monitor state programs.

Court Decisions

Payment hearings upheld. The Supreme Court, in a 5–3 decision March 23, 1970, ruled that welfare recipients have the constitutional right to formal hearings, complete with constitutional safe-guards, before officials can terminate their benefits. Under the court's order, procedures in use in California and New York City were declared unconstitutional.

The ruling marked the first time the Supreme Court had said that welfare officials must satisfy the Constitution's "due process of law" requirement before ending payments to welfare recipients.

The majority decision was entered by Justice William J. Brennan Jr. and joined by Justices Byron R. White, Thurgood Marshall, William O. Douglas and John M. Harlan.

Justice Hugo L. Black delivered a dissenting report and was joined by Chief Justice Warren E. Burger and Justice Potter Stewart.

Under the court order, welfare payments could not be terminated until the recipient had been given notice of the reasons he was considered to be ineligible for further benefits and an opportunity to appear with counsel at a hearing before "an impartial decision-maker" to testify and cross-examine all witnesses. The court said the welfare recipients who appeared before the hearing were entitled to counsel, but ruled that the state did not have to furnish it. After completion of the hearing, the decision-maker was required to submit a written ruling, explaining why the benefits had been terminated, if he so ruled.

The Justice Department had joined welfare officials in warning the Supreme Court that a decision in favor of the nearly nine million persons reported receiving welfare benefits could engulf welfare agencies with their demands for hearings while ineligible persons remained on relief rolls.

In his majority report, Justice Brennan said humanitarian considerations outweighed such administrative and fiscal concerns. He said welfare assistance was "not mere charity," but a means to "promote the general welfare and secure the blessings of liberty" as stated in the preamble to the Constitution. He concluded that the Constitution required that without due process of law, payments must be given without interruption to those who were eligible for them.

Justice Black, in the dissenting report, termed welfare a "gratuity" that was "nice for those who do not work but receive payments from the government— that is to say, those who do work."

Welfare ceilings upheld. The Supreme Court ruled, 5–3, April 6, 1970 that states could constitutionally limit the amount of welfare benefits a family could collect. The justices upheld a Maryland law that set a $250-a-month ceiling on welfare payments to one family, regardless of size. The case involved Mrs. Linda Williams of Baltimore who argued that she and her eight children were entitled to $296 a month.

Justice Potter Stewart, in the majority opinion, said federal courts should be reluctant to interfere with state distribution of welfare funds. Stewart argued that "the intractable economic, social and even philosophical problems presented by public welfare assistance programs are not the business of this court." Justices William O. Douglas, William J. Brennan Jr. and Thurgood Marshall dissented on the ground that a benefit limit violated the Social Security statute.

In another ruling, the justices held 6–2 that the New York State Legislature illegally scaled down benefits in 1969 under the Aid to Families with Dependent Children program by eliminating individual grants for such needs as laundry and telephones. But the majority, in an opinion by Justice John M. Harlan, said that "after recomputing its standard of need," the state might "pare down payments to accommodate budgetary realities by reducing the per cent of benefits paid or switching to a per cent reduction system."

Chief Justice Warren E. Burger and Justice Hugo L. Black dissented in the New York case, saying the courts should wait until the Health, Education and Welfare Department could rule on the case.

HEW upheld on 'man in house.' The Supreme Court April 20, 1970, in a 6–2 decision, upheld Health, Education & Welfare Department regulations prohibiting a state from cutting off welfare benefits to dependent children when there was a "man in the house" living with the mother without proof that the man contributed to the children's support. The case involved a California welfare rule.

Nixon & Welfare Reform

Nixon Presses Program

By early 1971 President Nixon's campaign for reform of the welfare system was well under way. He complained in his 1971 State-of-the-Union message Jan. 22, however, that of much Administration-proposed legislation "on which action was not completed" by Congress in 1970, the "most important" was welfare reform. Calling the current welfare system "a monstrous, consuming outrage," Nixon urged its replacement with a plan putting a floor under the income of every family with children and "without those demeaning, soul-stifling affronts to human dignity that so blight the lives of welfare children today." He also urged the establishment of "an effective work incentive, an effective work requirement."

Nixon's family aid plan rejected. After more than three years of effort, President Nixon in October 1972 conceded at least temporary defeat in a plan to reform the welfare system. The chief feature of the reform was the proposal of a Family Assistance Plan (FAP) that would guarantee a minimum income to a poor family of four and provide benefits for the working poor. (The original proposal was a minimum of $1,600 a year. The figure was later raised to $2,400.) Nixon's proposal, with modifications, was approved twice by the House of Representatives but finally rejected in the Senate.

Among major developments during 1970–72 in Nixon's struggle for FAP and welfare reform:

House approves measure—The Administration's welfare-reform legislation was approved by 243–145 House vote April 16, 1970. It was estimated that the plan would increase the federal share of welfare costs from $4 billion to $8.4 billion if it took effect in fiscal 1972.

The current program of aid to families with dependent children would be replaced under the bill with a family assistance program providing a minimum annual income of $500 for each parent and $300 for each child. Able-bodied adults, except mothers of children under the age of six, would be required to take job training and accept available work. Such families could earn $720 a year without losing their welfare benefits.

Above that figure, they would lose 50¢ for each $1 earned until their income reached $3,920 a year, when the welfare support would stop.

Poor families also would be eligible for $800 a year in food stamp aid plus supplementary state aid.

Three current adult welfare categories of aid for the aged, blind and disabled would be consolidated under the bill into one program providing a minimum monthly benefit of $110 (current average $68) for an adult and $185 for a couple.

The bill had been approved April 14 by the House Rules Committee and presented to the House April 15 by Chairman Wilbur D. Mills (D, Ark.) of the House Ways and Means Committee. Mills pointed out that half of the families expected to benefit from the bill lived in the South.

The House action was hailed April 16 by President Nixon as "a battle won in a crusade for reform" and by Robert H. Finch, secretary of health, education and welfare, as "the most significant shift in public assistance programs since their inception."

■A welfare committee of the Democratic Study Group, representing about 120 liberal members of the House, recommended the President's welfare plan as "a sound step toward the elimination of poverty," according to March 3 reports. A statement by the group being circulated in Congress said: "The Nixon welfare proposals contain a number of commendable initiatives, particularly with respect to coverage for all families with children and federal participation in setting standards." However, the panel recommended that the Administration measure be strengthened in several areas: to modify the requirement that mothers of school-aged children register for job training or employment; to progressively increase the minimum payment from $1,600 to the official poverty level; to automatically provide food stamps for participants in the family assistance program; to increase the guaranteed income minimum for the aged, blind and disabled to $150 a month; and to provide gradually for federal assumption of all welfare costs.

Senators seek changes—Hearings on the Nixon welfare-reform legislation were suspended May 1, 1970 by the Senate Finance Committee after objections by members of both parties to what they considered inadequacies. The bill was returned to the Administration for integration with other federal aid programs for the poor, such as food stamps, Medicaid and housing subsidies. The committee, in its third day of hearings with supporting testimony from Robert H. Finch, secretary of health, education and welfare, objected to the possibility that a man on welfare could reduce his family's overall income by earning more money.

Daniel Patrick Moynihan, counselor to the President, said May 5 the Administration would strengthen the work-incentive provisions of the program but it would be "the work of half a decade or more" to mesh it with other welfare programs.

Moynihan had chided the Chamber of Commerce April 27 for its "shrill opposition" to the Administration's welfare reform bill, which he described as this "magnificent, most radical legislation in two generations." The chamber's outgoing board chairman, E. Hornsby Wasson, April 28 restated the group's position—it supported 75% of the bill, particularly the concept of welfare reform, but opposed a guaranteed income and any expansion of the welfare program.

Nixon offers revisions—President Nixon submitted to Congress June 10 a new version of his bill. The revised program, with a reduced cost estimate of $4.1 billion compared with $4.4 billion original figure, retained the basic Administration proposal for a minimum income guarantee for poor families.

The President proposed in the revision to replace the Medicaid program for beneficiaries of his Family Assistance Plan with a new compulsory, contributory health insurance program for those earning less than $3,920 annually.

His revisions included an administrative change, not requiring Congressional consent, to have the food stamp formula taper off as the recipient's income increased. A simplified distribution system for food stamps also was introduced. The welfare recipient would receive the stamps with his benefit check.

A housing provision would permit tenants attaining a higher income to remain in subsidized apartments by paying more rent.

Daniel P. Moynihan, counselor to President Nixon and chief author of the family-assistance plan, said July 26 he believed that if the legislation were not passed in 1970 it would not be passed "this decade" because of the conservative political trend in the nation.

Senate Finance Committee Chairman Russell B. Long (D, La.), in committee, had suggested the possibility of an increase in the minimum wage to raise the living standard of the working poor and cut federal welfare costs. He also exhibited interest in a plan to pay welfare benefits to a working man through his employer so the recipient would not be aware of the reduction in welfare as his work increased. Both ideas—the minimum wage increase as an answer to the welfare problem and payment of benefits through the employer—were rejected by Labor Secretary James D. Hodgson during an appearance before the committee Aug. 6.

Long had resumed hearings on the legislation July 21 with a description of the Family Assistance Plan as "a massive and costly experiment which proposes adding 14 million Americans to the welfare rolls." He said it would cost $9.1 billion, $4 billion more than the federal cost of the existing system. As for the revised welfare proposals which the committee had requested from the Administration, the revised program was "in significant respects a worse bill" than the House-passed version, he said.

New York Mayor John V. Lindsay backed the Administration program Aug. 24 and said, based on the experience of New York and five other states with similar programs, no more than three to four million of the poor would apply for the aid. In New York State, he said, less than one-third of those eligible applied for state relief despite recruiting efforts.

Other testimony in support of the welfare plan came Sept. 1 from Cleveland Mayor Carl B. Stokes, who appeared before the panel as spokesman for the National League of Cities and the U.S. Conference of Mayors. He told them he came not "as a supplicant" but as a "representative of the people who create the money you spend."

Trial urged for Nixon plan—The Administration Aug. 28 announced support for a plan to hold a year of field tests on the proposed Family Assistance Program before the program went into full operation.

President Nixon let his approval of the testing be known as a spur to get action on his welfare reform legislation, which remained lodged in the Senate Finance Committee.

Committee Democrats advocated expansion of the President's program beyond the Administration's budget confines, and there was conservative Republican resistance within the committee to the principle of family assistance.

Nixon urged the committee Aug. 28 to give the Senate "a chance to work its will on this issue and this bill," which he called "the most important piece of domestic legislation of the past 35 years." The field-test proposal endorsed by the President was in the form of an amendment offered by Sen. Abraham A. Ribicoff (D, Conn.), a Finance Committee member.

Senate committee rebuffs bill—The Nixon reform program was rejected by the Senate Finance Committee Oct. 4 and Nov. 20, 1970.

The bill was defeated by 14–1 vote Oct. 8, the same day that the committee also voted, by 9 to 4, not to accept a substitute proposed by Sen. Abraham A. Ribicoff (D, Conn.) to test the FAP in selected areas and then put it into effect nationally Jan. 1, 1972. The Administration had proposed a July 1, 1971 starting date but had accepted the Ribicoff proposal to get the program to a floor vote.

The committee did approve by a 9-3 vote a bill permitting pilot testing of the program but no specific date was inserted.

The Nov. 20 rejection actually was a 10–6 vote against adding to the Social Security bill a revised version for a modest one-year test of FAP and other welfare proposals plus authorization to initiate a full-scale program pending results of the testing.

To gain support for its program after the initial rejection in the committee, the Administration had circulated a plan to replace food stamps with money and to raise the base national income for a welfare family of four from $1,600 a year to $2,200. An Administration spokesman, Robert E. Patricelli, a deputy assistant secretary of the Health, Education and Welfare Department, said Nov. 5 while the Administration did not want "to jeopardize" the $1,600 minimum "if the Senate likes the alternative then we would support it."

After the Nov. 20 vote, the Administration expressed disappointment, through White House Press Secretary Ronald L. Ziegler, that Democratic committee members had dropped support of the Administration plan. The reference was to Sen. Fred R. Harris (Okla.), who said Nov. 19 he had reconsidered his position and was inclined to vote against the program—his primary objection was that the $1,600 figure was too low—and Sens. Eugene J. McCarthy (Minn.) and Clinton P. Anderson (N.M.), whom the Administration had counted as committed to the plan. All three voted against it Nov. 20, along with three other Democrats and four Republicans. The President's position was supported in committee by three Republicans and three Democrats.

In a later vote Nov. 20, the committee approved 13–3 a proposal to undertake a test plan only, but with authority to initiate a full-scale program without Congressional approval withheld. Harris, McCarthy and Sen. Albert Gore (D, Tenn.) voted in opposition. HEW Secretary Elliot L. Richardson said afterwards "we would rather have no bill in this Congress than a test-only bill, because a test will mean delaying real welfare reform for at least four years" and "we'd rather start again in the next Congress."

Committee Chairman Russell B. Long (D, La.) had observed Nov. 18 that the Nixon welfare reform plan was "in bad shape" and "leaves a lot to be desired." He made the remarks during an unofficial hearing where McCarthy was taking testimony from members of the National Welfare Rights Organization. The welfare representatives were critical of the Nixon plan (because of its work requirement and low annual minimum) and Long (because he had not taken testimony from welfare recipients during his committee hearings).

Fresh Nixon revision offered—The Nixon Administration, under pressure from Congressional critics, offered a revised Family Assistance Plan Feb. 24, 1971 that would include an $800 million program to put 225,000 welfare recipients into city and state public jobs. The re-

vision was presented by Health, Education and Welfare Undersecretary John G. Veneman at a closed meeting of the House Ways and Means Committee.

Rep. Wilbur D. Mills (D, Ark.), chairman of the committee, had told the Administration Feb. 10 that it must revise its FAP proposal to meet what he called the "legitimate criticism" raised during 1970 hearings by the Senate Finance Committee. Senate critics objected that the plan lacked work incentive provisions and would add too many people to relief rolls.

Under the proposal presented by Veneman, able-bodied welfare recipients would have to sign up for jobs. If private jobs were not available, they would be assigned to work in city parks, hospitals, garbage collection departments or other public service jobs that would pay at least $1.20 per hour. The federal government would pay the full cost of the program for the first year. The states would pay 25% the second year and 50% the third in an arrangement that Veneman said would encourage states to move workers to jobs in the private sector.

Veneman also proposed that the basic family-of-four allotment be increased to $2,200 a year and that food-stamp benefits be eliminated. The Administration also proposed a penalty for welfare cheaters of a $1,000 fine and a maximum one-year prison sentence.

In announcing his demand for a revision of the FAP proposal, Mills said Feb. 10 that if the revised bill were not presented promptly, he would separate welfare reform from Social Security legislation and push through Social Security increases, a proposal that enjoyed general Congressional support.

Nixon urges reform plan—President Nixon addressed a meeting of Republican governors in Williamsburg, Va. April 19, 1971 on welfare reform plans. His effort to bring "greater benefits for those Americans, and there are many, who can't care for themselves," he said, would be "White House priority No. 1."

He stressed the work requirements of his welfare plan, upholding "the dignity and the value" of hard work. The success of his plan, Nixon said, would be measured "by the dignity it promotes and not by the dole it provides." The best way to reform the system, he said, was "to quit helping those who can help themselves and refuse to do so." He did not consider it menial or demeaning no matter what the job if it provided a living and "lets you look everyone else in the eye."

Republican Govs. Ronald Reagan (Calif.) and Nelson Rockefeller (N.Y.) were singled out by the President for praise because of their efforts to reduce the costs of the current welfare program.

House passes omnibus bill—The House, by 288–132 vote June 22, 1971, passed a bill (H.R.1) incorporating reform of the welfare system and major changes in Social Security, Medicare and Medicaid programs. A move to delete the welfare reform provision, the Family Assistance Plan, was defeated June 22 by a 234–187 vote.

The House considered the omnibus bill under a procedure barring floor changes except those proposed by the House Ways and Means Committee. But a separate vote on the welfare reform section had been authorized by the House Rules Committee June 15, a procedure opposed by Ways and Means Chairman Wilbur D. Mills (D, Ark.). He yielded, however, to prevent delay in house consideration of the bill. A move in the House June 21 to open the welfare section to modification or substitution was defeated 200–172.

President Nixon urged the House to approve the welfare reform bill in a letter read June 22 by House Speaker Carl Albert (D, Okla.) calling the bill "the most important social legislation in 35 years." After passage, Nixon lauded the House action as "a major legislative milestone" and thanked those supporting the bill "for their careful and responsible action." Expressing hope the Senate would "move with dispatch" on the legislation, Nixon said "we cannot afford to delay" replacement of the current welfare system with one "designed to build people up rather than pull them down."

The Family Assistance Plan approved by the House would guarantee a family of four an annual income of $2,400 and establish uniform national standards for eligibility and benefits. States would be relieved of some current welfare costs and any cost increases over the next five

years. The welfare provisions encountered opposition from liberals viewing the income floor as inadequate and conservatives objecting to the concept of an income floor.

Other provisions of the bill would increase Social Security benefits by 5% in 1972 and provide an automatic increase tied to cost-of-living increases; extend Medicare benefits to 1.5 million disabled persons; federalize welfare programs for the elderly, blind and disabled, providing $1,800 a year for a single person and $2,400 for a couple.

The House bill was modified by the Ways and Means Committee prior to passage June 22 to require state legislative action to eliminate supplemental welfare payments or food stamp procedure. Liberals had objected that the original bill had no remedy if states accepted the increased federal contributions and reduced their own investment and the amount allotted to poor families. The final provision froze state benefit levels unless positive legislative action were taken by the states.

Nixon stresses 'work ethic'—President Nixon stressed the American "work ethic" and increased productivity in a Labor Day radio address Sept. 6, 1971.

The work ethic, or competitive spirit, "the inner drive that for two centuries has made the American workingman unique in the world," he said, was "ingrained in the American character" and "that is why most of us consider it immoral to be lazy or slothful—even if a person is well off enough not to have to work, or deliberately avoids work by going on welfare."

Nixon & Ribicoff reach accord—The Nixon Administration and Sen. Abraham Ribicoff (D, Conn.) Feb. 2, 1972 compromised in a dispute over a guaranteed income for the working and non-working poor.

The Administration, denying that its support was wavering, said it would accept provisions for a pilot program, and Ribicoff said he would support permanent authorization for a full-scale national plan. Previously, the Administration had rejected suggestions that the income floor program be tested before it was enacted.

Ribicoff, in a surprise announcement

Jan. 28 at a Finance Committee hearing, had withdrawn his support of a national Family Assistance Plan, asking instead for a pilot program in selected localities, "to see if this kind of scheme really works." He had previously supported a proposal with more liberal benefits than the bill officially backed by the Administration, which had already passed the House.

Ribicoff, former secretary of health, education and welfare (HEW), had been the only prominent member of the conservative Finance Committee to support income supplements for the working poor. He had been expected to lead the floor fight for its passage.

Ribicoff said he was "trying to salvage something out of this," but said the Administration had failed to work for the bill in the committee, since "the President doesn't really believe in it."

President Nixon assured Ribicoff Jan. 31 of continued support for the bill. According to the White House Press Secretary Ronald L. Ziegler, Nixon told the senator that Administration aides would work with all committee members to find "common ground." Ziegler further reported Feb. 1 that Nixon had met with California Gov. Ronald Reagan and "reiterated his support" of the welfare plan, after Reagan had testified that morning before the Finance Committee that Nixon "no longer believes in" his own bill.

Ribicoff met with HEW Secretary Elliot L. Richardson and Presidential domestic aide John Ehrlichman Feb. 2. Both sides agreed to support permanent authorization along with an initial pilot program. No agreement was reached on proposed income levels. Richardson noted in a press conference Feb. 3 that federal income supplement experiments were already being conducted in eight states.

The Administration bill would provide a national income guarantee of $2,400 for a family of four, and would allow recipients to keep all earned income up to $720 a year, and one third of additional earned income up to the cutoff income of $4,320 a year. Ribicoff's bill would set the minimum at $3,000, to rise within three years to nearly $4,000, and allow recipients to keep 40% of earned income above $720 a year.

In committee hearings beginning Jan. 20, the Family Assistance Plan picked up the support of several governors, including Republicans Richard Ogilvie (Ill.), Nelson Rockefeller (N.Y.), Daniel Evans (Wash.), and Thomas Meskill (Conn.), and Southern Democrats Jimmie Carter (Ga.) and Preston Smith (Texas).

Beulah Sanders and George Wiley, chairman and executive director of the National Welfare Rights Organization, opposed the Nixon bill in testimony Feb. 2. They called the $2,400 minimum inadequate and said that forcing mothers with children over three years old to work would destroy families.

Senate committee's changes—With welfare-reform and Social Security proposals joined in a single bill (H.R.1), the Senate Finance Committee completed its months-long consideration of the measure June 13, 1972.

The committee had voted to eliminate the House-passed minimum income plan in favor of a series of changes to reduce welfare rolls and require many recipients to work at government or government subsidized jobs.

Major increases were approved in Medicare payments, in benefits for the aged, blind or disabled, and in pensions for long-term low-paid retirees. A minimum income plan for the aged and infirm was approved.

The decision to substitute a tough work requirement for the House minimum-income plan was made by a 10–4 vote April 28, with six Republicans supporting the version proposed by Long and four liberal Democrats in opposition.

The plan would require all able-bodied parents on welfare with no children under age 6 to accept work from a new federal employment corporation at $1.20 an hour, if they could not find jobs in the private sector. The corporation could employ its workers at public service jobs, or hire them out as domestics at the $1.20 wage rate. Recipients working for private employers at rates of $1.20–$1.60 an hour would receive rebates on Social Security tax payments, and the lower-paid private-sector workers would receive additional federal subsidies of up to $12 per week. (The federal minimum wage for most workers was $1.60 an hour.)

The House bill had included a work

provision, but did not cut off benefits to the children of non-complying parents, as did the Senate bill. The committee modified its stand June 1, by voting to refer such children to local child welfare agencies for support.

Other tough provisions approved by the committee would require recipient mothers to give written permission to state governments to track down non-supporting husbands; bar federal poverty lawyers from aiding welfare suits against the government; cut grants to states found to have a large proportion of ineligible recipients on welfare lists and provide bonuses to local governments that uncovered welfare frauds.

Senate action—The Senate further revised H.R.1 before approving it in modified form and sending it to joint Senate-House conference committee Oct. 6, 1972.

The Senate did not revive the nationwide minimum income plan, shorn from the bill during its 15-month stay in Sen. Russell Long's (D, La.) Finance Committee. Although the House had twice passed a minimum income plan submitted by the Nixon Administration, the Administration's refusal to join Senate liberals on a compromise plan allowed conservatives of both parties to defeat the concept, which Long said Oct. 3 "would destroy this country."

But the Senate also deleted the Finance Committee's "workfare" proposal to require recipient parents of school-age children to work at government or private jobs at less than the federal minimum wage, voted for a program of bonuses to low-wage workers, and provided more extensive increases in Social Security benefits than did the House.

Under a $400 million test plan adopted by 46–40 Senate vote Oct. 4, three proposed reform plans would be tried for two-four years by the Department of Health, Education and Welfare in selected areas to be approved by the Senate Finance Committee and the House Ways and Means Committee. The plans included: the Administration's proposal to provide a minimum income for those unable to work and for low-income workers, at a level of $2,400 annually for a family of four, rising to a combined maximum of earning and benefits of $4,200; a plan proposed by Sen. Abra-

ham Ribicoff (D, Conn.) for a $2,600 annual minimum for a family of four, with cost of living increases and full minimum wage levels for those required to work; and the Finance Committee plan, requiring employable aid recipients to work at wage rates as low as $1.20 an hour. New legislation would be required at the end of the test period before any permanent plan was adopted.

Immediate nationwide welfare reform was doomed when the Senate rejected by a 50–35 vote a compromise plan, offered Oct. 4 by Sen. Adlai Stevenson 3rd (D, Ill.), that was largely identical to the Administration plan but lobbied against by the Administration. Although White House Press Secretary Ronald Ziegler said Sept. 29 that President Nixon would refuse to support any alternative to the House-passed plan, the House plan was not even introduced on the floor after its sponsor, Sen. Hugh Scott (R, Pa.), decided to support the Stevenson plan instead.

Ribicoff charged in debate Oct. 3 that Nixon's refusal to compromise was an indication that he preferred a "campaign issue to a bill." But the President told reporters at an Oct. 5 press conference that he still favored a family assistance plan and would consider resubmitting the proposal to the new Congress if re-elected.

Among other major provisions in the bill, the Senate approved a 10% work bonus for families with up to $4,000 in annual earned income, plus supplements of 30¢ an hour to breadwinners earning $1.20 an hour. In conjunction, the two provisions could raise earnings of $2,400 to $3,300 a year.

The bill provided for federal takeover of state welfare programs for the aged, blind and disabled, with new minimum standard benefits, and for benefits to retirees with 17–30 years low-wage work experience higher than their contributions would merit. Both programs had been approved by the House, but money differences remained to be settled in conference.

Both House and Senate bills raised widows' benefits to 100% of deceased husbands' benefits, and extended Medicare coverage to 1.7 million recipients of disability benefits under 65.

Other provisions appearing only in the

Senate bill would bring certain out-patient prescription drugs under Medicare, allow tax deductions for child care expenses and prevent states from using the recent 20% Social Security increases to reduce various welfare benefits.

To finance these improvements, the Senate approved a $6 billion annual increase in Social Security taxes, to 6% from both employes and employers, up from the current 5.5%.

Income plan defeated—The version of H.R.1 produced by the joint conference committee excluded any form of minimum family income plan. The measure was then passed by both houses of Congress Oct. 17, 1972 and signed by President Nixon Oct. 30.

The conference committee bill was approved by the House, 305–1, and by the Senate, 61–0.

The conferees dropped the House version of President Nixon's family assistance plan, as well as the Senate's $400 million test plan, which the Administration had opposed. But a provision for a federal takeover by 1974 of welfare assistance to the aged, blind and disabled was retained, with a minimum monthly payment of $130 to single persons and $195 to couples, supplemented by up to $20 in Social Security payments, $65 in earnings, and any additional supplements paid by states with already higher benefits.

The conferees dropped a series of restrictive welfare rule proposals, including a plan to trace deserting fathers of welfare families and a restoration of residency requirements. A Senate provision to pay bonuses to low-income workers was also eliminated, as well as provisions to extend Medicare to cover some drugs for non-hospital patients and glasses, dental and podiatric devices. Also dropped were proposals to reduce the age at which workers or widows could retire at reduced benefit levels. A Senate prohibition against state reduction of various benefits to those receiving increased Social Security payments was also dropped.

Among the new benefits:

Medicare coverage for 1.5 million persons receiving disability benefits for at least 24 months; Medicare payments for some chiropractic and kidney dialysis treatments; increase from $1,680 to $2,100 in the amount an elderly person could earn without losing benefits (benefits would be reduced by $1 for each $2 earned above $2,100); benefits to widows were increased to 100% of their husband's benefits, up from 82.5%. Minimum monthly payments of $170 were approved for low-income beneficiaries who had worked at least 30 years, and lesser increases for those working at least 17 years; a change was made in the method of computing retirement payments, resulting in an increase for most recipients; and an increase in benefit rates was made of 1% for each year a worker over 65 chose to delay receiving payments. The bill also set up doctor "peer review" groups to hold down Medicare and Medicaid inefficiencies.

Agnew on relief problems. Vice President Spiro T. Agnew said Jan. 14, 1971 that the welfare problem would not be resolved until officials faced such issues as whether taxpayers should finance illegitimate children or keep terminal patients alive or whether the government should take children away from unfit mothers. Agnew spoke of rising welfare costs to Gov. Ronald Reagan and 300 local officials meeting in Sacramento, Calif.

The vice president said: "I have a theory that these problems will never be subject to complete solution until somebody in public life is willing to take on the hard social judgments that very frankly no one that I know in elective office is willing to even think about."

He said: "If a woman has not taken care of her children properly, who is going to say to that woman, 'We are going to take that child from you?' . . . Who is going to say to a welfare mother who has had three or four illegitimate children who are now charges of the state, 'We're very sorry but we will not be able to allow you to have any more children?'"

Citing as an example the $20,000 or $30,000 it might cost the taxpayers to extend the life of a terminal patient, Agnew asked: "Who decides . . . whether he's to be allowed for his terminal illness to run to the end or whether he's going to be allowed to die of natural causes before that time?"

Antipoverty Program Continued

3-year OEO extension. After vetoing a two-year extension of the Office of Economic Opportunity (OEO) at the end of 1971, President Nixon in September 1972 signed into law a bill providing for a three-year continuation of the antipoverty agency's existence.

Developments during 1971–72 preceding the decision to continue the OEO for three years:

2-year extension sought—Pending the implementation of Nixon Administration plans to reorganize the OEO, the Administration asked Congress March 18, 1971 for a simple two-year extension of OEO. Acting Director Frank Carlucci asked for the extension in letters to the House and Senate labor committees

OEO officials said the Administration still intended to implement previously announced plans to change the agency into an organization primarily for research but that the extension was needed to keep alive the war on poverty. The current OEO programs were to expire June 30.

The following were among Administration plans in various statements and legislative proposals: abolish special manpower training programs funded under OEO—Job Corps, Neighborhood Youth Corps, Operations Mainstream and the Opportunities Industrialization Centers—and allow states and cities to provide the services with funds from the President's special revenue sharing proposal on manpower; transfer OEO Legal Services to a new, quasi-public corporation; shift jurisdiction over Community Action Programs and let cities fund the programs with money from revenue sharing.

In a hearing by the House Education and Labor Committee March 22 on the proposed OEO extension, Rep. Carl Perkins (D, Ky.) expressed concern for the continued existence of rural community action programs if they were not directly funded by the federal government. Carlucci said he thought the urban programs had sufficient local support to survive but he admitted that some rural agencies might have problems.

Rep. Augustus Hawkins (D, Calif.) charged that the Administration would eliminate the OEO's role as "advocate for the poor." He asked Carlucci, "Why don't you say what you're doing? You are dismantling the OEO, stripping it of all its programs, and there won't be any agency to coordinate the programs for the poor."

Senate bill—The Senate Sept. 9, 1971 approved a $6 billion bill extending the OEO for two years. It contained a comprehensive child development program with day care centers available for children of working mothers and a provision for an independent National Legal Services Corporation to take over the functions of the program operated by OEO.

President Nixon had asked for the two-year OEO extension and for the legal services plan. But the Nixon Administration gave only lukewarm support to the bill that emerged from the Senate Labor and Public Works Committee. The committee version contained a $2 billion authorization for a child development program which would expand the Head Start concept by offering services, on an ability-to-pay basis, to middle-income as well as poor children.

The Senate rejected several amendments offered on the floor by Sen. Robert Taft Jr. (R, Ohio) to bring the bill more in line with Administration views. One Taft amendment, rejected 31–26, Sept. 9, would have deleted a provision denying the President authority to transfer functions out of OEO without Congressional approval. In an amendment defeated 44–20, Taft sought to change the provision providing free child-care for families of four with annual incomes of up to $6,960 by allowing the secretary of health, education and welfare to set the figure. Taft voted for the bill on final passage.

In addition to the $2 billion child-development authorization, the bill authorized $950 million for each of fiscal 1972 and 1973 for other OEO programs; $900 million for Labor Department manpower training programs in fiscal 1972; $500 for fiscal 1972 expansion of the Neighborhood Youth Corps; and $500 in fiscal 1972 for Head Start.

House bill—The House Sept. 30, by a 251–115 roll-call vote, passed a two-year OEO extension authorizing $5 billion for antipoverty programs. Like the Senate one, the House bill included a comprehensive child care and development program, added on the House floor, and a provision for transfer of the OEO legal services program to an independent corporation.

The child care provision was offered as an amendment to the bill by Rep. John Brademas (D, Ind.). Brademas asked free child care for children of families with incomes of up to $6,960 with graduated fees for families with higher incomes. The Brademas proposal was similar to the provision passed by the Senate and to a separate bill approved Sept. 25 by the House Education and Labor Committee.

House Republicans, citing Administration figures estimating that child care costs could reach $20 billion a year, succeeded in lowering the eligibility for free child care to families with incomes not above $4,300. According to government statistics, existing licensed day care facilities could serve less than 700,000 children, but there were 3.7 million working mothers with children under 5 years old.

The plan, as accepted by the House, would authorize 80% federal matching funds to build and operate child care centers. A Brademas amendment approved by the House lowered the population requirement for communities seeking to sponsor day care centers under the bill from 100,000 to 10,000. The Senate version set no population limit.

Compromise version—The OEO extension bill, adjusted in Senate-House conference committee, was passed by 63–17 Senate vote Dec. 2 and 210–186 House vote Dec. 7.

The compromise bill would have provided free day care to all children in families with incomes up to $4,320, reduced cost day care for families earning up to $6,960, and full cost care for all other children.

Between one and two million children aged 3–5 would have taken part in fiscal 1973 at a cost of $2 billion. The bill would also have authorized meals, education, medical care and social services.

The cost of the bill was estimated at $6 billion.

Sen. Strom Thurmond (R, S.C.) said Dec. 2 the bill would allow the federal

government to "mold the characters of our nation's young," while Sen. James Buckley (R-Conservative, N.Y.) said it "threatens the very foundation of personal liberty."

Nixon veto—President Nixon vetoed the compromise OEO extension bill Dec. 9, 1971. The Senate voted by 51–36 Dec. 10 to override the veto, but the vote was seven short of the two-thirds majority needed.

In a strongly worded veto message, Nixon said the child care provisions would "commit the vast moral authority of the national government to the side of communal approaches to child rearing against the family-centered approach," and would create "a new army of bureaucrats." While he affirmed support for day care provisions of the House welfare reform bill and other federal child care programs, Nixon said "good public policy requires that we enhance rather than diminish both parental authority and parental involvement with children."

The OEO programs also would have been operated by local government units of at least 5,000 population, leaving the states, in Nixon's words, "relegated to an insignificant role."

House passes new bill—In the face of Republican threats of a presidential veto, the House, by a 234–127 vote Feb. 17, 1972 passed and sent to the Senate a new two-year OEO authorization measure which included a major expansion of the Head Start pre-school program.

The new House bill replaced the day care provision with a two-year expansion of Head Start, from its current budget of $376 million to $1 billion, and opened the program to families above the poverty level, who would pay tuition on a sliding scale.

The bill retained a provision for an independent poverty legal services corporation, backed in principle by Nixon, but the House refused his demand to appoint all 17 corporation directors at his discretion, instead mandating that 11 be chosen from lists drawn up by legal and poverty organizations.

Total authorizations would be $2.3 billion for fiscal 1972 (for which money had already been appropriated by Congress) and $3 billion for fiscal 1973. Before adopting the final bill, the House rejected by a 206–159 vote a Republican move to substitute a simple two-year OEO extension without new provisions.

The bill included an amendment sponsored by Rep. James H. Scheuer (D, N.Y.) to set aside $50 million for programs to aid the elderly poor, and a provision that local community action boards be comprised one-third by elected officials, if they so desire.

Other provisions of the OEO bill criticized by Nixon were the mandatory fund levels for 15 categorical programs, which Nixon claimed would vitiate the OEO's function as innovator, and the creation of an independent national legal services corporation outside the poverty agency. The Administration had favored an independent agency, but Nixon opposed the bill's requirement that 11 of 17 board members, all to be named by the President, be selected from lists drawn by the American Bar Association and other private groups.

Nixon had been urged to sign the bill by a wide range of legal, educational, labor, welfare, religious and women's organizations, and bipartisan groups in both Houses. Opponents claimed that costs would eventually soar, and that the day care program was unnecessary on such a scale.

Senate revises bill—After making major revisions of the House bill, the Senate passed by a 74–16 vote June 29 and sent to a House-Senate conference committee a three-year $9.6 billion authorization bill for the Office of Economic Opportunity, and voted to transfer the legal services program to an independent corporation.

Before passing the measure, the Senate defeated June 29 by a 56–34 vote a proposal by Sen. Roman L. Hruska (R, Neb.) to delete the legal services provision, which he contended would not adequately prevent abuses by poverty lawyers, including radical political activity and broad class action suits against government agencies. Another amendment offered by Sen. Peter H. Dominick (R, Colo.) and accepted by an 89–1 vote would bar lawyers employed by the Legal Services Corp. from engaging in voter registration, illegal demonstrations or violence.

Sen. Gaylord Nelson (D, Wis.), chief sponsor of the bill, said that President Nixon's objections when he vetoed an earlier version of the bill in 1971 were met by the bill's provision that the President appoint 10 of 19 directors of the legal services corporation. But the bill would authorize about $1 billion more in fiscal 1973 than Nixon requested, and would not allow him as much scope in administering and transferring programs as he had asked.

Final version enacted—Following final compromise action on the bill by Congress, President Nixon Sept. 20, 1972 signed a $4.75 billion measure extending the life of the OEO for three years.

The bill had been passed by both houses of Congress Sept. 5, by a 223–97 vote in the House and voice vote in the Senate. A Senate-House conference committee had capitulated to Administration objections by dropping entirely a provision approved by both houses to set up an independent legal services agency for the poor.

The committee had earlier modified the bill to allow the President to name all the agency directors, although two would have been selected from the poor and two from among poverty lawyers. But when rumors persisted that Nixon might repeat his 1971 veto of an earlier version of the bill, Sen. Gaylord Nelson (D, Wis.), chief Senate conferee, had the bill recommitted in a rare parliamentary move, and the independent agency was dropped.

The legal services program thus remained within the OEO, where it was subject to limited veto power by state governors. Vice President Spiro Agnew, in the September issue of the American Law Association Journal, renewed his criticisms of the program, saying "while most programs now turn away individual poor clients with routine legal problems, many nevertheless find time to engage in practically every cause celebre that comes along," including attempts to "effectuate major political changes." The bill authorized a record $71 million for the program.

In other provisions, the bill prohibited any charge for Head Start participation by children from families with incomes below $4,320 a year. The secretary of health, education and welfare would determine fees for other families. At least 10% of Head Start enrollment was to be offered to handicapped children.

The bill authorized a new environmental works program to employ poor people, and a consumer action and education program for the poor.

Administration Proposals

Revenue sharing. President Nixon Jan. 22, 1971 delivered to Congress a State-of-the-Union message in which he proposed the annual sharing of $16 billion of federal revenues with state and local governments. Welfare reform was one of the major concerns to be dealt with. Specific plans for various aspects of aid to the poor were dealt with later in special messages.

Manpower training—The President proposed March 4 in his second revenue sharing message that states and cities be permitted to use federal funds to develop temporary public service jobs to train the unemployed.

In December 1970 the President had vetoed a manpower bill with a similar provision for a public service program, which, he had charged, would only create "dead-end jobs in the public sector." The new proposal stipulated that a public service job could be held no longer than two years and should be regarded as a "transitional opportunity" leading to a regular job with a public or private employer.

Under the proposal a number of existing programs would be consolidated into an annual $2 billion program of unearmarked grants to state and local governments representing 100,000 or more persons. The President stressed that his proposal was not intended to supplant or terminate any program, but to enable the "continuation, expansion or modification of each program [to] be determined . . . by the test of performance alone—and determined by the state or community which the program serves."

The President based his proposal on the idea that manpower programs were best devised and controlled at local lev-

els free from the "bureaucratic jungle." He stressed that the plan (1) was optional, (2) allowed state and local governments to devise their own works plans, (3) freed city, county and state budgets from matching and maintenance-of-effort restrictions, and (4) dispensed with stringent accountability requirements, except for annual audits and publication of spending plans.

Of the proposed $2 billion for the program—a one-third increase over existing manpower outlays—85% would be divided among state and local governments by statutory formula according to proportionate numbers of workers, unemployed persons and low-income adults. The Labor Department would retain 15% for research, development of computerized job banks, experimental manpower programs and local staff training assistance. The proposal also contained a "trigger" feature to automatically release additional funds if the nation's unemployment level ranged 4.5% or higher for three straight months or more.

Urban assistance—The President's urban assistance program sent to Congress March 5 would merge several major housing and urban development programs into one $2 billion plan to enable local governments to develop their own plans for urban and community redevelopment.

In an accompanying fact sheet, the President said "proliferation of separate urban development programs have brought into being independent, local bureaucracies which frequently operate outside the control of elected local officials. This has fragmented local effort and made it difficult for cities to frame a community-wide development strategy. In addition, lengthy federal reviews of applications, and the imposition of federal categorical requirements have excessively delayed renewal activities and distorted local priorities."

Of the proposed $2 billion, $1.6 billion would be allocated to the nation's 247 urban areas with 50,000 or more persons according to a statutory formula taking into account population, degree of substandard housing and proportion of families below the poverty level. The residual $400 million would be distributed at the discretion of the Department of Housing and Urban Development, chiefly to insure that a recipient received no less under the new program than under the old. Any leftover funds would be distributed to reward communities with outstanding programs and help those with exceptional problems.

The President said his proposal would eliminate numerous federal requirements that would free local communities to write their own rules. Matching of federal funds would also be cut out under the new plan.

Rural aid—The President's rural aid message signed March 10 would create a $1.1 billion program for rural development that would replace 11 aid programs but add $179 million in additional funds. The purpose of the program would be to help stem the tide of people to the cities and to create a "dynamic balance" betweeen city and town that "would no longer siphon off one another's strengths and resources nor shunt problems and burdens from one to the other."

The 50 states, as well as Puerto Rico, the Virgin Islands and Guam, would receive funds on the basis of such criteria as the state's rural population, rural per capita income relative to the national average and the state's change in rural population. Each state would be required to submit a budget to the Department of Agriculture and the Department of Housing and Urban Development outlining the state's plans for urban and rural development, thereby focusing on the interrelationship of the two areas. The plans would not have to have federal approval.

In his message, the President also proposed to add $100 million to his $2 billion urban program to assure continued aid to cities with populations ranging from 20,000 to 50,000.

Revenue sharing enacted. Congress completed action Oct. 13, 1972 on a compromise revenue sharing bill, as the Senate voted 59–19 to accept the conference committee report. President Nixon signed the bill Oct. 20.

The House had approved the measure Oct. 12 by a 265–110 vote, after defeating an amendment to delete a $2.5 billion annual limit on various social services programs by a 281–86 vote. The amendment had been proposed by New York representatives, since New York state would be the largest loser under the limit. The state, which had received $498 million in aid under the programs in the past fiscal year, and had expected to receive $855 million in the current year, would receive only $223 million under the new bill.

The bill would distribute $30.2 billion over five years in almost untied aid to states and localities.

The final legislation compromised between the Senate formula for allocating the funds, which favored the smaller states, and the House version favoring the more populous states, by allowing each state to choose the more advantageous of the two.

Funds would be distributed within the states according to the Senate formula, with one-third going to state governments and two-thirds to localities, based on tax effort, population and per capita income. Large cities and rural areas were expected to benefit at the expense of more affluent suburbs.

The funds, which could not be used by localities to meet operating costs of education or general administration needs, could be spent on almost any capital project, or for operating expenses in the areas of public safety, environmental protection, transportation, health, recreation and libraries, social services for the poor or elderly or financial administration. There would be no restrictions on the state government share of the funds.

The $2.5 billion social services authorization limit, compared with a $1.6 billion limit set by the Senate and none by the House, would curb a rapidly expanding program begun in 1962 to aid people currently, recently or potentially on welfare to become self-sufficient. Under previous law, the Department of Health, Education and Welfare (HEW) had provided unlimited funds on a 75% federal-25% state basis for a variety of services. Costs had totaled $1.5 billion for fiscal 1972, but had been expected to rise to $4.7 billion in fiscal 1973 without the new limit.

Under the compromise plan, the social services money would be distributed on a straight population basis and would be retroactive to July 1. The money could be spent in any proportion on child care, family planning, aid to the retarded, foster care or treatment of narcotics or alcohol victims. Other programs could be covered, with a proviso that 90% of spending in such programs be for actual welfare clients.

Volunteer agencies reorganized. President Nixon, in a special message to Congress March 24, 1971, proposed a detailed reorganization plan to merge the Peace Corps, VISTA and seven other volunteer service agencies. The idea for the new agency, called Action, was first offered by the President in a speech at the University of Nebraska Jan. 14.

The plan, which took effect after Congress failed to object within the requisite 60 legislative days, merged programs with 15,000 full-time and 10,000 part-time volunteers.

The National VISTA Alliance, composed of VISTA volunteers, issued a statement March 24 calling the plan "a staggering blow to the war on poverty and the idealism of the American youth." The organization had previously objected to the proposal, which it said would dismantle Volunteers in Service to America. A draft of the merger plan, circulated March 5 to agencies involved, appeared to replace VISTA with four new corps and to direct its activity away from the needs of the poor.

Peace Corps Director Joseph Blatchford, whom the President had designated to head Action, denied March 24 that VISTA's work for the poor would be impaired under the new plan. He said present poverty efforts would be "not only maintained, but expanded."

Nixon inaugurated the new Action agency July 1.

Welfare rule on fathers revised. The Administration proposed Feb. 5, 1971 a welfare rule revision governing the amount of work a welfare father could accept while still receiving aid. The Department of Health, Education and Welfare said the proposal, to take effect in 30 days, "will help to eliminate from the welfare rolls those individuals who are in reality working full time."

It was estimated that the rule change would effect 5% of the men in 119,000 families—or the fathers in 6,000 families—who received aid under a program designed to keep families together. Currently, a welfare father was considered unemployed and eligible for aid if he worked less than 30 hours a week (35 hours in some states). Under the proposed change, a jobless welfare father would be one who worked less than 100 hours a month. More than 100 hours a month would be permitted if the total hours were expected to drop below 100 in future months, such as in cases of migrant or farm workers.

In eight states, the persons dropped from welfare rolls would also lose Medicaid benefits. In those states, Medicaid only covered welfare clients.

Mrs. Johnnie Tillmon, chairman of the National Welfare Rights Organization, said Feb. 5 that the proposed change would actually increase welfare rolls. She said a working father currently receiving some aid "is going to just up and leave [his family], and they're going to have to support the whole family."

Income support plan tested. Preliminary results from a federally-financed welfare test, released May 8, 1971, indicated that a guaranteed minimum income for the working poor would not cause poor people to quite their jobs and live on welfare. Reporting on an experimental program in five Eastern cities, the study said, "There is no evidence indicating a significant decline in weekly family earnings as a result of the income assistance plan."

The Office of Economic Opportunity project, which began in August 1968, paralleled features of President Nixon's proposed Family Assistance Plan in that income assistance was extended to about 700 poor families regardless of whether they continued to work or not. The working habits and incomes of the families given assistance were compared with a control group of unaided poor families.

The experiment, to be completed in 1973, included poor families in Trenton, Paterson, Passaic and Jersey City, N.J. and in Scranton, Pa.

Hunger & Food Aid

Nixon cites program's gains. President Nixon said Jan. 21, 1971 that the number of persons participating in the food stamp program had tripled in 1970, but he added "this is no time to sit back or ease off in our efforts." The President's comments were released with a White House report on accomplishments in the year following the White House Conference on Food, Nutrition and Health.

The report said those participating in the food stamp program rose from 3.6 million to 9.3 million between December 1969 (when the conference was held) and November 1970. It said nearly 300 cities and counties had joined the program during the year and that all but 10 of the nation's cities and counties had established some kind of food program. Federal expenditures for the program were $248 million in 1969, $576 million in 1970 and were budgeted at $1.25 billion in the current fiscal year, ending June 30, 1971.

■ South Carolina Gov. John C. West (D), who had pledged in his inaugural address to end hunger and malnutrition in the state, toured poverty communities on John's Island and in Charleston Feb. 3. West was accompanied by Sen. Ernest F. Hollings (D, S.C.), who said 15 million people in the U.S. suffered from malnutrition. He said the purpose of the tour was to "bring the problem to the public's attention." Hollings said conditions had improved since his last tour two years before. He said: "Now they at least know about the food stamp program."

■ An Agriculture Department spokesman said Feb. 3 that federal school lunch aid had been cut off from 92 school districts in January because of failure to provide "policy statements" of terms under which needy children would be eligible for free or token-priced lunches. Officials said that some of the districts, serving more than 40,000 students, may have since complied with the requirement and had aid restored.

Inaction on hunger charged. Leaders of a national hunger conference said Feb. 5, 1971 that despite "real progress" in the fight against hunger in the U.S., the Nixon Administration's response to the conference's recommendations had been inadequate. The critique of the nation's actions to eliminate hunger came during a one-day follow-up meeting in Williamsburg, Va. of 79 panel chairmen and vice chairmen at the 1969 White House Conference on Food, Nutrition and Health.

Mrs. Patricia Young, who had chaired the Women's Task Force at the conference, said: "I assumed this job with the understanding that our real work would begin after the first conference ended—to press for public, private and governmental action against hunger. But we've had almost no support at all for this from the Administration." She said the delegates had "to put pressure on the White House even to have the follow-up meeting.

Dr. Jean Mayer, general chairman of the 1969 conference, lauded the "gigantic progress" toward eliminating hunger, but he spoke of groups of people "who somehow fall between the cracks of existing progress." He described migrant workers as "men who are killing their wives and their children trying to get work—and subsidizing both the food industry and the consumers out of their misery." He said their "wives and children could receive better care, better housing and better education if they moved north and went on welfare."

Yvonne Perry, who said she came to the meeting uninvited to represent the Virginia branch of the National Welfare Rights Organization, read a statement charging that the meeting had been "quietly stashed away in remote Williamsburg, Va., with no representations from the ranks of the poor."

Hunger session held. Witnesses from 12 states testified at a public meeting in Washington Feb. 16 staged to call attention to hunger in the U.S. by the Citizens Board of Inquiry into Hunger and Malnutrition.

Leslie W. Dunbar, executive director of the Field Foundation and chairman of the meeting, said testimony from the 100 participants demonstrated "a pattern of official lawlessness, at that point where government comes most into contact with poor people."

Many of the witnesses recounted incidents of official callousness and bureaucratic bottlenecks confronting persons seeking relief. Dunbar said, "I have a feeling, and I think it's widely shared, of despair. . . . A feeling that we—our institutions—don't know where we're going. We make the poor fight, clutch and claw for everything they can get."

■ Assistant Secretary of Agriculture Richard E. Lyng said Feb. 19 that the federal government would not undertake food distribution centers in 10 "holdout" counties that had refused to establish federally aided food programs. Lyng said efforts to induce voluntary cooperation in the 10 counties would continue and "I think we'll get most of them." When the Nixon Administration took office, 480 counties and cities had not established locally administered food programs. By Aug. 31, 1970, all but 10 had established programs.

School lunch aid. In response to a protest from 40 senators who had accused the Administration of reneging on a commitment to fund expanded summer free lunch for 2 million children in inner city areas, the Administration agreed to release an additional $15 million in funds. George P. Shultz, director of the Office of Management & Budget, revealed the decision in a letter July 8, 1971 (published July 10) to Sen. Clifford P. Case (R, N.J.). Case had written a July 7 letter bearing the signatures of the bipartisan group.

The protest arose over an announcement by the Agriculture Department June 28 that it would operate the lunch program under an $18.1 million budget, despite requests from states that reportedly totaled $33 million. The same day, Congress cleared a bill (HR 5257-PL 92/32) authorizing an additional $135 million through June 30, 1972 to provide free or reduced-price meals for needy children.

New food stamp rules. The Agriculture Department July 22, 1971 issued revised food stamp program regulations that would make 1.7 million persons eligible for the first time but would eliminate or decrease benefits for more than 2 million other persons currently participating in the program. The rules, which implemented the 1970 Food Stamp Reform Act, also included a new "work requirement" that would make registration for and acceptance of jobs by able-bodied adults a prerequisite for food aid.

The regulations set a uniform national eligibility standard, which would allow a family of four with a monthly income of $360 or less to receive some aid. Of the 45 states participating in the program, only New York, New Jersey and Alaska had eligibility levels at or above the new standard. Other states had ceilings ranging down to $180 per month for a South Carolina family of four.

The Administration changed the final rules from a version proposed April 15 so that a family on welfare could get food stamp aid even if its household income exceeded the national eligibility level. In announcing the regulations, Assistant Agriculture Secretary Richard E. Lyng said the revised rules would particularly benefit "the poorest of the poor"—the estimated 900,000 persons who would receive free food stamps for the first time. For example, a family of four with less than $30 monthly income could now receive free stamps where formerly the stamps cost $2 a month.

However, the new rules cut off aid altogether for some 600,000 current participants with incomes above the new national standard. In addition, others would become ineligible because the new rules denied benefits to unrelated groups living in the same household, a provision mandated by Congress to cut off aid to hippie communes.

Answering protests that the household provision would work against migrant workers who lived in communal situations, Lyng said: "More migrants will be eligible simply because of the fact that they are families and can be certified wherever they move."

The new rules raised the monthly food stamp allocation for a family of four by $2 to $108. However, families with incomes near the maximum eligibility level would have to pay more for their stamps. For example, a family of four earning $360 a month formerly paid $82 for stamps valued at $106. Under the new rules, this family would have to pay $99 for $108 in stamps.

Stamp cutback reversed—The Nixon Administration Jan. 16, 1972 reversed the planned cutback in the food stamp program after the change had drawn protests from senators and governors.

While the July 1971 rules would have allowed an additional 1.7 million people, most of them in Southern and Western states, into the program, it would have eliminated, or reduced benefits to, about 2.1 million people, mostly in Northeastern states, where the cost of living was higher.

The change had been protested Dec. 19, 1971 by 28 senators in a letter to the Agriculture Department.

Sens. George McGovern (D, S.D.) and Clifford P. Case (R, N.J.), in separate statements Jan. 3, warned that they would take legislative action, if necessary, to counter the change.

The protest gained momentum when it was joined by the governors of 15 states and New York Mayor John V. Lindsay, whose representatives met in Hartford, Conn. Jan. 7 to mount an effort to preserve current benefits. They demanded that no family be dropped from the program and that benefits be increased to reflect the cost of an adequate diet.

The New York Times reported from confidential budgetary documents Jan. 12 that the Nixon Administration had impounded $202 million of funds allocated for food assistance, almost 10% of the $2.2 billion appropriated by Congress for the food stamp program. The Administration's budget request for food stamps was $2 billion for fiscal 1972, and Congress had added $200 million to the program.

Sen. Hubert H. Humphrey (D, Minn.) and McGovern protested the impounding Jan. 12. Assistant Agriculture Secretary Frank B. Elliott said that day the $202 million had not been impounded, except in a technical sense, and the money, while not requested by the department for its budget, was "available from the Office of Management and Budget any time we need it."

The policy reversal was announced Jan. 16 by Agriculture Secretary Earl L. Butz, who said he had issued new regulations to insure that "the benefits available to each household are as high or higher than they were under the old regulations." He made clear that the "impounded" funds would be used.

A department report Jan. 1 put enrollment in the food stamp program at 10.9 million persons in November 1971. The combined enrollment in the food stamp program and the program of distributing surplus commodities to needy families was estimated at 14.4 million in November. This compared with a 13.1 million combined enrollment a year earlier and 7.1 million two years previously.

Stamp money unspent—The Agriculture Department reported June 7, 1972 that $400 million of $2.3 billion appropriated for the food stamp program would not be spent because of errors in projecting program growth, delays in implementing new rules and delays by states in bringing new counties under the plan.

Witnesses at a June 7 hearing of the Senate Select Committee on Nutrition criticized the department's action.

Sen. Charles Percy (R, Ill.), chairing the hearing, criticized government rules that penalized recipients who entered work-training programs, while a New York City food stamp program official said more than one out of three recipients in his city would have benefits reduced or eliminated by new rules to be enforced July 1.

Communes to get stamps—A three-judge federal panel ruled in Washington May 30 that a 1971 law denying food stamps to unrelated persons living in the same household, aimed at "hippie" communes, was unconstitutional. Not only did the "hasty last-minute Congressional action" penalize other recipients unintentionally, the court argued, but the law violated Supreme Court decisions on privacy and freedom of association.

School lunch aid increased. The House by 353–0 vote Oct. 18, 1971 and the Senate by unanimous voice vote two days later passed and sent to the President a school lunch aid bill prohibiting Administration cutbacks in the number of eligible children and increasing the federal per-meal subsidy to a minimum of 46¢ for each needy child. President Nixon signed the measure as Public Law 92-153 Nov. 5.

The Agriculture Department Oct. 18 had revoked an Oct. 6 order which had ended subsidies to children of families above the official poverty line.

The order would have eliminated between 584,000 and 1.5 million children in states with eligibility limits above the federal poverty guideline of $3,940 for a family of four. The cutback had been designed to compensate for a per-meal subsidy rise to 45¢ from the previously issued figure of 35¢, which had aroused Congressional and public criticism. (The 1970–71 payments had averaged 42¢ for each of 7.3 million children receiving free or reduced price meals.)

Congress had reacted to the Oct. 6 move as an attempt to circumvent the intent of the 1970 law funding the program. In an Oct. 15 letter to President Nixon, 59 senators of both parties asked him to overrule "what we must consider an unlawful interpretation" of a law "passed by Congress and signed by you as a fulfillment of our pledges to put an end to hunger in America's schoolrooms." Two days later a White House spokesman reported that Nixon had ordered the department to "clarify its regulations."

In Senate hearings Oct. 14 Dr. Jean Mayer, President Nixon's special consultant on hunger, criticized the cutback, which he said had been ordered by the Office of Management & Budget, as "a narrow, legalistic approach at the meanest possible level."

The new bill differed from the latest Agriculture Department regulations in setting 46¢ as a minimum, rather than average, figure. The bill would also prevent the department from restricting the growing school breakfast program, designed for severe poverty areas. (The Department reported Oct. 13 that it had ordered states not to add to the 952,000 children who received breakfast aid in 1970.)

In a related development, Democratic Sens. Hubert Humphrey (Minn.) and George McGovern (S.D.) Oct. 13 asked for a universal free school lunch system. At a hearing of the Senate Select Committee on Nutrition, Humphrey claimed that the means test for lunch aid had encouraged "an economic caste system." McGovern said free lunches should be "an integral part of and prerequisite of the educational process."

Nixon requests further aid—President Nixon asked Congress May 6, 1972 for increased funds for school breakfast and summer lunch programs for poor children, and for revision of the formula for distributing school meal funds.

Nixon asked for $25 million to double the 1972 summer lunch budget, raising the number of recipients to 2.1 million, and requested a $19.5 million rise in the 1972–73 breakfast plan to $52.5 for 1.9 million children.

The proposed new rules would require states to provide free lunches to all children from families with incomes below the poverty line—$4,110 for a family of four in the 1973 fiscal year. Federal subsidies would be denied for any free lunches to children from families with incomes more than 15% above the poverty line. Reduced price lunches would be allowed for children whose families' income was up to 30% above the line.

Another rule change would guarantee federal subsidies to states based on average per-pupil expenditures, apparently replacing the current provision guaranteeing a minimum subsidy for each participating child.

Assistant Secretary of Agriculture Richard E. Lyng said May 6 an additional one million children could be covered. About 8.1 million currently received free or reduced price lunches, out of 25.4 million children in the federally-aided lunch program.

The proposed revision in eligibility rules was criticized May 6 by Sen. Hubert Humphrey (D, Minn.), who said two million children currently on the rolls would be excluded, and by Sen. George McGovern (D, S.D.), who said the fund increase was "not sufficient to make up for the funds authorized by Congress but unspent by the Administration over the past several years." McGovern claimed that three million needy children were still excluded, and warned that subsidy averaging, rather than per-pupil minimums, would harm children in affluent areas, since states would concentrate aid in poor areas. Furthermore, he said, stricter income eligibility rules would hurt children in high-price regions.

Agriculture Department officials had said before appearing at the Senate

Select Committee on Nutrition and Human Needs April 7 that the summer lunch program would be adequately funded by a total of $25.5 million, prompting criticism by McGovern and by Sen, Alan Cranston (D, Calif.).

The Senate committee heard further charges April 10 that the Agriculture Department had "knowingly misled" Congress in underreporting the number of additional schools wanting to join the breakfast program. The department had reported that a survey ordered by Congress had turned up only 1,100 such schools (7,200 currently participated), but Ronald F. Pollack of the Food Research and Action Center in New York said his own survey found 4,903 schools willing to join even at current subsidy levels.

The committee also heard a report by the Action Center that the effect of the breakfast program showed improvements in pupil health, behavior and achievement, and a decrease in absenteeism of up to 10%.

School programs again expanded—Both houses of Congress Sept. 13, 1972 passed and President Nixon Sept. 26 signed a bill providing, in modified form, some of the school-meal requests made by Nixon.

Federal reimbursement for each school lunch would rise from 6¢ to 8¢, with an additional 40¢ for needy children, defined as those from families with incomes less than 125% of the official poverty level. The changes entailed an $85 million fund increase.

An $115 million increase was provided for school breakfast and nonschool food programs. A new two-year program was approved to aid undernourished children and pregnant or lactating mothers.

Cash food aid urged. A public interest organization urged that federal food programs to aid the poor be replaced by direct cash payments, it was reported Oct. 26, 1972.

The Citizens' Board of Inquiry into Hunger and Malnutrition, whose reports in 1967 and 1968 had prompted Congress to pass legislation increasing food aid, said that while vastly increased federal food stamp and school lunch programs

now reached 57% of the nation's poor, bureaucratic waste, private profit and budget-cutting by the Department of Agriculture had kept individual payments to a minimum.

The report said the programs had spawned a "vast bureaucratic mechanism" with a large payroll and high profits to companies providing supplies and help, following a pattern set in antipoverty and defense programs. Nevertheless, the report charged, the Department of Agriculture had returned $418 million in 1972 food aid money to the Treasury, and would have curtailed several programs if Congressional and public pressure had not materialized.

Total federal food aid had risen to $4.3 billion a year, to provide food stamps for 11.8 million recipients and school lunches to 8.4 million poor children. But 43% of the nation's 27 million poor people received no food assistance, and an additional 12% "receive less than three-fourths of the recommended dietary allowances."

Poverty & Welfare Statistics

Number of poor up. The Census Bureau reported May 7, 1971 that the number of the U.S. poor had risen by 5% in 1970, reversing a 10-year trend during which the number of poor decreased by an average of 5% a year. "This is the first time that there has been a significant increase in the poverty population," the bureau said, since it began keeping such statistics in 1959.

The bureau reported 25.5 million poor persons in 1970, an increase of 1.2 million over 1969. John O. Wilson, research chief of the Office of Economic Opportunity, said a major factor in the rise was unemployment, which averaged 4.9% in 1970 and 3.5% in 1969. Government analysts also cited inflation as a contributing factor, particularly among families on fixed incomes. The poor accounted for 12.6% of the population in 1970, as compared to 12.2% in 1969.

Despite the increase in poverty in 1970, the bureau reported far fewer poor people than in 1959 when the poverty population numbered nearly 40 million. The government defined the poverty level as $2,973 for a family of four in 1959, $3,743 in 1969 and $3,968 in 1970, paralleling cost of living increases.

In a racial breakdown, the bureau reported that the white poverty population was 17.5 million in 1970, 67% of the total, and black poor people numbered 7.7 million. However one in three Negroes lived in poverty, compared with one in 10 white persons.

Families headed by women, accounting for 14% of the total population, represented 44% of the poverty population. Poverty was about evenly divided between rural and urban areas, but about 90% of the increase in poor families in 1970 came in metropolitan areas.

(A study released March 18 by two Census Bureau officials showed that a balancing of taxes paid in to the government and benefits paid out to the population resulted in a progressive redistribution of income from rich to poor. Taking direct and indirect taxes into account, the report said families with annual incomes of under $2,000 paid an average of 50% of their incomes in taxes. However, the study showed that returned to them was 106.5% in government benefits—such as welfare, Medicaid and Social Security payments—so that their "net" tax was negative, a benefit of 57%. In comparison, the highest income group, families earning more than $50,000 a year, paid 45% of their incomes in taxes and got back less than 1% for a "net" tax of 44.7% of their incomes. The study was conducted by Herman P. Miller, director of the bureau's population studies, and Roger A. Herriot, a bureau statistician. The report was based on 1968 statistics.)

The bureau reported July 17, 1972 that the number of people classified as poor in 1971 in the U.S., 25.6 million, was unchanged from 1970. (A 200,000 increase from the previous year was described as statistically insignificant.) In 1960, nearly 40 million persons were classified as poor. Overall, 13% of the nation's families in 1971 had incomes below the official poverty level of $4,137 for an urban family of four, about the same percentage as in 1970.

An estimated 42% of the elderly and about 15% of all children under 18 were classified as poor in 1971.

While female-headed households represented only 12% of all families, they accounted for 40% of poor families.

The bureau had reported July 13 that 31.8% of black families were headed by women in 1972, a rise from 28% in 1970, and that median black family income continued to be about 60% of white family income in 1971.

The report found no significant change in the number of black or white families living below the poverty level ($4,137 a year in 1971 for a nonfarm family of four), with 7.4 million blacks in that category in 1971. Unemployment among nonwhites averaged 9.9% in 1971, while the rate for whites was 5.4%.

In one category of families, those in the North and West in which both husband and wife worked, black income reached 104% of white income in 1970, partly because more black women worked year-round.

10% on relief in big cities. A new Health, Education and Welfare Department study, reported by the Washington Post July 16, 1971, showed more than one of 10 residents in the 26 largest U.S. cities received welfare aid. The study, based on February 1971 data, showed a 22.5% increase nationwide in the number of relief clients since the year before. The total number of persons on welfare in the U.S. was reported to be 14.2 million.

The study was the first made by HEW that focused on big-city relief rates. The closest comparable study, one based on February 1970 statistics of the 20 largest metropolitan areas, had shown 6.5% on welfare in the metropolitan areas.

The report said 10.3% of the residents of the 26 largest cities or the counties that contained them were on relief, compared with 6.9% of the entire U.S. population. Large increases in the big-city relief rolls were shown, with Washington, D.C. leading with a 58% increase over February 1970.

The report listed the following relief dependency rates for nine of the 26 largest cities:

Baltimore, 15.2%; New York, 15%; New Orleans, 14.8%; Philadelphia, 14.8%; St. Louis, 14.7%; San Francisco, 14.2%; Washington, 10.5%; Denver, 10.1%; and Jacksonville, 7.5%.

The following relief dependency rates were listed for counties containing the remaining 17 of the 26 largest cities:

Suffolk (Boston), 16.6%; Los Angeles, 12.7%; Shelby (Memphis), 9.8%; Wayne (Detroit), 9.1%; Cuyahoga (Cleveland), 8.8%; Cook and DuPage (Chicago), 8.1%; San Diego, 7.4%; Allegheny (Pittsburgh), 7%; Bexar (San Antonio), 6.7%; Franklin (Columbus, Ohio), 6.7%; Milwaukee and Washington (Milwaukee), 6.2%; Clay, Jackson and Platte (Kansas City, Mo.), 5.5%; King (Seattle), 5.2%; Dallas, 5%; Fort Bend, Harris and Montgomery (Houston), 4.2%; Maricopa (Phoenix), 4%; and Marion (Indianapolis), 3.4%.

'72 welfare data reported. The Department of Health, Education and Welfare reported May 2, 1972 that 14.8 million persons were receiving some form of welfare or medical assistance payments at the end of 1971, 7.2% more than a year earlier. Total payments reached $17.7 billion, nearly $7 billion of that total for medical costs.

But HEW reported that tougher state eligibility rules had slowed the increase in recipients of Aid to Families with Dependent Children in the second half of the year. Some 10.6 million persons were in that category by year end.

The HEW report of June 6, 1972 said that despite an increase of 65,000 in the number of persons receiving some form of welfare in January, total payments declined by $12.4 million, attributed to unpredictably lower medical costs. It was the fifth time in six months that costs declined, although a $100 million increase in October 1971 canceled out the accumulated savings of $57.7 million for the other months. Total January costs were about $900 million in cash payments and $640 million for medical assistance.

Rolls had dropped—The HEW Aug. 25, 1971 had reported the first monthly decline in the size of the nation's welfare rolls in three years. In May there was a .3% drop in the number of relief recipients, a decline of 37,000 persons to 14.4 million on welfare.

The HEW report said the largest welfare category, Aid to Families with Dependent Children (AFDC), showed the first relief roll drop since June 1968, when 5.6 million persons received aid under the program. A total of 10.23 million received AFDC aid in May 1971, 16,000

fewer than in April. The average monthly check for a family also declined $1.65 to $183.75, following a $1.10 average decline the previous month.

In releasing the April figures Aug. 1, HEW had reported the smallest monthly increase in AFDC rolls in two years. John D. Twiname, administrator of the department's social and rehabilitation service, had said then the "April figures reflect in some instances the efforts of states to cut back on the eligibility of applicants for welfare due to the states' financial difficulty. . . . We are concerned about this situation because the needs of welfare recipients have not lessened." Twiname reiterated these comments in releasing the May figures Aug. 25.

In May, 19 states and Puerto Rico reported drops in benefits or eligibility according to the Aug. 25 report. The largest decreases: Alabama, 28,700 recipients; Puerto Rico, 24,300; California, 13,200; Oregon, 5,600; New York, 4,800; Washington, 4,000; and New Jersey, 3,200. Four of these states and Puerto Rico had reported drops the month before: Puerto Rico, 14,000; California, 14,000; Oregon, 5,600; Washington, 3,000; and New York, 2,000.

HEW's report on June data, released Sept. 23, showed a decrease in welfare rolls for the second consecutive month and a three-month decrease in welfare spending. However, the 1971 fiscal year, which ended June 30, showed the biggest annual welfare increase in history: a 27% increase in costs and a 17% increase in welfare rolls. HEW reported total fiscal 1971 welfare costs at $16.3 billion and relief rolls at the end of June at 14.3 million.

The HEW report of March 22, 1972 disclosed that the aggregate number of welfare recipients nationally rose for four consecutive months from August to November 1971, when 14.6 million people received $871.8 million in benefits, an increase of 94,000 people and $14 million over October.

The increase, which followed a three-month decline in May, June and July 1971, occurred in 42 states and jurisdictions in November 1971.

Relief growth slows in '72—HEW said Oct. 17, 1972 that the rate of growth in welfare rolls and in total welfare-Medicaid payments had slowed in fiscal 1972 to the lowest levels since 1966.

In the year ending June 30, slightly more than 15 million persons were on public assistance rolls, a 5% increase over the previous year. Federal-state-local costs reached $18.2 billion, a 17.4% increase in the year. The corresponding fiscal 1971 figures had been 17.2% and 28.3%. HEW attributed the slowdown to rising employment, and to stricter state eligibility and cost controls.

The rolls rose a further 16,000 to 15,-071,000 in July, but costs fell $13 million to $1.6 billion, HEW reported Nov. 24.

HEW reports little welfare fraud. The Health, Education and Welfare Department reported July 7, 1971 that fewer than 1% of the nation's welfare recipients were suspected of fraud by state officials in 1970. HEW's National Center for Social Statistics reported that state agencies were able to document fraud in only about half of the 33,900 suspected cases.

The HEW report said there were more cases of suspected fraud in the family program—1.7%—than in aid programs for the aged, blind and disabled—0.2%. Fraud involved deception about income, resources and need.

The 33,900 suspected cases represented an increase of 200 over suspected fraud in 1969 but a decrease of 5,000 from five years before. The report said state agencies had referred only 8,600 of the 15,500 documented fraud cases for prosecution and only 3,000 cases were actually prosecuted.

■ Rep. John M. Murphy (D, N.Y.) said Jan. 29 that more than $144 million in federal and state antipoverty funds allocated to various agencies across the nation over the last three years was missing. Murphy said General Accounting Office auditors uncovered the loss of the funds and attributed it to shoddy bookkeeping practices rather than fraud. Murphy said he asked for the GAO audit after $7.7 million in funds for New York City antipoverty agencies was reported missing Dec. 14, 1970.

5% said ineligible. Health, Education and Welfare (HEW) Deputy Undersecretary Richard P. Nathan reported Jan. 3, 1972 that 4.9% of all U.S. welfare recipients were ineligible, according to an April 1971 survey, resulting in annual government losses of about $500 million.

Nathan, at a news conference at which Administration officials pressed for Congressional action on President Nixon's welfare reform program, said "most of the errors were honest," and "more than half were agency errors," which could be eliminated by "transfering responsibility and making payments to a new, uniform and automated national system."

The figures were based on a survey of 2.85 million cases in 39 states, Puerto Rico and the District of Columbia, excluding some of the largest states. In the aid to dependent children category, the survey said 5.6% of recipient families were ineligible, 14.6% overpaid, and 9.6% underpaid.

Suspected cases of fraud remained at less than .4% of recipients, Nathan said.

Jobs for Those on Welfare

Welfare-work test announced. President Nixon announced a demonstration project Aug. 20, 1971 under which welfare clients in parts of Illinois, New York and California would be required to take public service jobs or forfeit part of their relief grants. A work requirement formed part of the President's family assistance welfare reform proposal.

Health, Education and Welfare Undersecretary John G. Veneman said Nixon had discussed the experiment with New York Gov. Nelson A. Rockefeller and Illinois Gov. Richard B. Ogilvie Aug. 18. California Gov. Ronald Reagan had met with the President Aug. 20.

New York and California had both enacted recent welfare-work legislation. The California legislation included welfare mothers and unemployed fathers.

The New York law, which took effect July 1, applied only to clients receiving general assistance, a state program not funded by the federal government. Veneman said the demonstration project would extend the New York program to include Aid to Families with Dependent

Children (AFDC) clients. He said, however, that HEW foresaw no work requirements for mothers with children who needed daytime care unless daycare facilities were available.

New York City Human Resources Administrator Jules M. Sugarman said Oct. 3 that the state work-relief law had had "only a marginal effect" in reducing city welfare rolls. Sugarman said that although 20% (5,911 persons) of the city's eligible recipients had failed to comply with the work requirement according to first reports, 2,400 of these were found to have had legitimate reasons.

He said an analysis of the August relief rolls showed only a 4% drop (1,152 persons) related to noncompliance with the new law. Sugarman said 1,331 others had been taken off relief rolls for "normal" reasons.

Sugarman said he was concerned because the initial reports left a "grossly untrue" impression that 20% of the recipients were improperly on relief rolls. He said U.S. congressmen, now considering welfare reforms, had been "besieging us for information, and people who normally defend public welfare are scared to death."

New York plans approved—Health, Education & Welfare (HEW) Secretary Elliot L. Richardson Nov. 24, 1971 approved two experimental welfare plans proposed by New York state that would require some recipients to accept public service jobs, and would penalize others for failing to utilize counseling or work services. The plans were approved on condition that the state provide further financial and administration data.

The New York plan included two parts, labeled "Public Service Work Opportunities Project" and "Incentives for Independence." In the work project, all employable members of 88,500 families, one fourth of those in the Aid to Families with Dependent Children category, would be required to work off their grants in public agencies at prevailing wage rates, accept training, or provide day care for the children of other working recipients.

The incentive plan, which was confined to three localities and was to last one year, would penalize families that refused work and counseling services, provide some full-time public sector jobs for recipients, and set up $1.50 an hour jobs for 15–18-year-old welfare schoolchildren.

HEW approved the experiment after New York state confirmed Nov. 4 that it had dropped a controversial "Brownie point" system. The system, which would have been imposed in an inner city neighborhood, a suburban and a rural county, would have sharply reduced payments to recipient families. The families could then have recouped the money by earning points for children's regular school attendance, participation in community projects or membership in Scout groups, cleaning or repairing residences or reporting the whereabouts of missing fathers.

New York City Mayor John V. Lindsay and Human Resources Administration chief Jule M. Sugarman contended that the "Brownie point" plan would substantially increase administrative costs. In an Oct. 21 letter to Richardson, Lindsay called the proposal "a step back to the dark era of 19th-century Poor Laws."

The plan was also opposed by the AFL-CIO, whose president, George Meany Nov. 1 said that "the Big Brother philosophy behind this proposal involves the most detailed scrutiny of the private lives of those who would be forced to participate."

The work-relief project also ran into criticism. Meany charged that the plan "would carry an onus of second-class nonemployment," would undermine labor and child care standards, and would "exploit" recipients.

Sugarman, according to the Oct. 21 New York Times, claimed that work relief would be more wasteful than hiring recipients for full-time Civil Service jobs, where salary costs would be largely offset by tax collection and elimination of welfare administration costs.

Rep. William Fitz Ryan (D, N.Y.) said Nov. 25 he would join a legal challenge by welfare groups against the entire project, which he called "regressive and punitive," and which he charged was discriminatory, since only some areas within the state were involved.

In a suit filed Oct. 19 by the National Welfare Rights Organization (NWRO), a federal district court judge in Washington refused Nov. 16 to prevent Richardson from approving the plan until HEW released relevant internal government documents. The suit had been filed under the Freedom of Information Act.

George Wiley, NWRO executive director, charged Nov. 10 that "a deal had been made between President Nixon and Gov. Nelson Rockefeller in which rights and needs of welfare mothers and children were being sacrificed on the altar of political ambition."

Reapproval of state plans—HEW announced June 6, 1972 that it had reapproved the experimental New York and California welfare reform plans.

After HEW's approval of the New York plan in November 1971, a federal court in Washington had delayed implementation in March to give welfare rights groups an opportunity to comment. The plan went into effect June 1.

The California plan would place 30,000 welfare recipients in jobs and training. The first group of recipients was summoned to discuss employment alternatives June 15. An earlier California proposal that would reportedly have covered all the state's welfare recipients had been dropped due to HEW opposition.

Work rule enacted for welfare. Congress, by voice votes of both houses Dec. 14, 1971, approved a bill to establish a national work registration requirement for almost all adults receiving welfare aid, many of whom were mothers with dependent children.

The legislation originated in the Senate Dec. 11 as amendments introduced by Sen. Herman Talmadge (D, Ga.) to a minor Social Security bill. They were accepted by a Senate-House conference committee and adopted with little discussion by both houses Dec. 14.

The welfare work plan would require, effective July 1, 1972, all those receiving benefits under Aid to Families with Dependent Children to register for work or training unless they were children (under 16), elderly, ill, mothers with children under six years of age, or supporting someone incapacitated.

Under current law, each state determined the registrants and referred "appropriate" welfare recipients for employment.

The federal government would assume 90% of the cost of day care services for children of working mothers, and 100% of the cost of public service jobs for the employable adults in the first year of the new program, 75% in the second year and 50% in the third year.

The National Welfare Rights Organization Dec. 14 called the work requirement bill "an act of stupidity."

President Nixon signed the bill Dec. 28.

Nixon said the so-called "workfare" provisions, in his judgment, reflected the national interest. "We are a nation that pays tribute to the working man and rightly scorns the freeloader who voluntarily opts to be a ward of the state," he said. "No task, no labor, no work is without dignity or meaning that enables an individual to feed and clothe and shelter himself and provide for his family."

Public jobs bills. A public service jobs bill, approved by the House Aug. 4, 1971 by a 321–76 vote and the Senate Aug. 6 by a 68–10 vote, was signed by President Nixon Aug. 9. The $1 billion appropriation was designed to provide 150,000 jobs in state, county and city governments for the unemployed. The jobs would be in health, education, law enforcement, sanitation and public works.

The triggering mechanism, whenever the nation's jobless rate exceeded 4.5% for three consecutive months, was effective immediately. Labor Secretary James D. Hodgson had announced July 23 the Administration was ready to start disbursing the funds pending Congressional action.

Nixon July 12 had signed an Emergency Employment Act authorizing $2.25 billion to provide public service jobs in the next two years for the unemployed at the state and local levels. Although Nixon had vetoed two previous public service job bills in December 1970 and June 29, 1971, he said the bill he signed July 12 had been written in a way that removed his objections to the earlier measures. He said that while the bill vetoed in December might have led to "dead-end" jobs, the new bill provided work that could lead to permanent employment. He added that the job opportunities opened up by the new bill would not lead to "entrapment in permanent public subsidy."

Nixon said that the July 12 bill would provide 150,000 jobs. He said the new law would go into effect immediately in high unemployment areas such as those affected by layoffs in the aerospace industry.

The jobs provided by the July 12 law would be similar to those envisaged under the two vetoed measures. A key difference, however, was that under the new law, state and local governments would be required in their applications to give the federal government assurances that the jobs would lead to permanent employment. In addition, the new law would expire in two years. The earlier measures would have been permanent.

A bill essentially the same as the one he had vetoed June 29 was signed by Nixon Aug. 5, 1971. The measure, authorizing $2,445,500,000 for public works and economic development and $1,547,000,000 for Appalachian regional development had been passed by the House July 28 and by the Senate July 30. It differed from the vetoed bill by the deletion of a $2 billion authorization for accelerated public works projects, a feature to which Nixon objected as a "costly and time-consuming method of putting unemployed persons to work." (The Senate upheld the veto July 14.)

(President Nixon announced a $303 million federal program June 2 to provide summer jobs for 674,000 teenagers. An additional 150,000 jobs would be underwritten by the National Alliance of Businessmen. The jobs would be as tutors, office aides, antipollution and recreation workers.)

Job training program resubmitted. President Nixon renewed a request to Congress Feb. 7, 1972 for a $2 billion manpower program. In a special message stressing a shift of control in manpower programs from federal to local government, the President called for enactment of an Administration program proposed in 1971 for distributing $1.7 billion in unearmarked grants to states, cities and counties for training the unemployed and underemployed.

Current manpower training programs would be consolidated under the revenue sharing plan and some programs commanding powerful support in Congress, such as Neighborhood Youth Corps, JOBS and Operation Mainstream, would be replaced.

Another $300 million would be administered by the Labor Department for national job training programs.

JOBS program questioned. The Job Opportunities in the Business Sector (JOBS) program, the major Nixon Administration job training effort, was criticized as ineffective and wasteful in a March 23, 1972 report (released May 29) by the Department of Labor program review and audit section.

The report charged that businesses had been paid for "excessive costs in those cases where an enrollee only required placement assistance," that fixed-unit-price contracts had not been reexamined when businesses failed to abide by all the terms, that the Manpower Administration had not verified information supplied by contractors, and that the Administration had ignored 584 audit reports on contracts. The audit section decided, in view of past results, to suspend future audits in the program.

The JOBS program, which paid private businesses to train and employ disadvantaged workers, had trained more than half a million persons, according to government figures, at a cost of over $1 billion.

Manpower Administrator Malcolm R. Lovell Jr., in reply to the charges May 29, said the Administration was satisfied with the overall program, and reported that a new type of contract was being developed.

Work disincentives cited. A study prepared for the Joint Congressional Subcommittee on Fiscal Policy, reported Dec. 21, 1972, said rules reducing benefits in a wide range of federal aid programs when family income rose strongly discouraged recipients from finding new or better jobs.

Reductions in welfare, Medicaid, food stamp, unemployment or Social Security payments and increases in rents for public housing amounted in many cases to "confiscatory tax rates," according to subcommittee chairman Rep. Martha W. Griffiths (D, Mich.), who said the findings showed that reform of the welfare program alone would fail without "comprehensive revision of our entire system of public benefit programs."

Problems of the Aged

'Crisis' for aged reported. The Senate Special Committee on Aging, in a report of Jan. 17, 1971, said the "retirement income problem in the United States has become a retirement income crisis." Sen. Harrison A. Williams Jr. (D, N.J.), chairman of the committee, prefaced the report entitled "Economics of Aging."

The report said: "A most distressing fact—a disgrace in a nation pledged to an all-out war on poverty—is that there was an increase in both the number and the proportion of aged poor between 1968 and 1969." The study said poverty among Americans over 65 increased by 200,000 people between 1968 and 1969 while it decreased by 1.2 million for all other age groups.

The committee said poverty was most acute among the minority group elderly. It reported a 50.2% poverty rate among older blacks compared with 23.3% for elderly white Americans.

The report said health costs for persons over 65 averaged $692 in 1969 and that Medicare covered less than half the costs. Health costs for the aged were six times that for young people and $2\frac{1}{2}$ times that for the 19–64 age group.

The committee said older Americans had been particularly hard hit by unemployment and that the problem was aggravated because thousands lost not only their jobs but also their pensions "even though they may have worked most of their lives to provide a 'nest egg' for retirement." Unemployment among workers over 45 had risen from 596,000 to 1,017,000 since January 1969.

Programs for aged assessed. The Senate Special Committee on Aging, in a report of April 4, 1971, said federal housing, health and retirement income programs for older Americans continued to be "fragmented" and "haphazard." The report, prepared for the White House Conference on Aging to be held in November, called 1970 "a year of frustration" for the elderly.

The report said the Administration on Aging, set up in 1965, failed to coordinate programs adequately for the 20 million Americans 65 years old and over. It said the elderly poor increased by 200,000 in 1970 and that 25% of older Americans lived in poverty.

Citing housing problems, the committee said six million persons 65 and over lived in substandard housing in 1970 and that many of the one million older persons currently in nursing homes or mental institutions could be released if they had someplace to go. The report recommended that the government build 120,000 new housing units each year for the elderly, double the current level.

Noting that the cost of premiums for the part of Medicare paid for by the elderly had nearly doubled since the program began in 1965, the report recommended that Medicare be entirely financed through payroll taxes and general revenues. The report also supported automatic cost-of-living rises in Social Security benefit levels.

A federal advisory council, in a report issued April 3, also recommended that the entire Medicare program be paid for through payroll taxes and federal revenues and that Social Security laws be changed to permit automatic cost-of-living adjustments.

The panel asked that Medicare be expanded to cover partial payment of prescription drugs for out-of-hospital use. It urged that Medicare be extended to persons receiving disability benefits under Social Security. The report also recommended extended Medicare coverage at a lower cost for persons with long illnesses.

Aged poverty rises. The Senate Committee on Aging said Nov. 25, 1971 that 4.7 million elderly Americans, one quarter of those over 65, lived in poverty, an increase of 100,000 since 1968. The figure reversed a trend from 6 million in 1959 to 4.6 million in 1968. Some 6 million aged persons still lived in unsatisfactory housing.

The committee blamed forced early retirement as one cause of poverty, citing an increase in the number of Social Security pensioners under 65, despite reduction in benefits for early retirees. In addition, nearly 20% of the nation's unemployed were over 45.

The committee called for big increases in Social Security benefits and for federal help in building 120,000 housing units a year for the elderly.

Conference on aging. Delegates to the White House Conference on Aging, held in Washington Nov. 28 to Dec. 2, 1971, heard a variety of proposals to bolster income and health care for the nation's 20 million people over 65.

The conference had been authorized by Congress in 1968, called by Nixon in 1969 and preceded by about 6,000 local meetings. Dr. Arthur S. Flemming, former secretary of health, education and welfare (HEW) and Nixon's special consultant on aging, chaired the conference, as he had the previous conference in 1961.

In his Dec. 2 address to the 3,500 delegates, Nixon promoted the welfare reform bill passed by the House, which would provide a minimum income of $1,800 for single elderly persons and $2,-400 for elderly couples, and increase Social Security and Medicare benefits. The White House conference's income committee voted Dec. 1 for a $4,500 per couple minimum, while a meeting of blacks, one of 17 "special concerns sessions," Dec. 1 backed a $9,000 figure.

Nixon promised relief from rising property taxes through an unspecified overhaul of the nation's school finance system, and said he would propose a private pension reform bill to expand coverage and require vesting of employes to protect their benefits.

The President expressed continued concern with unsatisfactory conditions in nursing homes, and HEW Secretary Elliot L. Richardson told a conference luncheon Nov. 30 that HEW would initiate Medicaid cutoff procedures against 7,000 nursing homes in 37 states and the District of Columbia if the states failed to correct "substantial deficiencies."

Some Administration spokesmen sparked debate by emphasizing voluntary action. Dr. Jean Mayer, former Nixon nutrition adviser, Nov. 30 questioned Housing and Urban Development Secretary George Romney's statement that "self help is vital," in the case of "someone who is deaf, who is partly blind, whose children have moved away."

A Cabinet-level committee on aging and a special post-conference board would review the recommendations, according to Nixon.

Migrant Farm Workers

Senators hear plight of migrants. In testimony before the Senate Select Committee on Nutrition Feb. 23, 1971, a pediatrician said malnutrition among the children of migrant workers was 10 times greater than among the nation's children generally. The hearing was the first of a series called to review the results of the 1969 White House Conference on Food, Nutrition and Health.

Sen. George S. McGovern (D, S.D.), chairman of the committee, said the testimony of Dr. H. Peter Chase of the University of Colorado medical center was "among the most dramatic and disturbing evidence" heard by the committee since its inception in December 1968. Chase, 34, was conducting his third study of Mexican-American migrant children in Texas and Colorado.

Chase reported instances of severe cases of malnutrition and disease among the children he examined. He said that while extreme cases were rare, malnutrition serious enough to stunt growth and endanger mental development "definitely exists in this [migrant] population and must be corrected."

In a letter to the committee, Dr. Jean Mayer, chairman of the 1969 conference, said "the biggest deficiencies at the federal level" of the fight against hunger "are the underfunding of practically every program, and the lack of clearcut, unambiguous federal directives to local authorities."

Migrants' plight. The 1971 Manpower Report of the President gave this description of the plight of migrant farm workers:

The migratory workers and their families may be away from their home base for several months out of the year. Their itinerary may span thousands of miles, many different employers, and a variety of crops. Jobs are intermittent, and slack periods with little or no earnings are common.

Migratory farmworkers travel out of economic necessity, not because of preference for nomadic life. Seasonal farm activities in the southern parts of Florida, Texas and California, which are the home base areas for the largest groups of migrants, do not provide sufficient employment and earnings. Workers depending on seasonal farm jobs must move with the crops in the hope of lengthening their periods of work and increasing their annual incomes. Migrants begin their annual trek northward in the early spring, following a cycle of activities in a number of crop areas. In California, they typically cultivate cotton and vegetables and then move into the harvest of a variety of spring vegetable and fruit crops. In other Western and North Central States, they find spring jobs in sugar beet cultivation and in the strawberry harvest. During the spring, migratory workers also are found in fruit and vegetable harvest activities in the Atlantic Coast States. Summer and fall are the most active seasons; migratory workers are relied on to supplement local labor in harvesting tomatoes, grapes, peaches, pears, melons, cherries, blueberries, cucumbers, apples, tobacco and other crops.

The peak employment of migratory workers in areas reporting to the Department of Labor usually occurs in August . . . Nearly three-fourths of these were interstate migrants. Virtually every state uses migratory workers at some time during the year, with the largest numbers in California, Michigan, Texas, and Florida. Other states with significant numbers of these workers were Ohio, Oregon, New York, Washington, and New Jersey.

Migratory workers basic problem is, of course, irregularity of work, despite efforts by the public employment service to coordinate and regularize their employment. Harvest timetables may be upset by the vagaries of weather and crop failure. The number of workers needed may be overestimated, or the unexpected arrival of crews may upset prior plans and create labor surpluses in some areas while others are short of workers. And workers receive no pay for time spent in travel or waiting for work. In effect, some of the risks associated with the weather and other circumstances are shifted from

employers to hired workers to a much greater extent than in other industries where the labor supply is less flexible and workers are protected by collective bargaining agreements. Furthermore, housing and sanitary conditions are often unsatisfactory in the migrant workers' camps, and adequate health services and child care are generally lacking.

The majority of migratory farmworkers come from seriously disadvantaged groups. Many are Mexican-Americans and Negroes, whose employment problems are compounded by discrimination.

The average level of education is low. Since families are constantly on the move, the schooling of children is often interrupted. Large numbers of migrant children who are in school are below the grade level normal for their age. Many drop out of school at an early age to help supplement family earnings and thus further handicap themselves in future efforts to enter more stable, better paid fields.

Dr. Robert Coles, Harvard research psychiatrist, had told the Senate Subcommittee on Migratory Labor July 18, 1968:

It is one thing to get poor food, never see a doctor, and live in a brokendown shack—indeed, at times in enlarged chicken coop without running water, screens, plumbing or even electricity. It is quite another order of human experience when children are moved from one place to another, within States and across State lines. These children eventually become dazed, listless, numb to anything but immediate survival—which is also in jeopardy, because the infant mortality rate among such children can be three or four times higher than it is among nonmigrant people. I am saying that constant mobility, constant moving and more moving, damages the physical and mental health of children in special ways—so that migrants present us with a special and awful problem even when compared to other underprivileged groups.

An OEO study found that the average migrant family of six had a total income of $2,021 in 1971 at a time when the poverty level for such a family was $4,800.

Relief ordered in Florida. President Nixon acted March 15, 1971 to extend disaster relief to include migrant workers in Florida who were unemployed as a result of freeze and drought that ruined commercial tomatoes and other crops. The President declared the crop failure a major disaster and allocated $2.5 million to pay unemployment compensation to the workers, who were ineligible for state benefits.

Press Secretary Ronald L. Ziegler said the action was "unprecedented" but emphasized that similar applications in the future would be considered on a "case-by-case" basis. In the past, federal disaster relief only applied to such occurrences as floods, hurricanes and earthquakes.

Hundreds of migrants had demonstrated peacefully March 13 outside the President's Key Biscayne home seeking relief. The migrants, who estimated that more than 15,000 were out of work, cited U.S. aid to Pakistan and said, "if this country can provide relief for starving people over 15,000 miles away, surely it can take care of its own people who find themselves, through no fault of their own, in a disaster situation here in Florida." Florida Gov. Reubin Askew had asked the President for federal disaster relief March 11.

In addition to unemployment compensation, the President's emergency declaration would permit additional relief to the migrants under the federal food stamp program.

Camp access blocked. Attorney General John N. Mitchell announced March 11, 1971 that the government had filed suit seeking access to migrant worker camps for agents of federal assistance programs. The suit, the first of its kind, was filed in federal district court in Kalamazoo, Mich. against John Hassle, owner of the largest farm and orchard in Van Buren County.

The suit said Hassle had tried to keep representatives of federal, state, local and private assistance programs from entering the camps, thus depriving the migrants of information about aid programs open to them. Van Buren and its neighboring counties had the largest concentrations of migrant workers in the U.S. From May to September each year, more than 21,000 workers harvested fruit and vegetable crops in the area. Most of the workers were Mexican-Americans, but some were poor whites and blacks.

In a related development, Gov. William T. Cahill (R, N.J.) proposed a migrant-labor bill March 15 that would guarantee what he called "reasonable" access to migrant camps in New Jersey, many of which had been sealed by farmers posting "no trespass" signs. Cahill said, "Refusal to permit federal and state antipoverty, health and education officials to visit migrant labor camps has at times frustrated the lives of seasonal workers."

The proposals, which also included a $1.50 an hour minimum wage guarantee and a provision for interpreters to help Puerto Rican workers, were based on an investigation by Cahill's administration following a 1970 controversy between New Jersey farmers and federal antipoverty officials. Two antipoverty workers were arrested on trespass charges in August 1970, and the officials contended that farmers were misusing trespass laws to perpetuate alleged squalor and deprivation in the camps.

The N.J. Supreme Court ruled unanimously May 11 that farmers could not invoke trespass statutes to keep qualified visitors from migrant work camps. The ruling struck down trespass convictions of two federal antipoverty officials—Peter K. Shach, a legal services lawyer, and Frank Tejeras, a caseworker.

The opinion by Chief Justice Joseph Weintraub said: "The employer may not deny the worker his privacy or interfere with his opportunity to live with dignity and to enjoy associations customary among our citizens. These rights are too fundamental to be denied on the basis of an interest in real property and too fragile to be left to the unequal bargaining strength of the parties."

State legislation to improve the working and living conditions of migrant workers was signed by Gov. Cahill June 7.

One of the new bills guaranteed wages equal to the state's $1.50 per hour minimum for seasonal farm workers who did piece-rate work. Another provided for registration of migrant crew leaders and prohibited hiring of crew leaders not certified by the state.

Another bill required water and sanitary facilities for work sites. The legislation also provided $50,000 for interpreters to assist non-English speaking migrants.

Aid to education mismanaged? A private study charged March 19, 1971 that $17 million of $97 million appropriated for educational aid for migrant children had been returned unused by states in fiscal years 1967-69. The National Committee on the Education of Migrant Children, in a 15-month study funded by the Ford Foundation, said the Office of Education program, "as presently conceived and administered, . . . cannot meet the needs of migrant children."

Sen. Walter F. Mondale (D, Minn.), at a Washington news conference where the report was released, said the study showed that even Congressional action was no guarantee that migrants would receive the intended benefits. Sen. Adlai E. Stevenson III (D, Ill.), who succeeded Mondale as chairman of the Senate Subcommittee on Migratory Labor, said the report was "shocking" and that he had sent letters to the secretary of health, education and welfare and the U.S. commissioner of education asking for their comments.

The study, written by Cassandra Stockburger, also charged that many migrant children were found to be enrolled in segregated classes or schools. The report said that in 42 states surveyed, only 22% or less of migrant children were enrolled beyond the sixth grade—a proportion half that for the nation as a whole and only 1% higher than the number enrolled beyond the sixth grade in 1952. Miss Stockburger estimated that 300,000 migrant children were affected by the federal program.

Child labor conditions deplored. The American Friends Service Committee, in a report on a five-state investigation conducted in the summer of 1970, said March 21, 1971 that child-labor abuse in American agriculture compared with "the sweatshop scene in 1938." Quaker investigating teams, aided by the National Committee on the Education of Migrant Children, had conducted these studies in Ohio, Maine, California, Oregon and Washington.

The report said many migrant families lived in shacks without plumbing and worked in fields sprayed with DDT. The study said that child labor in industry was outlawed in 1938 but that one-fourth of the farm wage workers in the U.S. were under 16, and some were as young as six.

The study contended, "As long as farm workers are not covered by the same legislation as industrial workers, especially as such legislation relates to children, the farm labor supply will be increased by the employment of these children. As a consequence, wages for all farm labor will remain low."

The study found pay for children ranging from piecework wages such as 12¢ a crate for strawberries to an average hourly wage of $1.12 in California. Among other findings: 35% of the potato crop in Aroostook County, Me. was hand-harvested by crews consisting mainly of children; 4,500 children picked berries, beans and cucumbers in Skagit County, Wash., including 99% of all children over six in migrant families there.

Migrant aid called inadequate. A two-year study issued May 28, 1971 by the Migrant Research Project showed that fewer than one in 10 of the migrant families surveyed received welfare assistance of any kind. The report said the average income of the families in 1970 was only $2,021—less than half the federal poverty level for families of their size.

Margaret Garrity, project director, said federal assistance programs were ineffective for migrants because of the mobility of the families, their ignorance of available benefits and bureaucratic conflicts. The project's annual report said the Nixon Administration's family assistance plan was a step in the right direction but added, "unless the proposed legislation takes into consideration the sporadic and erratic income pattern of migrants, they will be as successfully eliminated from that type of assistance as they are from current programs."

Manpower program for migrants. Labor Secretary James D. Hodgson announced a $20 million manpower program for migrant farm laborers June 19, 1971. The plan was immediately denounced by several migrant groups.

Critics cited a Labor Department probe that had found the Farm Labor Service, in charge of the new program, to be "a de facto institutional discriminator."

Hodgson said the $20 million allocation, to run through June 30, 1972, would be in addition to the $23 million regular budget for the Farm Labor Service. He said the new money would provide health care, educational, food stamp and housing services. Training and job development would be provided for seasonal workers who wanted to leave the migrant work force.

Hodgson said a "comprehensive manpower program" for migrants was "long overdue." He said the migrant worker's "plight has been studied excessively, but not dealt with effectively."

The Migrant Legal Action Program Inc. issued a statement June 19 criticizing Hodgson for placing the new program under the "one agency which his own department has labeled an institutional discriminator." Mario Obledo, executive director of the Mexican-American Legal Defense and Educational Fund, said "doubling the Farm Labor Service budget is a little like giving $20 million to the Ku Klux Klan to find jobs for blacks." Robert Gnaizda of California Rural Legal Assistance urged Hodgson to "express his faith in the farm worker by giving the farm worker an opportunity to run his own manpower program."

Sixteen organizations and 398 individual farm workers had petitioned Hodgson April 22 to replace the Farm Labor Service with a migrant-staffed Worker Service. The petition called the Farm Labor Service "a grower-staffed and oriented network that cycles migrants into poverty." The suit charged the service with "sending an oversupply of migrants to the worst paying jobs" and "housing them in condemned barns." It charged "wholesale violations of the civil rights of black and brown workers." The groups said the program, which had been set up during the Depression to find jobs in the interstate market for persons unable to find jobs locally, now functioned to guarantee growers a cheap supply of labor.

In another development, a bipartisan group of 38 representatives from Northeastern and Middle Atlantic states protested to the Labor Department June 30 that the new migrant manpower program excluded 30,000 migrants who came into their states to work each year. At a Washington news conference, Rep. Herman Badillo (D, N.Y.) said he failed to see how the department could describe the new program as comprehensive.

Health & Education

Nixon health plan. President Nixon Feb. 18, 1971 submitted to Congress a 17-page message outlining his proposals for "a comprehensive national health insurance program, one in which the public and the private sectors would join in a new partnership to provide adequate health insurance for the American people."

The major feature concerning the poor was a Family Health Insurance Plan. The plan, to be "fully financed and administered by the federal government," would cover "all poor families (with children) headed by self-employed or unemployed persons whose income is below a certain level. For a family of four persons, the eligibility ceiling would be $5,000." Charges would be based on income—for the poorest there would be no charges, and as "family income increased beyond a certain level ($3,000 in the case of a four-person family) the family itself would begin to assume a greater share of the costs."

This proposal would cost about $1.2 billion in additional federal funds in the first year. "Since states would no longer bear any share of this cost, they would be relieved of a considerable burden," Nixon said. He added that as an encouragement to states "to use part of these savings to supplement federal benefits, the federal government would agree to bear the costs of administering a consolidated federal-state benefit package."

In addition, the message added that the "federal government would also contract with local committees to review local practices and to ensure that adequate care is being provided in exchange for federal payments. Private insurers, unions and employes would be invited to use these same committees to review the utilization of their benefits if they wished to do so."

Under the Family Health Insurance

Plan, the parts of the current Medicaid program designed to help most welfare families would be eliminated; the Medicaid provisions covering the aged poor, the blind and the disabled would continue.

HEW moves to curb Medicaid fraud. The Department of Health, Education & Welfare issued final regulations March 26, 1971 to prevent fraud by doctors dentists and other dispensers of medical services under Medicaid. The regulations had been published in proposed form in 1969, following hearings by the Senate Finance Committee on charges of fraud in the Medicare and Medicaid programs.

Under the regulations, states would have to spot-check clients from among the 17 million participants in the $6 billion Medicaid program to determine whether reported services had actually been received. States would also have to file annual information returns with the Internal Revenue Service showing amounts paid to providers of Medicaid service, who would be identified by name, address and Social Security number. The regulations also provided for state and federal prosecution for Medicaid fraud.

Free hospital care ordered. Health, Education and Welfare (HEW) Secretary Elliot L. Richardson announced new rules April 18, 1972 to enforce requirements that all hospitals and health care facilities that have received federal aid provide a minimum amount of free services to poor people.

Under the rules, to go into effect within 30 days, any institution that had ever accepted funds under the Hill-Burton Act would have to provide free services to poor people equivalent to at least 5% of its operating cost and at least 25% of its net income, or face penalties ranging to revocation of its license. Institutions in financial difficulties, or in areas with few poor people, would be exempted.

The order was issued after five class action suits were filed against HEW, mostly by poverty lawyers working with Office of Economic Opportunity funds, in the District of Columbia, West Virginia, Florida, Louisiana and Colorado. Nationally, 3,608 non-profit hospitals and 2,700 other facilities were affected.

Long-term poverty funding asked. An American Public Health Association study panel concluded that long-term funding of health care centers in poor areas was necessary to improve stability and quality of care, it was reported Nov. 13, 1972.

The study had been requested by four U.S. senators, with the support of Mississippi Gov. William Waller, to investigate charges surrounding the Delta Health Center in Mound Bayou, Miss. Although "there were problems surrounding the operations of the Delta" center, the panel found, they were not "irreversible or unique," and resulted largely from the lack of long-term funds, leading to difficulties in staff recruitment, and from failure to recognize the specific problems of operating in poverty areas.

Office of Economic Opportunity (OEO) Director Phillip V. Sanchez had decided Sept. 17 to overrule Waller's veto of a $4.15 million nine-month grant to the center. It was the second Mississippi health center to receive OEO funds in 1972 over Waller's objections; the other was in Jackson.

Waller had charged that the Delta center had delivered insufficient care for the money spent, but Owen Brooks, Delta's board chairman, claimed that Waller's vetoes were prompted by opposition to community control.

Medicaid cut warning. HEW warned Nov. 22, 1972 that thirteen states and the Virgin Islands faced cutbacks in federal Medicaid assistance because they had failed to begin preventive medical and dental screening programs for the children of Medicaid-eligible parents, as required by the 1967 Social Security Act.

In addition, the states faced losses of 1% in AFDC payments under a provision of the 1972 Social Security Act requiring states to inform welfare recipients that the screening programs were available.

Title I inefficiency charged. A survey prepared for the U.S. Office of Education (released April 10, 1972) said the Title I program to improve education for poor children "has never been implemented" as intended in the 1965 Elementary and Secondary Education Act. It concluded that "there is little evidence at the national level that the program has had any positive impact on eligible and participating children."

The report, prepared by the private American Institutes for Research in Palo Alto, Calif. and based mostly on federal and state evaluation data and audits, said that after six years of operation and early public criticism, 37 states (as of June 1971) were violating Title I rules, according to the Department of Health, Education and Welfare (HEW). Among the major deficiencies were the use of funds for routine school expenses, improper accounting and auditing and failure to involve parents.

HEW had requested in September 1971 that the District of Columbia and six states return $5.6 million in misspent funds. At the time of the April 1972 report, none but Wisconsin had complied. A HEW spokesman said April 10 that 26 more states would be asked to return $28 million–$30 million. Total aid was running at the rate of $1.6 billion a year.

"No hard evidence" was uncovered linking the cost of the special programs with results, or indicating any "minimum necessary expenditure" as a prerequisite for success. In the five states reporting average costs of their most and least successful programs, the least effective were often substantially more expensive. In very few cases was the difference between achievement by poor children and the national average on standard tests substantially narrowed as a result of a Title I program.

The report recommended a maximum per-pupil aid figure, to prevent "expensive programs that deny services to many deserving children." Such non-academic services as food, health and "cultural enrichment" should be covered by other federal programs, with Title I concentrating on reading and mathematics.

Voucher test. The Office of Economic Opportunity April 24, 1972 announced a two-year experiment of the educational voucher system for 4,000 elementary and junior high schoolchildren in a San Jose, Calif. school district.

Parents of the children, chosen as a cross-section of the mixed Mexican-American, black and white Anglo district, would receive vouchers equivalent in value to the funds currently spent by the district for each pupil. They would turn the voucher over to any of six public schools in the district, each of which would develop a separate curriculum centered on such concerns as reading, the arts, ethnic studies or bilingual studies.

The OEO would provide a supplement of one-third the voucher value for each of 2,000 poor children in the district, as an incentive for the schools to develop programs attractive to poor parents.

The OEO pledged $2 million for the supplements and for administration and training expenses.

State & Regional Action

Residency requirements under fire. Despite a Supreme Court ruling in 1969 that residency requirements for welfare benefits were unconstitutional except in cases of "compelling state interests," legislatures in four states passed one-year residency requirements in June and July 1971. The High Court had held that such requirements violated the Constitution's equal protection clause as well as the "freedom to travel."

Hawaii Gov. John Burns signed legislation setting up the residency requirement June 7, to take effect June 22. The Hawaii bill was passed partly due to fear that many applicants from among an estimated total of 6,000 young people expected in the islands as part of an annual summer influx would apply.

New York Gov. Nelson Rockefeller's office announced June 23 that a welfare residency requirement bill had been signed and would take effect immediately. Responding to an appeal by the New York Civil Liberties Union, however, U.S. District Court Judge John T. Curtis in Buffalo issued an injunction July 12 against enforcement of the new law until a trial could be held to determine if the requirement were constitutional.

One-year welfare residency requirements were approved by the Connecticut and Illinois legislatures July 1.

*Courts act against residency laws—*A three-judge federal panel in Buffalo ruled Aug. 9 that New York's newly enacted welfare residency law was unconstitutional.

The law had taken effect June 22 but had only applied for one month because enforcement was halted by a federal restraining order. The new ruling ordered a permanent statewide injunction against the requirement.

The state had argued that New York was getting back only 43% from the federal government for its $8 million a year welfare program while Mississippi, with much lower benefits, was getting 78% federal reimbursement. The American Civil Liberties Union (ACLU) said relief rolls in New York increased 11% in fiscal 1971, the lowest proportionate rise in all 50 states.

A three-judge federal panel in Hartford had voided a Connecticut welfare residency law July 29. The Connecticut legislation had been modeled on the New York law.

The Supreme Court Jan. 24, 1972, unanimously and with no hearing, upheld the court rulings barring one-year welfare residency laws in New York and Connecticut.

The court had ruled in 1969 that a welfare residency law was an unconstitutional restriction on free interstate travel and made "invidious distinctions" between poor persons who were long-term residents and those who were not. Such a law could be justified, the court said, only by "compelling governmental interest." The two state laws, enacted after that decision, cited budgetary problems as meeting that criterion. However, federal panels in both cases said the 1969 ruling excluded fiscal problems as a justifying factor. (Opponents of the bill said that fewer than 1% of New York recipients had resided in the state for less than a year.)

Chief Justice Warren Burger, who had criticized the 1969 ruling in an earlier opinion, concurred in the latest decision.

(The Supreme Court Oct. 12, 1971 had upheld a lower court ruling invalidating a five-year residency requirement for applicants for publicly supported housing in New Rochelle, N.Y.)

States cut welfare funds. A Health, Education and Welfare Department (HEW)

survey, reported by the Associated Press July 8, 1971, said 22 states were cutting welfare benefits or planning to effect reductions by the end of the year. The survey, submitted to HEW Undersecretary John G. Veneman, said the findings indicated a reversal of a long trend of higher assistance for the poor.

The study of family welfare programs said cuts of up to 20% had been ordered in 10 states and reductions by the end of 1971 were possible in 12 additional states. Moves to cut benefits failed in the legislatures of four states. The study listed 1971 aid increases in four states and the District of Columbia and increases were said to be possible in three other states.

The 10 states slated for definite reductions were Alabama, Georgia, Kansas, Maine, Nebraska, New Jersey, New Mexico, New York, Rhode Island and South Dakota. The 12 states listed for possible reduction were Arizona, California, Connecticut, Delaware, Idaho, Illinois, Minnesota, New Hampshire, Oregon, Pennsylvania, Texas and Vermont.

U.S. threatens welfare cuts. The Department of Health, Education & Welfare said Dec. 4, 1972 that it would withhold up to $689 million in welfare payments in 1973 to states that had failed to institute adequate procedures to eliminate ineligible recipients and overpayments. (But HEW agreed Dec. 13 to delay the holdup from Jan. 1, 1973 to April 1 after state welfare officials had protested that they had inadequate notice of the new policy.)

HEW said it had moved in order to "restore public confidence" in the welfare program. John D. Twiname, administrator of the Social and Rehabilitation Service of HEW, cited a March survey which estimated that 6.8% of families in the Aid to Families with Dependent Children (AFDC) program were ineligible, as were 4.9% of adult blind, disabled and aged beneficiaries. Some 13.8% of AFDC families were found to be receiving overpayments, as were 9.7% in the other programs. Underpayments were found in the cases of 7.6% and 5.6% of recipients respectively.

In the 21 states that had not investigated the required percentage of cases to determine ineligibility rates, funds would be reduced according to the national average. HEW said it expected that as many as 700,000 persons in the AFDC program and 147,000 in the other programs would be cut from the rolls, if the new policy were fully effective.

Twiname said "we can't continue in a business as usual way," since "during the [election] campaign ... all political spectra were getting ... heat about welfare spending." He said Caspar W. Weinberger, HEW secretary-designate, fully supported the new policy.

Indiana & Nebraska cutoff averted—A cutoff of federal welfare funds to Indiana and Nebraska was averted in 1971.

HEW Social & Rehabilitation Service Director John D. Twiname had said Jan. 19 that the U.S. would stop the flow of $54 million in federal welfare aid to Indiana and Nebraska April 1 because of violations in the states' AFDC programs. HEW said both states failed to make cost-of-living adjustments. Indiana, with $39 million in federal funds at stake, also allegedly failed to make payments to persons who furnished food and shelter to children on AFDC.

Twiname said: "It is a step we take with great reluctance because of its potentially serious impact on needy families. . . . But we must uphold the law and insure that assistance to the poor provided by law is made available in fact." Bills to comply with federal regulations were before the legislatures in both states.

Both states enacted legislation in March to bring their welfare systems in compliance with federal law before the HEW's April 1 deadline.

Indiana, in a measure signed March 26 by Gov. Edgar D. Whitcomb, made its first increase in payments for dependent children in three years. The bill provided payments of $115 a month for a mother and one child and $30 for each additional child. The old schedule was $100 for a mother and one child and $25 for each additional child.

The Nebraska measure, enacted March 31, made cost-of-living adjustments in maximum payments authorized for dependent children. In addition to raising the authorization, the Nebraska legislature voted to increase welfare payments.

HEW cancels California cutoff—HEW had said Jan. 8, 1971 that a decision to cut off $684 million in federal welfare funds to California had been reversed because of a "personal positive step" by Gov. Ronald Reagan. At a news conference originally called to announce the cutoff, HEW said Reagan had moved to expedite a court case blocking the state's compliance with federal welfare regulations.

The California Supreme Court ruled March 25 that Reagan had violated the state law in November 1970 when he cut welfare grants to 69% of the official level of need established by the state. The court said only the California legislature had authority to impose such a payment limit.

In the November action, the Reagan administration had adopted higher grant schedules for aid to families with dependent children, a move required to bring the state into technical compliance with federal regulations. However, at the same time, Reagan ordered the 69% cut in actual grants. In a March 26 letter to the California welfare department, federal welfare administrator John D. Twiname noted that a threatened cutoff of federal funds had been rescinded only "on the basis of the governor's commitment to implement the regulation updating the family maximums as soon as the court acted."

Reagan met with President Nixon at San Clemente, Calif. April 2, and the President then agreed to a second temporary delay in the threatened cutoff of $684 million in federal welfare aid to California. Nixon said the talk, which he described as a "summit meeting on welfare," was "one of the most constructive meetings on the problem of welfare reform that I have attended."

As a result of the "summit meeting," the cutoff was postponed, at least until July 1, and the President and Reagan directed subordinates to work out details of a plan to put the state in compliance with federal law.

(The California Welfare Rights Organization filed suit in federal court in San Francisco April 9 charging President Nixon and Reagan with conspiring to violate federal welfare laws.)

HEW notified California June 21 that the state was in compliance with federal law requiring cost-of-living adjustments in welfare payments. John D. Twiname, administrator of the Social and Rehabilitation Service, said the government would authorize grants to California July 1, the date of the threatened welfare funds cutoff.

Twiname said he had been notified June 4 that the state had adjusted its maximum payments by 21.4%. He said the adjustment, ordered by Sacramento County Superior Court Judge William A. Gallagher April 15, was "acceptable." Twiname said other California regulations dropping those recipients with outside income from relief rolls were under review by the state courts. He said "We'll give the California court a reasonable time to stay the regulations before we act" to determine if they violated federal standards.

Nevada relief cuts voided. A federal judge ordered Nevada March 19, 1971 to restore welfare benefits to 3,000 recipients who had been cut from the state relief rolls in December 1970. Without judging the merits of Nevada's claim of massive welfare cheating, District Court Judge George P. Foley in Las Vegas said the procedures used in the cuts "ran roughshod over the constitutional rights of eligible and ineligible recipients alike."

Foley was ruling on a suit brought by the National Welfare Rights Organization (NWRO), which had sponsored marches down the famous Las Vegas Strip March 6 and March 13. Foley backed the NWRO claim that Nevada violated notice and hearing requirements in making the cuts. The judge said some recipients did not receive notice until their checks had been stopped.

The March 6 demonstrators, numbering 1,000 and led by NWRO leader George Wiley and the Rev. Ralph D. Abernathy of the Southern Christian Leadership Conference, ended their march with an invasion of the $25 million Caesars Palace Hotel. The protesters, who included pacifist David Dellinger and actress Jane Fonda, left the hotel under the discipline of parade marshals 20 minutes later. About 250 marchers were barred from the Sands Hotel a week later, and 100 protesters were arrested for blocking traffic in front of the hotel.

George Wiley said March 19, "We look on this as a major national campaign. We want this to serve as an example to other states that the welfare rights movement won't sit by and watch welfare recipients get brutalized."

Nevada welfare administrator George Miller also viewed the Nevada confrontation in national perspective. He reportedly sent letters announcing the cutoffs to U.S. congressmen and welfare officials throughout the country. According to one account of the letters, quoted by the Washington Post March 7, Miller said, "if a state the size of Nevada has this high incidence of cheating, what is the situation in larger states, especially in urban areas?"

Nevada officials and NWRO lawyers signed an accord April 1 to restore to welfare rolls 1,000 recipients whose aid had been cut off and to increase benefits to 1,000 others whose aid was reduced.

In a stipulation for judgment, which was approved by a three-judge federal panel April 8, the state also agreed to a federal system to oversee future attempts by the state to alter relief checks. The state had cut off or reduced benefits to the 2,000 recipients involved in the court action on grounds that they had not reported all outside income.

Missouri payments okd. The Health, Education and Welfare Department said Sept. 29, 1971 it would not withhold $8.7 million a year in federal welfare reimbursement to Missouri. In July, HEW had warned that the money would be withheld after Oct. 1 unless the state made prompt payments to recipients, as required by federal regulations.

Connecticut developments. Federal District Court Judge M. Joseph Blumenfeld Oct. 28, 1971 enjoined the Connecticut Welfare Department from enforcing proposed cuts in welfare payments of 13%–22% in the Aid to Dependent Children program.

Blumenfeld said he would base his final decision on whether the state complied with federal regulations. That in turn would depend on whether the new "standard of need" took into account current prices for necessities, and whether it excluded any items formerly part of the standard.

HEW March 31, 1972 approved a proposal by Connecticut to distribute the money on a flat grant basis depending only on family size.

Under the plan, every family of four in the program would get $310 a month, which was the average payment under the old system based on individual family needs. The state expected to save as much as $3 million from the $10 million cost of administering its welfare programs, although no savings in total grants would occur.

HUD program resumed in 21 areas. Housing and Urban Development Secretary George Romney said Feb. 5, 1971 that a HUD home-ownership program that had been suspended Jan. 14 was being resumed in selected areas across the country. The mortgage subsidy program for existing low and moderate income housing had been suspended after a House committee reported fraud and speculation in the program.

Romney said 21 regional HUD and Federal Housing Administration offices would resume issuance of mortgage commitments. The suspension remained in effect for the rest of the country. The offices served the following states: Maine, Rhode Island, New Mexico, Iowa, Nebraska, Montana, North and South Dakota, Utah, Wyoming and Idaho. The remaining offices covered by the order served Puerto Rico and the following cities: Albany, Hempstead and New York, N.Y.; Tampa, Fla.; Memphis; Shreveport, La.; Tulsa, Okla.; and Houston and Lubbock, Tex.

HUD freezes NY slum clearance aid. Charging that New York City failed to provide "decent, safe and sanitary" housing for persons displaced by urban renewal, HUD announced Feb. 11, 1971 an immediate "embargo" of federal contributions to the city's slum clearance programs. HUD regional administrator S. William Green charged that staff audits had shown "widespread deficiencies" in city relocation efforts.

Green said he hoped the embargo would be "shortlived" but he said it would not be lifted "until the city demonstrates it has adequate relocation facilities and is complying with all federal requirements governing relocation."

Albert A. Walsh, New York housing administrator, denounced the action as "precipitous, unfounded and potentially destructive." Simeon Golar, chairman of the city Housing Authority, admitted that some families were relocated into faulty city-owned housing, but he added, "with all our problems, our [relocating] performance has been unprecedented in this city and the nation."

Appalachia failure reported. A study prepared by the General Accounting Office (GAO) of the effects of federal antipoverty programs on a typical rural Kentucky County during 1965–69 found that "extensive federal expenditures had not made a significant impact on alleviating poverty and unemployment." The report was published Feb. 10, 1971.

The $21.5 million spent in Johnson County through a variety of federal programs averaged $243 for each resident, yet, GAO reported, "no federal organization has overall responsibility to coordinate the wide range of federal programs in a specific locality." The agency recommended that the Appalachian Regional Commission play a larger role in planning and coordination.

California Developments

Reagan promises welfare reform. Gov. Ronald Reagan (R, Calif.), in his inaugural address in Sacramento, Calif. Jan. 4, 1971, criticized the entire welfare situation.

Reagan, beginning his second term, said welfare, "mandated by statute and federal regulation, . . . has grown into a leviathan of unsupportable dimensions." He said, "We have economized and even stripped essential public services to feed its appetite."

In an outdoor speech hampered by a faulty public address system and a group of hecklers, Reagan said California spent more than double the national average on welfare. He said the costs "have been increasing more than three times as fast as revenues" and attributed the rising costs to lax regulations and court decisions that struck down state residency requirements.

Reagan rejected tax increases as the answer to the rising costs of welfare. He said, "Common sense and simple fairness suggest reducing grants to those with outside income in order to increase our ability to help the totally dependent." Contending that nearly a million California children "are growing up in the stultifying atmosphere of programs that reward people for not working," he said welfare programs "separate families and doom these children to repeat the cycle in their own adulthood."

Reagan Feb. 2 submitted a $6.7 billion budget that would avoid a tax increase by cutting welfare and health expenditures by $700 million. The legislature approved a $7.3 billion budget July 2, but Reagan then vetoed $503 million for education, welfare, medical care and salary increases.
■ Gov. Reagan issued his third veto of federal funds for California antipoverty projects Feb. 18. He vetoed a $1.6 million grant to the Oakland Economic Development Council Inc. on grounds that the staff had engaged in politics and had withdrawn policy-making authority from its citizen governing board. Reagan's December 1970 veto of $308,000 for an antipoverty coordinating agency in Santa Cruz County had been withdrawn after local officials removed "material of a revolutionary nature" that they admitted had been found in the center.

Reagan proposes welfare reforms— Gov. Reagan proposed a welfare reform program March 3 that he estimated would save the state $740 million in the next year, allowing him to balance the 1971–72 budget without a tax increase. A staff member estimated that the proposal would drop 300,000 persons from the aid to families with dependent children program.

Reagan proposed tightened eligibility requirements, an assigned work program, limits to the amount that could be earned by welfare recipients, a plan to force fathers to support deserted welfare fam-

ilies and reduced benefits under California's Medicaid program. Reagan claimed some of the proposals had the support of the Nixon Administration and 23 state governors.

The proposals, planned for presentation to the state legislature, were unveiled at a luncheon meeting in Los Angeles after Democratic leaders refused to convene the legislature to hear Reagan's plan. After bills incorporating the program were introduced March 15, State Sen. Mervyn M. Dymally, chairman of the Democratic caucus, said the Reagan plan meant "levying of $1.1 billion in taxes on the blind, the poor, the disabled, the disadvantaged."

California enacts welfare reform. The California legislature enacted a welfare reform bill Aug. 11, 1971 following a compromise between Gov. Ronald Reagan and Democratic leaders of the legislature who had fought his proposals. The legislation stiffened eligibility rules, established residency requirements and tightened controls on fraud in the state's $2 billion annual welfare system.

In a major concession, Reagan accepted the need for a tax increase. He had originally proposed to avoid new taxes by saving $700 million through reform. The final measure was expected to save $184 million in federal, state and county welfare funds.

Reagan also agreed to a provision for a cost-of-living increase mechanism for Aid to Families with Dependent Children (AFDC) recipients. AFDC clients had received no increase in California from 1957 until earlier in 1971 when courts ordered a 21% increase.

Other provisions would increase basic AFDC grants while decreasing checks for families with outside incomes. A provision made it possible to attach the wages of a father who had deserted a welfare family, and state income tax records of recipients would be open to welfare officials.

Reagan signed the welfare measure and a companion Medi-Cal reform bill Aug. 13. Savings to the state from the Medi-Cal bill were estimated at $200 million a year. Both measures would take effect Oct. 1.

California work plan OKd. California Gov. Reagan announced March 1, 1972 that about 30,000 welfare recipients would be required to work off their grants in part-time jobs or lose their benefits. The Department of Health, Education and Welfare had approved the test proposal, originally presented early in 1971.

The three-year plan, which began April 1 and was applied in 35 counties, mostly in Northern California, would exempt only the handicapped or mothers with children under six. Mothers with older children would work during school hours.

Participants would work up to 80 hours a month at such unskilled jobs as kitchen helpers, parking lot attendants and day care aides for schools, government and private agencies.

Court Decisions

Welfare inspections valid. In a 6–3 ruling Jan. 12, 1971, the Supreme Court upheld the right of state and local welfare officials to visit the homes of recipients and to cut off funds from persons who refused to let them enter their homes. The justices overturned a federal district court ruling in New York that welfare caseworkers without search warrants could not force their way into the homes of persons on public assistance.

Justice Harry A. Blackmun, writing his first majority opinion since joining the Supreme Court, said the "caseworker is not a sleuth but rather, we trust, is a friend in need." He gave as a parallel one who dispenses private charity, who "naturally has an interest in and expects to know how his charitable funds are utilized and put to work."

Dissenting Justices William O. Douglas, Thurgood Marshall and William J. Brennan Jr. argued that the ruling violated the spirit of a 1967 high court decision that housing and fire inspectors did not have the right to force their way into business premises without a warrant. They said the difference in the cases was that welfare recipients are "the lowly poor."

The case involved Mrs. Barbara James of New York City, who had refused to allow a city caseworker to enter her home in connection with welfare payments to support her young son. Welfare officials decided to cut off her payments. She brought suit and won a 1969 ruling that the cutoff was illegal.

In his dissent, Justice Douglas asked, "If the welfare recipient was not Barbara James but a prominent, affluent cotton or wheat farmer receiving benefit payments for not growing crops, would not the approach be different?"

Child aid rulings. The Supreme Court Jan. 18, 1971 unanimously upheld a federal law that was designed to encourage welfare recipients of aid to dependent children to take jobs. The law contained an "income disregard" provision that permitted welfare parents to deduct a portion of their income in determining whether they earned more than the state "need level."

The law was challenged by Mrs. Lula Mae Connor of Chicago who argued that it was discriminatory because the "income disregard" deduction extended only to persons who were already welfare recipients and not to those who were applying for benefits.

In another ruling Jan. 18, the court upheld without a hearing a lower court ruling that states did not violate the law by granting higher welfare payments to dependent children living in foster homes than to children living with their natural parents. A lower court had ruled that the higher payment was a valid way for states to encourage persons to become foster parents. Justice William O. Douglas argued that the court should have heard the case.

The court Oct. 12 sustained a lower court ruling against Oregon's denial of welfare aid to dependent children in cases where the mother refused to file non-support complaints against the father.

Rights of the poor. The Supreme Court ruled unanimously March 2, 1971 that poor people could not be jailed solely because they could not pay fines. In another ruling, over the dissent of Justice Hugo L. Black, the court held that people who wanted divorces but were too poor to pay filing fees and court costs must have those costs borne by the states.

The jail-or-fine case involved a Houston laborer, Preston A. Tate, who accumulated $425 in traffic fines and was sentenced to jail to work off the fines. Writing for the court, Justice William J. Brennan Jr. said states and localities could adopt "alternative" ways of collecting fines, such as installment payments. He said a person could still be sent to jail if he refused or neglected to pay fines. Justices Black, John M. Harlan and Harry A. Blackmun concurred in the ruling but did not join Brennan's opinion.

The divorce case was brought by five Connecticut welfare mothers who had tried to file divorce suits but could not pay filing fees and court costs of about $60 each. Justice Harlan wrote that the women's right to due process of law had been violated. He said they were effectively denied the opportunity to be heard since the state maintained a monopoly over marriage and divorce. In concurring opinions, Justices Brennan and William O. Douglas said the court should have based the ruling on the 14th Amendment guarantee of equal protection under the law.

In his dissent, Black said the effect of the ruling would be to use taxpayers' money to encourage divorce.

Housing project bar upheld. The Supreme Court April 26, 1971 upheld the constitutionality of state referendum laws that allowed a majority of voters in any city, state or county to block low-rent public housing in their community.

By a 5–3 vote the court sustained California's referendum law, on the books since 1950, which required public approval of the low-rent projects before they could be built.

California voters had used the law to block construction of almost half the low-rent housing proposed for the state since its passage.

In the opinion written by Justice Hugo L. Black, the court described the law as consistent with "devotion to democracy, not to bias, discrimination or prejudice."

Chief Justice Warren E. Burger and Justices John M. Harlan, Potter Stewart and Byron White joined Black in the majority decision. Justices Harry A. Blackmun, William J. Brennan Jr. and Thurgood Marshall dissented. Justice William O. Douglas did not take part in the case.

The court had been asked in a host of friend-of-court briefs to strike down the California law on the ground that it frustrated efforts to erect low-rent public housing for the poor. Among those filing briefs were the National Urban Coalition, the National Association of Home Builders, the American Institute of Architects and the Justice Department.

The Urban Coalition said the ruling "may have rendered meaningless" the Supreme Court's unanimous April 20 decision approving busing to dismantle dual school systems. The organization's statement said development of "black and poor central cities and white and affluent suburbs" will frustrate such "piece-meal approaches" as busing.

The California law was challenged in a suit brought by 41 welfare families in San Jose after the city's voters reversed a decision by the city council in 1968 to build 1,000 low-rent apartments. San Jose's voters turned down the proposed construction, 68,000–58,000. A three-judge federal district court in San Francisco struck down the law as unconstitutional, saying that it violated the equal protection clause of the 14th Amendment by discriminating against the poor.

Black said for the court that the 14th Amendment's principal thrust was to outlaw legal distinctions based on race and that there was no evidence that the California referendum law was prejudicial against any racial minority. He said "this procedure for democratic decision-making" gave the voters a voice in decisions that would raise their taxes and affect the future of their community.

Welfare for strikers. The Supreme Court April 26, 1971, by refusing to review, left undisturbed a lower court ruling that welfare benefits could not be denied to striking workers on an employer's claim that the benefits gave strikers an unfair advantage and upset the collective-bargaining process. The court denied an appeal by the ITT Lamp Division of the International Telephone and Telegraph Co. in a case involving a 1970 strike in Massachusetts.

The court Oct. 16, 1972 upheld a lower court ruling overturning a Maryland law that denied welfare payments to families of workers on strike.

At issue was a federal district court order that voided the Maryland law and in effect struck down similar laws in six other states. The lower court had held that Maryland could not withhold aid-to-dependent-children assistance to the families of whose who were either on strike or who had been dismissed for misconduct.

Lower benefits illegal. The Supreme Court May 21, 1971 upheld lower court rulings that New York state violated federal welfare rules by paying upstate recipients lower benefits than paid in New York City. According to the ruling, the state had to pay retroactive benefits to some 250,000 welfare clients who had received lower compensation from October 1970 to May 1971, when the differentials were eliminated by the state legislature.

Welfare for aliens. The Supreme Court, ruling unanimously June 14, 1971, held that states could not deny welfare benefits to needy aliens. In an opinion by Justice Blackmun, the court tied its ruling to a 1969 decision striking down state residency requirements for welfare applicants.

Ruling against restrictions against aliens in Arizona and Pennsylvania welfare laws, Blackmun said "a state's desire to preserve limited welfare benefits for its own citizens is inadequate" to justify exclusions based on residence or citizenship. He said "a concern for fiscal integrity is no more compelling a justification for the questioned classification" in the present cases than it was in the 1969 case.

Justice John M. Harlan concurred in the outcome of the case, but he based his vote on national immigration policy, which set no restrictions against aliens who become public charges after settling in the U.S.

California school tax case. The California Supreme Court ruled, 6–1, Aug. 30, 1971 that the state's school financing

system based on property taxes favored affluent districts and discriminated against children in poorer neighborhoods. The ruling, written by Justice Ralph L. Sullivan, examined a series of U.S. Supreme Court decisions and held that the property-tax system "must fall before the equal protection clause" of the 14th Amendment, which guaranteed every citizen "the equal protection of the laws."

The California system, followed in virtually every state, raised 56% of the school revenues from local property taxes, 35% from the state and about 9% from federal grants. The California court held that affluent districts could spend more per pupil and, at the same time, have lower property taxes. The ruling objected that the system "makes the quality of a child's education a function of the wealth of his parents and neighborhoods."

Similar suits had been filed in Illinois, Michigan, Texas and Virginia but had met with little success.

Non-uniform aid upheld. The Supreme Court ruled May 30, 1972 that neither the Constitution nor federal welfare laws prohibited states from granting lower benefits to child welfare recipients than to the aged and disabled.

In a 6–3 decision, the court rejected the contention that such non-uniform relief aid violated the Constitution's equal protection guarantee.

At the same time, the court ruled 5–4 that states did not violate federal law when they made sharper cutbacks in certain assistance programs than in others.

By virtue of the two votes, the court upheld the public assistance program in Texas under which the state paid families with dependent children, a majority of whom were black and Spanish-speaking, 75% of the estimated need while paying aged and disabled recipients, almost all of whom were white, 95%–100% of the estimated need.

In both votes, the Nixon appointees to the court fashioned the backbone of the majority opinions.

On the constitutional question the President's nominees, Chief Justice Warren Burger, Justices Harry A. Blackmun, Lewis F. Powell Jr. and William H.

Rehnquist, joined Justices Potter Stewart and Byron R. White in upholding the Texas system.

Dissenting were Justices William O. Douglas, Thurgood Marshall and William J. Brennan Jr.

The majority opinion, written by Rehnquist, rejected the assertion that cutbacks in public assistance to dependent children discriminated against non-whites.

Rehnquist termed it a "naked statistical argument" that discrimination was involved because 87% of the child welfare cases in Texas were black or Mexican-American, while 62% of these receiving old age benefits and 53% receiving disability aid were white.

In the 5–4 vote, Stewart changed sides to vote with Douglas, Marshall and Brennan. On the question of federal law, the court upheld the method used by Texas and 18 other states to cut benefits paid to recipients with some outside income. At issue was a system in which welfare payments were reduced by the amount of outside income brought into the family. In other states, the family could keep some of the earned money in addition to its regular welfare payment.

Counsel right extended. The Supreme Court June 12, 1972 extended its landmark 1963 Gideon v. Wainwright decision entitling poor defendants to free lawyers in felony trials to apply to cases involving misdemeanors as well.

The ruling assured that no poor person could lawfully be jailed unless he had been given a free lawyer or had waived his right to counsel. It was the first time the court had held that the Sixth Amendment's guarantee of counsel applied to misdemeanor trials.

In an opinion written by Justice William O. Douglas, the court held that henceforth judges would be precluded from jailing indigent defendants unless they had been offered free counsel. The ruling did not, however, prevent judges from imposing money fines in misdemeanor trials.

Douglas noted that the ruling could tax the legal profession and place some strains on state treasuries in covering the cost of free legal aid. But Douglas added that in many instances misde-

meanor cases would still be handled without counsel because the judges would have no intention of jailing the defendant.

At issue in the case was the conviction of Jon R. Argersinger, who had been convicted of carrying a concealed weapon and sentenced to pay a $500 fine or serve three months in a Florida county jail.

The entire court agreed in overturning the conviction. But Justices Lewis F. Powell Jr. and William H. Rehnquist said in a concurring opinion that the states should not be bound to a rigid rule under the Sixth Amendment.

The 1972 Elections

Richard M. Nixon was reelected President Nov. 7, 1972 by a landslide victory over Sen. George McGovern (S.D.), the Democratic nominee. The issue of welfare and the poor played an important but not crucial rule in the campaign.

McGovern proposes $1,000 grant for all. While seeking the Democratic Presidential nomination early in 1972, McGovern made a controversial proposal that haunted him throughout the campaign. This was that everybody in the U.S. be given a $1,000 annual grant.

Sen. George McGovern's original plan to replace the welfare program with a minimum income grant program was contained in an economic policy statement Jan. 13 at Iowa State University at Ames. He proposed that every person, including children and regardless of income, receive or be credited with an annual minimum income grant. The current $750 personal income tax exemption would be eliminated, as would the current welfare system. The grant would be taxable as income to families with incomes above poverty levels. Revenue to finance the plan would come from elimination of the personal exemption, from reduction of current welfare payments and costs and from taxes on the grants to those with income above a designated break-even point.

McGovern contended the personal exemption system provided more tax relief for the high-income person than those with low incomes. An example used was that the personal exemption, to a person in the 50% tax bracket, was worth $375 for himself and each dependent but worth only $150 to a person in the 20% bracket and nothing to a person too poor to pay a tax.

While stressing that an essential feature of his plan was that the grant must not vary with the income of the recipient, McGovern said the plan itself could be implemented by a number of methods. "These methods require full examination by the best economic talent available," he said, "and the plan chosen must have the support of the President, if it is to have any chance of adoption. For those reasons, the present proposal is not designed for immediate legislative action. Instead, it represents a pledge that, if elected, I would prepare a detailed plan and submit it to the Congress."

McGovern used three plans to illustrate his idea, one based on a proposal by Professor James Tobin of Yale University. The Tobin plan was later singled out more often than the others, where the grant might be smaller for children or in sum.

The Tobin plan was to provide a grant of $1,000 to each man, woman and child, or $4,000 for a family of four, approximately the poverty level according to government statistics. Recipients with no other income would retain all of the grant. Those with income up to a designated break-even point would retain a portion of the grant that would decline with increased income. While adding to their taxable income, these recipients would receive a net benefit. Persons with income above the break-even point also would pay taxes on their grants according to their incomes, and some would pay less and some more than under the current tax system. The point at which the new plan would represent a tax increase was generally set at incomes of $20,000 or more. At this level, the grants actually would not be paid but credited. McGovern said:

"As redistribution of income, the minimum income grant would represent no additional cost to the Treasury. Funds to finance the grant would be expected to come from those above a designated break-even income and would take the form of additional taxes. If the break-even income for a family of four were set at $12,000, about 20% of federal taxpayers would experience a tax increase, while about 80% would be able to keep all or part of the grant. It is expected that those below the poverty line and the break-even point would keep a gradually decreasing amount as their incomes rose. The loss of grant benefits would thus be sufficiently gradual as not to discourage those on welfare from seeking a job (in fact, it would encourage them to seek work) and would provide a significant income supplement to the millions of Americans in the medium income range. Thus, for example, a family of four with its own income of $8,000 would be able to retain an additional $2,000 of the minimum income grant. . . .

"This credit income tax proposal would imply a redistribution of income of some $14.1 billion for those above the poverty line to those below it. The redistribution from those above the break-even income line to those below it but still above the poverty line would amount to $29 billion. These figures demonstrate that while the minimum income grant would represent a total reform of the present welfare system, it would actually provide more money to medium income taxpayers than it would to the poor."

McGovern, Humphrey debate. Sens.
George McGovern (S.D.) and Hubert H. Humphrey (Minn.) confronted each other in nationally televised debates from Los Angeles May 28 and 30 in their intense duel for victory in the California Democratic presidential primary.

The confrontations, each before a panel of news interrogators, were held as special hour-long versions of CBS'

"Face the Nation" broadcast (May 28) and NBC's "Meet the Press" program (May 30).

Humphrey attacked McGovern's welfare bill as too costly—some $72 billion, he said. McGovern said the bill was one he had submitted as a courtesy to the National Welfare Rights Organization so it would gain consideration, with a specific attachment to it that he did not support it. Humphrey outlined his own $11.5 billion welfare reform plan—a 25% increase in Social Security benefits, a minimum income for a family of four of $3,000, transfer of aid to the aged and disabled from local and state financing to federal financing.

McGovern pointed out the minimum support figure was only $1,000 less than his own, which called for $1,000 per person. He conceded he could not estimate the cost of his plan but said the funds, in any event, would not come out of the Treasury.

On welfare reform, Humphrey said McGovern's minimum-income proposal would cost at least $60 billion and "you're going to have to take it out of somebody." McGovern said his proposal would benefit every family of four earning under $12,000 a year and those earning up to $20,000 a year would pay only a minimal tax increase.

Following his victory in the California primary, McGovern discussed several aspects of the contest with New York Times personnel June 7.

He said "it may have been a mistake" to specify that $1,000 be provided to every American as a welfare allotment. He had used a definite figure "for illustrative purposes," he said, to show "the impact of the program."

Poor at Miami convention. The Democratic National Convention in Miami Beach drew many non-delegates, including representatives of the poor, who rallied peacefully for two hours July 11 in their only major demonstration.

Protesters were allowed to sleep at campgrounds near the convention hall by a 4-2 vote of the Miami Beach City Council July 5. A Poor Peoples Coalition, formed by members of the Southern Christian Leadership Conference, the National Tenants Organization and the National Welfare Rights Organization (NWRO), established a "tent city" at the campsite for all non-delegates attending the Democratic National Convention and the NWRO's five-day conference in Miami Beach which concluded July 9.

The NWRO meeting, called to "confront the politicians and the Democratic party," failed to win its demand for 750 non-voting delegate seats at the convention or the party's adoption of a minority platform plank calling for minimum income assistance of $6,500 for a family of four.

Party platforms. The platform adopted by the Democratic National Convention included the following statements on the issues of welfare and poverty:

Jobs, Income and Dignity. Full employment—a guaranteed job for all—is the primary economic objective of the Democratic Party. The Democratic Party is committed to a job for every American who seeks work. Only through full employment can we reduce the burden on working people. We are determined to make economic security a matter of right. This means a job with decent pay and good working conditions for everyone willing and able to work and an adequate income for those unable to work. It means abolition of the present welfare system.

To assure jobs and economic security for all, the next Democratic Administration should support: . . .

■ Tax reform directed toward equitable distribution of income and wealth and fair sharing of the cost of government. . . .

■ Overhaul of current manpower programs to assure training—without sex, race or language discrimination—for jobs that really exist with continuous skill improvement and the chance for advancement. . . .

■ Economic development programs to ensure the growth of communities and industry in lagging parts of the nation and the economy.

■ Use of federal depository funds to reward banks and other financial institutions which invest in socially productive endeavors. . . .

■ Assurance that the needs of society are considered when a decision to close or move an industrial plant is to be made and that income loss to workers and revenue loss to communities does not occur when plants are closed.

■ Assurance that, whatever else is done in the income security area, the social security system provides a decent income for the elderly, the blind and the disabled and their dependents, with escalators so that benefits keep pace with rising prices and living standards.

■ Reform of social security and government employment security programs to remove all forms of discrimination by sex; and

■ Adequate federal income assistance for those who do not benefit sufficiently from the above measures.

The last is not least, but it is last for good reason. The present welfare system has failed because it has been required to make up for too many other failures. Millions of Americans are forced into public assistance because public policy too often creates no other choice.

The heart of a program of economic security based on earned income must be creating jobs and training people to fill them. Millions of jobs—real jobs, not make-work—need to be provided. Public service employment must be greatly expanded in order to make the government the employer of last resort and guarantee a job for all. Large sections of our cities resemble bombed-out Europe after World War II. Children in Appalachia cannot go to school when the dirt road is a sea of mud. Homes, schools and clinics, roads and mass transit systems need to be built.

Cleaning up our air and water will take skills and people in large numbers. In the school, the police department, the welfare agency or the recreation program, there are new careers to be developed to help ensure that social services reach the people for whom they are intended.

It may cost more, at least initially, to create decent jobs than to perpetuate the hand-out system of present welfare. But the return—in new public facilities and services, in the dignity of bringing a paycheck home and in the taxes that will come back in—far outweigh the cost of the investment.

The next Democratic Administration must end the present welfare system and replace it with an income security program which places cash assistance in an appropriate context with all of the measures outlined above, adding up to an earned income approach to ensure each family an income substantially more than the poverty level ensuring standards of decency and health, as officially defined in the area. Federal income assistance will supplement the income of working poor people and assure an adequate income for those unable to work. With full employment and simpler, fair administration, total costs will go down, and with federal financing the burden on local and state budgets will be eased. The program will protect current benefit goals during the transitional period.

The system of income protection which replaces welfare must be a part of the full employment policy which assures every American a job at a fair wage under conditions which make use of his ability and provide an opportunity for advancement.

H.R. 1, and its various amendments, is not humane and does not meet the social and economic objectives that we believe in, and it should be defeated. It perpetuates the coercion of forced work requirements. . . .

Rights of Poor People

Poor people, like all Americans, should be represented at all levels of the Democratic Party in reasonable proportion to their numbers in the general population. Affirmative action must be taken to ensure their representation at every level. The Democratic Party guidelines guaranteeing proportional representation to "previously discriminated against groups" (enumerated as 'women, young people and minorities') must be extended to specifically include poor people.

■ Political parties, candidates and government institutions at all levels must be committed to working with and supporting poor people's organizations and ending the tokenism and cooptation that has characterized past dealings.

■ Welfare rights organizations must be recognized as representative of welfare recipients and be given access to regulations, policies and decision-making processes, as well as being allowed to represent clients at all governmental levels.

■ The federal government must protect the right of tenants to organize tenant organizations and negotiate collective bargaining agreements with private landlords and encourage the participation of the tenants in the management and control of all subsidized housing. . . .

Rights of the Elderly

Growing old in America for too many means neglect, sickness, despair and, all too often, poverty. We have failed to discharge the basic obligation of a civilized people—to respect and assure the security of our senior citizens. The Democratic Party pledges, as a final step to economic security for all, to end poverty—as measured by official standards—among the retired, the blind and the disabled. Our general program of economic and social justice will benefit the elderly directly. In addition, a Democratic Administration should:

■ Increase social security to bring benefits into line with changes on the national standard of living;

■ Provide automatic adjustments to assure that benefits keep pace with inflation;

■ Support legislation which allows beneficiaries to earn more income, without reduction of social security payments;

■ Protect individual's pension rights by pension re-insurance and early vesting;

■ Lower retirement eligibility age to 60 in all goverment pension programs;

■ Expand housing assistance for the elderly; . . .

■ Pending a full national health security system, expand Medicare by supplementing trust funds with general revenues in order to provide a complete range of care and services; eliminate the Nixon Administration cutbacks in Medicare and Medicaid; eliminate the part B premium under Medicare and include under Medicare and Medicaid the costs of eyeglasses, dentures, hearing aids, and all prescription drugs and establish uniform national standards for Medicaid to bring to an end the present situation which makes it worse to be poor in one state than in another. . . .

Health Care

Good health is the least this society should promise its citizens. The state of health services in this country indicates the failure of government to respond to this fundamental need. Costs skyrocket while the availability of services for all but the rich steadily declines.

We endorse the principle that good health is a right of all Americans.

America has a responsibility to offer to every American family the best in health care wherever they need it, regardless of income or where they live or any other factor.

To achieve this goal the next Democratic Administration should:

■ Establish a system of universal National Health Insurance which covers all Americans with a comprehensive set of benefits including preventive medicine, mental and emotional disorders, and complete protection against catastrophic costs, and in which the rule of free choice for both provider and consumer is protected. The program should be

federally-financed and federally-administered. Every American must know he can afford the cost of health care whether given in a hospital or a doctor's office . . .

■ Set up incentives to bring health service personnel back to inner-cities and rural areas;

■ Continue to expand community health centers and availability of early screening diagnosis and treatment . . .

The platform adopted by the Republican National Convention made these statements on the welfare and poverty issues:

Welfare Reform

The nation's welfare system is a mess. It simply must be reformed.

The system, essentially unchanged since the 1930's, has turned into a human and fiscal nightmare. It penalizes the poor. It provides discriminatory benefits. It kills any incentives its victims might have to work their way out of the morass.

Among its victims are the taxpayers. Since 1961 the Federal cost of welfare has skyrocketed over 10 times—from slightly over $1 billion then to more than $11 billion now. State and local costs add to this gigantic expenditure. And here are things we are paying for:

■ The present system drains work incentive from the employed poor, as they see welfare families making as much or more on the dole.

■ Its discriminatory benefits continue to ensnare the needy, aged, blind and disabled in a web of inefficient rules and economic contradictions.

■ It continues to break up poor families, since a father's presence makes his family ineligible for benefits in many states. Its dehumanizing life-style thus threatens to envelop yet another "welfare generation."

■ Its injustices and costs threaten to alienate taxpayer support for welfare programs of any kind.

Perhaps nowhere else is there a greater contrast in policy and philosophy than between the Administration's remedy for the welfare ills and the financial orgy proposed by our political opposition.

President Nixon proposed to change our welfare system "to provide each person with a means of escape from welfare into dignity." His goals were these:

■ A decent level of payment to genuinely needy welfare recipients regardless of where they live.

■ Incentives not to loaf, but to work.

■ Requiring all adults who apply for welfare to register for work and job training and to accept work or training. The only exceptions would be the aged, blind and disabled and mothers of preschool children.

■ Expanding job training and child care facilities so that recipients can accept employment.

■ Temporary supplements to the incomes of the working poor to enable them to support their families while continuing to work.

■ Uniform Federal payment standards for all welfare recipients.

In companion actions, our efforts to improve the nutrition of poor people resulted in basic reforms in the food stamp program. The number of recipients increased from some three million to 13 million, and now 8.4 million needy children participate in the school lunch program, almost three times the number that participated in 1968.

Now, nearly 10,000 nutrition aides work in low-income communities. In 1968 there were none.

Since 1969, we have increased the Federal support for family planning threefold. We will continue to support expanded family planning programs and will foster research in this area so that more parents will be better able to plan the number and spacing of their children should they wish to do so. Under no circumstances will we allow any of these programs to become compulsory or infringe upon the religious conviction or personal freedom of any individual.

We all feel compassion for those who through no fault of their own cannot adequately care for themselves. We all want to help these men, women and children achieve a decent standard of living and become self-supporting.

We continue to insist, however, that there are too many people on this country's welfare rolls who should not be there. With effective cooperation from the Congress, we pledge to stop these abuses.

We flatly oppose programs or policies which embrace the principle of a government-guaranteed income. We reject as unconscionable the idea that all citizens have the right to be supported by the government, regardless of their ability or desire to support themselves and their families.

We pledge to continue to push strongly for sound welfare reform until meaningful and helpful change is enacted into law by the Congress. . . .

Children

We believe, with the President, that the first five years of life are crucial to a child's development, and further, that every child should have the opportunity to reach his full potential as an individual.

We have, therefore, established the Office of Child Development which has taken a comprehensive approach to the development of young children, combining programs dealing with their physical, social and educational needs and development.

We have undertaken a wide variety of demonstration programs to assure our children, particularly poor children, a good start in life—for example, the Parent and Child Center program for infant care, Home Start to strengthen the environment of the preschool child, and Health Start to explore new delivery systems of health care for young children.

We have redirected Head Start to perform valuable fullday child care and early education services, and more than 380,000 preschool children are now in the program. We have doubled funds for early childhood demonstration programs which will develop new tools and new teaching techniques to serve children who suffer from deafness, blindness and other handicaps.

So that no child will be denied the opportunity for a productive life because of inability to read effectively, we have established the Right to Read Program.

To add impetus to the entire educational effort, our newly-created National Institute of Education ensures that broad research and experimentation will develop the best educational opportunities for all children. Additionally, we have taken steps to help ensure that children receive proper care while their parents are at work.

Moreover, as stated elsewhere in this platform, we have broadened nutritional assistance to poor children by nearly tripling participation in the food stamp program, more than doubling the number of needy children in the school lunch program, operating a summer feeding program for three million

young people, increasing the breakfast program fivefold, and doubling Federal support for child nutritional programs. We are improving medical care for poor children through more vigorous treatment procedures under Medicaid and more effectively targeting maternal and child health services to low-income mothers. We will continue to seek out new means to reach and teach children in their crucial early years. . . .

Older Americans

We believe our nation must develop a new awareness of the attitudes and needs of our older citizens. Elderly Americans are far too often the forgotten Americans, relegated to lives of idleness and isolation by a society bemused with the concerns of other groups. We are distressed by the tendency of many Americans to ignore the heartbreak and hardship resulting from the generation gap which separates so many of our people from those who have reached the age of retirement. We deplore what is tantamount to cruel discrimination—age discrimination in employment, and the discrimination of neglect and indifference, perhaps the cruelest of all.

We commit ourselves to helping older Americans achieve greater self-reliance and greater opportunities for direct participation in the activities of our society. We believe that the later years should be, not isolated years, not years of dependency, but years of fulfillment and dignity. We believe our older people are not to be regarded as a burden but rather should be valuable participants in our society. We believe their judgment, their experience, and their talents are immensely valuable to our country.

Because we so believe, we are seeking and have sought in many ways to help older Americans—for example:

■ Federal programs of direct benefit to older Americans have increased more than $16 billion these past four years.

■ As part of this, Social Security benefits are more than 50% higher than they were four years ago, the largest increase in the history of social security.

■ Social Security benefits have become inflation proof by making them rise automatically to match cost of living increases, a protection long advocated by the Republican Party.

■ We have upgraded nursing homes.

Expenditures under the Older Americans Act have gone up 800% since President Nixon took office, with a strong emphasis on programs enabling older Americans to live dignified, independent lives in their own homes. . . .

We have urged upon the opposition Congress—again, typically, to no avail—numerous additional programs of benefit to the elderly. We will continue pressing for these new initiatives to:

■ Increase the amount of money a person can earn without losing Social Security benefits.

■ Increase widow, widower, and delayed retirement benefits.

■ Improve the effectiveness of Medicare, including elimination of the monthly premium required under Part B of Medicare—the equivalent of more than a 3% Social Security increase. . . .

■ Give special attention to bringing full government services within the reach of the elderly in rural areas who are often unable to share fully in their deserved benefits because of geographic inaccessibility.

■ Upgrade other Federal activities important to the elderly including programs for nutrition, housing and nursing homes, transportation, consumer protection, and elimination of age discrimination in government and private employment. . . .

McGovern's views. Following his nomination, McGovern continued to explain his views on a variety of issues.

In a nationwide TV address Aug. 5, McGovern said, "Those who can work should have jobs, even if the government must provide them, and all our citizens, those who work and those who cannot, should be assured an adequate income." "Poverty cannot be ended by providing less than people need," he said, "even for the barest necessities of life. Every worker, and every merchant will do better when poverty gives way to new purchasing power."

Nixon's campaign director Clark Mac-Gregor assailed McGovern in a National Press Club talk Aug. 10 for advocating a "giveaway" welfare program, "massive and reckless" defense cuts and a "begging" foreign policy. He said McGovern's "$1,000-per-person giveaway program . . . would split America permanently into a welfare class and a working class."

McGovern presented revised proposals for welfare reform Aug. 29 in a New York speech, and he dropped his proposal of a $1,000-a-person grant.

In its place, he proposed a National Income Insurance plan to provide (a) public service jobs for the employable on welfare, (b) a $4,000 aid floor, consisting of cash and food stamps, for a family of four on welfare, and (c) a shift of care for the aged, disabled and blind from welfare to the Social Security system.

He estimated the cost of his revised welfare plan at $14 billion above current budgetary levels—$6 billion for the jobs portion, $3 billion—from general revenues—for the Social Security portion and $5 billion for the family-aid portion.

Elliot L. Richardson, secretary of health, education and welfare, Aug. 30 called the new welfare proposal "costly and scatterbrained." He criticized it for lacking details on its incentives for the working poor and work requirements for welfare recipients.

In Washington Sept. 23, the President addressed a group of young labor supporters at the White House on "the dignity of work" saying that "a man should work for what he gets and get what he works for," that it was "wrong for someone who works to get less than someone on welfare."

Nixon, speaking Sept. 22 at John B. Connally Jr.'s ranch in Texas, had said, "even though it might be politically, shall we say, somewhat appealing in some quarters to call for a redistribution of income . . . I say that it is vital for us to remember that in this country what brought us where we are is the fact that we have always recognized that an individual who works will receive what he is entitled to."

Nixon assails 'welfare ethic.' President Nixon upheld the "work ethic" and denounced the "welfare ethic" in a Labor Day statement issued Sept. 3. "We are faced this year," he said, "with the choice between the 'work ethic' that built this nation's character and the new 'welfare ethic' that could cause that American character to weaken." The former taught that "everything valuable in life requires some striving and some sacrifice," Nixon said, while the latter "says that the good life can be made available to everyone right now and that this can be done by the government."

In citing three areas in which the 'welfare ethic' posed challenges to traditional values, Nixon attacked (1) "a policy of income redistribution," (2) involuntary school busing to achieve "racial balance" and (3) what Nixon perceived as an increasing trend to assign quotas in politics as well as in jobs.

As for income redistribution, Nixon said such a policy "would result in many more Americans becoming poor because it ignores a human value essential to every worker's success—the incentive of reward."

McGovern urges more aid to elderly. Traveling to a senior citizens' rally in North Bergen, N.J. Sept. 20, McGovern deplored the plight of the elderly in America and proposed a number of specific boosts in aid. He had met senior citizens who paid half their income in property taxes, he said, others who were "forced to eat dog meat because they can't afford hamburger," others "who must wait years for decent housing" and others who were in nursing homes "where I would not want to stay 10 minutes, much less the rest of my life."

He said the elderly, the blind and the disabled should be provided a minimum monthly income of $150. McGovern proposed raising Social Security benefits to widows to 100% of their deceased husband's benefits, increasing the amount of income the elderly could earn without reduction of Social Security benefits (up to $8,000 a year for a single person, McGovern proposed), permitting men to retire at age 62 with reduced Social Security benefits, retaining a cost-of-living adjustment to make the income maintenance program "inflation-proof," expanding Medicare coverage to out-of-hospital prescription drugs, eliminating the monthly charge for doctors' bills under Medicare, reducing property taxes and providing guarantees that private pension plans actually paid benefits.

Nixon on 'welfare mess.' In a pre-election interview by Garnett D. Horner of the Washington Star-News Nov. 5 (the interview was published Nov. 9), Nixon assailed the "welfare mess."

The President said, "This escalation of the numbers on welfare, much of it is a result simply of running down what I call the work ethic." One thing the election was about, he said, "is whether we should move toward more massive handouts to people, making the people more and more dependent, looking to government, or whether we say, 'no, it is up to you.' The people are going to have to carry their share of the load."

"The average American is just like the child in the family," Nixon continued. "You give him some responsibility and he is going to amount to something. He is going to do something. If, on the other hand, you make him completely dependent and pamper him and cater to him too much, you are going to make him soft, spoiled and eventually a very weak individual."

Activists

NWRO convention. The National Welfare Rights Organization (NWRO) held its fifth annual convention at Brown University (Providence, R. I.) July 28–Aug. 1, 1971. 1,200 delegates came to represent the organization's 125,000 members in 50 states. While continuing to concentrate on welfare reform and the need for an adequate guaranteed annual income for the poor, the organization appeared to be moving towards an effort to organize a broad, populist coalition for political action.

In a speech July 29, Dr. George A. Wiley, 39, NWRO executive director, urged the group, already organized across racial lines, to seek a coalition with the working poor, the elderly, women's rights groups, the peace movement, tenants organizations, minority groups and farm, hospital and domestic workers. Workshops July 30 instructed the delegates in political organizing tactics, teaching how to run for office and influence candidates.

Reps. Donald V. Dellums (D, Calif.) and Bella Abzug (D, N.Y.) opened the convention with speeches July 28. Sen. George McGovern (D, S.D.) told the convention July 29 he would sponsor NWRO welfare reform proposals in Congress, calling for a guaranteed annual income of $6,500 for a family of four. McGovern said the proposal "rests on the hard rock of human dignity, on the essential business of giving every American a truly adequate income."

Wiley indicated July 29 that the NWRO was moving away from absolute opposition to President Nixon's family assistance program, which included a proposed $2,400 annual income for a family of four. He said NWRO would push for Congress to liberalize the bill and would support a measure with certain minimum concessions—guarantees against reductions of any recipient's present benefits, an increase in the proposed income and safeguards for the legal rights of welfare recipients. Wiley also faulted the Nixon plan for provisions he said would require recipients to work for less than a minimum wage, undermining the wages of the working poor.

30,000 in DC march. A predominantly black crowd of 30,000, about half of them children, rallied before the White House and the Washington Monument March 25, 1972, to protest Nixon welfare, education and child care policies. The rally, sponsored by the National Welfare Rights Organization, heard speakers demand a $6,500 guaranteed minimum income for a family of four, and call for President Nixon's defeat in the November election.

Arrangements by District of Columbia school officials to bring schoolchildren and parents to the rally were called "degrading and regretful" March 24 by Nixon special assistant Robert J. Brown.

Rural housing aid sought. A three-day conference on rural housing, attended by 600 delegates from antipoverty groups, rural cooperatives, labor and religious groups, was held in Washington Nov. 28–30, 1972. It urged more federal funds for housing in rural areas, which, conferees claimed, provided less adequate housing, medical and educational facilities to its poor people than urban areas.

The conference, organized by the Rural Housing Alliance (RHA) and the Housing Assistance Council, passed resolutions Nov. 30 asking for property tax exemptions for homes worth less than the national median ($17,000), stronger regulation of the mobile home industry, doubling of federal spending on migrant labor housing, now running at $2.5 million a year, and increased attention by the Farmers Home Administration to low-income housing.

End of Nixon Administration

Antipoverty Agency
Under Attack

The Watergate scandal, a lingering legacy of the 1972 Presidential election campaign, put an end to the Nixon Administration Aug. 9, 1974. Before his forced resignation as President, Richard Nixon had sought unsuccessfully to dismantle the Office of Economic Opportunity, the umbrella antipoverty agency created to run Lyndon Johnson's War on Poverty.

Budget plans OEO demise. President Nixon submitted his fiscal 1974 budget to Congress Jan. 29, 1973. It called for a final dissolution of the Office of Economic Opportunity (OEO), the coordinating agency for antipoverty programs since the Johnson Administration, ending the $384 million community action program. Some OEO programs would be transferred to other agencies, while legal services for the poor would be reorganized as an independent agency, funded at $71.5 million.

The budget justified the community action cutoff by a lack of evidence that the program was "moving substantial numbers of people out of poverty on a self-sustaining basis." An Office of Management and Budget official explained further that the Administration felt the program had alienated local officials without helping poor people very much.

OEO's migrant programs would go to the Labor Department, its Indian and health programs would go to HEW, and its community economic development programs would move to the Office of Minority Business Enterprise.

The budget did not mention a Family Assistance Plan to replace the welfare system, but HEW officials said a proposal was in the works. Meanwhile, the Administration hoped to save nearly $600 million in welfare payments through management reforms and removal of ineligibles from the rolls. HEW planned to add 700 enforcement employes.

HEW said expenditures on social services for welfare recipients, which Congress had limited at $2.5 billion a year, could be further limited to $1.8 billion. The services included counseling and day care.

Controversy over attack on OEO. Dispute flared in early 1973 over the Nixon Administration's proposals to dismantle the OEO. Much of the controversy was over Administration plans to restrict the scope of the legal services program.

A memorandum prepared in the OEO budget office and reported Feb. 16 recommended that the Administration "present Congress with a fait accompli before

129

critics" of OEO dismantling "can organize effective countermoves." The memo said conservative congressmen should be enlisted to divert consideration of the question to the conservative appropriations committees, and to delay appropriations bills until OEO was disbanded.

The memo said the Administration should avoid a confrontation on the constitutional issues of Congressional power, and said "at this point there probably is not much fight left in Congressional supporters of OEO and community action," although it admitted "legal services is probably another matter."

OEO Acting Director Howard Phillips said the memo reflected only the views of the individual who drafted it, but House Speaker Carl Albert called it an "arrogant attempt to surreptitiously manipulate the legislative process."

Another memo, prepared by the acting director of the legal services evaluation division at OEO, called for elimination of 13 "backup centers," mostly attached to universities, which served as legal services research and advisory groups. The centers had developed much of the rationale for class action test cases and other controversial litigation. The memo said the centers' functions should be transfered to Washington to "render the program more amenable to control by those who are the elected and appointed stewards of the funds used."

Theodore Tetzlaff, acting director of the legal services program for one year, was replaced Feb. 12 by Phillips, who had been named acting director Jan. 31. Tetzlaff charged Phillips with a number of "acts of political interference" with legal services, including the appointment of officials hostile to the program.

Phillips had abolished the National Advisory Committee to the Legal Services Program earlier in February. The 34-member committee had been a liaison between lawyers groups, poor clients of the program and the government.

Phillips, a former Young Americans for Freedom chapter chairman and a longtime critic of some legal services activities and other OEO programs, had issued an order limiting legal services grant renewals to 30-day periods.

An OEO evaluation of 591 community action agencies, completed in January and

disclosed Feb. 2, said the program had been "highly constructive." Phillips replied the same day that the report had been prepared by "various people identified with previous Administration policies," and had at any rate come too late to alter OEO budget requests.

The survey said the agencies were "becoming very positive forces in their communities" and could help local government respond effectively to the Administration's revenue sharing and decentralization philosophy. In addition, the agencies had improved their ability to mobilize outside funds, raising $396 million in 1972.

The report said the agencies had improved their relations with local governments, which had become "extremely supportive of community action" at least since 1968.

Cuts protested—Protesters estimated at 10,000–35,000 lobbied at the Capitol and rallied on the Capitol steps Feb. 20 to oppose Administration cuts in poverty and urban programs.

The predominantly black demonstration was sponsored by the National Association for Community Development, an organization of leaders of community action programs.

Suits oppose Phillips & OEO end. Four Democratic senators sued March 14, 1973 in U.S. District Court for the District of Columbia seeking removal of Howard J. Phillips as acting director of the Office of Economic Opportunity (OEO), on grounds that federal law required Senate confirmation of the heads of federal departments within 30 days of their appointment.

Aides of the four senators said the suit was aimed at delaying the dismantling of OEO. The senators were Harrison A. Williams (N.J.), chairman of the Labor and Public Welfare Committee, and Claiborne Pell (R.I.), Walter F. Mondale (Minn.) and William D. Hathaway (Me.), all members of the committee.

Three lawsuits had been filed in U.S. district courts in Chicago and the District of Columbia Feb. 26 by OEO employe unions, employes of some of the doomed community action programs and some poor beneficiaries of the programs, seek-

ing injunctions against further dismantling.

The suits charged that Phillips had
violated the law by conducting an executive reorganization without giving Congress 60 days to review the plans, by dele-
gating authority over OEO programs to
other agencies contrary to 1972 Congressional legislation, by ending programs
mandated by Congress to continue
through June 1975, and by impounding
$113.5 million in funds appropriated for
fiscal 1973.

Phillips had been sharply criticized at
a Feb. 27 hearing of the House Equal Opportunity subcommittee. Rep. Frank
Thompson Jr. (D, N.J.) said Phillips was
"subverting the national policy of the
United States." But Phillips told the committee his actions were designed to
strengthen the antipoverty program by
paring programs that had failed.

Phillips said legal services programs
would probably be granted one-year extensions until Congress could work out
new legislation. He said the community
action programs had been only one-third
funded by the federal government, and
could be continued through local funding.

Phillips announced March 12 that all
10 OEO regional offices would be closed
by April 28, and about 700 employes
would lose their jobs.

Court bars OEO breakup. U.S. District
Court Judge William Jones ordered Acting OEO Director Phillips April 11, 1973
to cease dismantling his agency and
continue funding antipoverty programs at
Congressionally appropriated levels "until
Congress changes that command."

In a suit brought by four community
action agencies and several labor unions
representing OEO employes, Jones said
Phillips actions were "unauthorized by
law, illegal and in excess of statutory
authority," and were therefore "null and
void."

Responding to the Administration's
argument that the executive power allowed the President to reorganize
agencies, Jones said "if the power sought
here were found valid, no barrier would
remain to the executive ignoring any and
all Congressional authorizations if he
deemed them, no matter how con-

scientiously, to be contrary to the needs
of the nation."

"The defendant [Phillips]," Jones ruled,
"really argues that the Constitution con-
fers the discretionary power upon the
President to refuse to execute laws
passed by Congress with which he disa-
grees."

The court also found that Phillips had
violated the Reorganization Act, which
required prior notification to Congress before an agency could be abolished.

Congress, Jones said, had authorized
continuation of the OEO through June 30,
1975. Although the Administration noted
that Congress had so far not appropriated
any new OEO funds for the fiscal year beginning July 1, the court ruled that the
executive must continue to spend remaining funds until Congress decides "to make
provisions for termination." The government had argued that fiscal chaos would
result if Congress did not appropriate new
funds by July 1, but Jones said he could
"not presume that Congress will act in
such an irresponsible manner."

President Nixon's Jan. 29 budget message, which ruled out new OEO funding,
was "nothing more," Jones said, "than
a proposal to the Congress to act upon
as it may please."

Jones agreed that the OEO could withhold funds from antipoverty agencies that
had been fiscally irresponsible, but specified that impounding could not be used
"for reasons unrelated to the purposes of
the Economic Opportunity Act."

Harold Himmelman, attorney for the
Lawyers Committee for Civil Rights Under Law, which represented the Community Action agencies in the case, said
the decision would bolster those in Congress trying to "fight against the Administration's use of executive power to
end programs voted by Congress." But
officials of antipoverty agencies were reported April 12 to be unsure of the effect
of the ruling.

Phillips had ordered OEO regional offices disbanded and many staffers dismissed by April 28, had ordered termination of federal aid to local Community
Action agencies, and had delayed approval of funding for some programs the
Administration said it would continue under the control of executive departments,
such as legal services units.

Shifts approved—The Administration's transfer of eight programs from the OEO to other federal agencies was approved in U.S. district court in Washington Aug. 3.

Rejecting a suit filed by the OEO employes' union, Judge Thomas A. Flannery ruled that the transfers were designed to achieve efficiency and were "not integral to the abolition of OEO or its programs." The programs remaining under OEO jurisdiction were community action, economic development and legal services, all of which the Administration had said it wanted abolished or transferred.

Flannery said OEO employes would be given the opportunity to transfer to the other agencies at the same job levels.

The programs affected included Head Start, the Job Corps, migrant farm workers' assistance, drug rehabilitation and birth control.

Legal services bill gains. Legislation to create an independent, federally-funded legal services corporation for the poor was adopted by the House Education & Labor Committee May 24, 1973 after significant changes were made in a version submitted to Congress May 11 by President Nixon.

The corporation would replace a program administered by the Office of Economic Opportunity (OEO). The OEO was scheduled to go out of existence June 30 unless Congress acted, but OEO Acting Director Howard J. Phillips had indicated that the legal services program might be extended pending new legislation.

The committee approved Nixon's proposal for an 11-member, bipartisan corporation board, including six lawyers, to be appointed by the President and confirmed by the Senate. Antipoverty lawyers would also be supervised by state advisory councils.

The Nixon bill's strict prohibitions against lobbying and political activity by legal services attorneys were modified to allow them to testify before legislative bodies as representatives of the poor. Lawyers would also be permitted, under guidelines to be drawn up by the corporation, to help the poor in organizing special interest groups, an activity which the Administration had sought to ban. The lawyers, however, would be barred from encouraging their clients to participate in riots, picketing, boycotts or strikes.

Eligibility standards providing free legal assistance to those with incomes less than twice the poverty level were modified to take into account family size, debts, expenses and the local cost of living. The committee also deleted a requirement for a fee schedule to be charged eligible clients who could afford to pay.

Action for Legal Rights, an organization backing a strong legal services program, expressed fear that the bill's provisions for regulating the activities of staff lawyers might improperly interfere with the traditional lawyer-client relationship and leave the attorneys open to political pressure.

Phillips May 30 and June 4 issued regulations for legal services programs extended beyond the potential June 30 date for the OEO's extinction.

The new rules, to be effective June 29 and July 5, were in direct opposition to provisions of the bill reported by the House Education and Labor Committee: staff lawyers would not be allowed to represent clients in "political and/or legislative aims;" representation of groups would be severely restricted; and programs to educate the poor on legal rights would be limited to generalities and could not advocate "reforms allegedly designed to make the legal system more responsive to the needs of the poor."

Robert W. Meserve, president of the American Bar Association, protested to Phillips that the rules were inappropriate while Nixon and Congress were trying to establish a new program, the Washington Post reported June 6.

The Post also said Phillips had given congressmen "speech material" used in denunciations of the bill on the House floor May 31. The Post cited three speeches as coming almost directly from material provided by the OEO.

Lawrence Straw, acting associate director of OEO, denied that Phillips was opposing the attempt to set up a legal services corporation or seeking to wreck the program with the new regulations. Straw said the speech material, highly critical of legal services in both concept and operation, would be given to congressmen on request.

House OKs amended legal services bill—
The House June 21 approved, 276–95, a
bill creating an independent legal services
corporation after attaching to the com-
mittee-approved   version   numerous
amendments designed primarily to bring
the bill into line with the original Administration proposals.

The final bill restored the Administration's prohibition on lobbying by legal
services lawyers. An amendment by Rep.
Edith Green (D, Ore.) barred outside legal
research   or   other   assistance.   Other
amendments would: prevent staff attorneys from bringing busing, desegrega-
tion or abortion suits; bar lawyers from
political activities, including voter registration drives; insure that no legal services
were offered to the "voluntary poor;" prohibit contracts with law firms who spent
more than half their time on "public interest" litigation; and give preference to
local attorneys in staff hiring.

Filibuster stalls bill—A similar bill
was stalled in December by a Senate
filibuster. The current legal services
program under the Office of Economic
Opportunity was due to expire July 1,
1974, and the Administration had
proposed a revision with curbs on lobbying
and political activities of poverty lawyers.

When the Senate took up floor
consideration of such a measure Dec. 10,
Sens. Jesse A. Helms (R, N.C.) and
William Brock (R, Tenn.) launched a
filibuster to defeat it. Helms contended it
would provide funds for "Naderesque"
law groups. Two cloture votes to cut off
debate, requiring two-thirds majority for
approval, were lost—the first Dec. 13 by
four votes, the second Dec. 14 by one vote.
Unanimous consent was given the Senate
leadership Dec. 17 to postpone further
consideration of the bill until 1974.

Legal services bill enacted. The bill
to transfer the legal services program
from the OEO to an independent Legal
Services Corp. was finally approved in
compromise version by action of both
houses of Congress July 16, 1974, and
Nixon signed the measure July 25.

**Before approving most of the
conference committee's version, both
houses deleted a provision that would have
allowed the corporation to award**
contracts and grants to outside poverty
law research centers in several law
schools. The rejected research programs
had been intended as back-up operations
for class action lawsuits on behalf of the
poor.

In a key preliminary vote, the Senate
rejected, 61–34, an amendment by Jesse
A. Helms (R, N.C.) which would have
prohibited research by the corporation itself and funding of public interest and
poverty law firms.

Establishment of the independent corporation removed legal services functions
from the moribund Office of Economic
Opportunity.

Among major provisions:

■ The corporation would have an 11-member board
of directors, appointed by the President and
confirmed by the Senate.

■ Employes would be exempt from laws and
executive orders affecting federal agencies.

■ The corporation could not lobby for or against
legislation at any government level, except in response
to formal requests from legislative bodies for
testimony.

■ Lawyers involved full-time in corporation-funded
activities could not engage in outside practice for
compensation.

■ Corporation funds could not be used for suits
involving criminal charges, political activities, school
integration, Selective Service laws or abortions.

The bill authorized funding of $90
million for fiscal 1975, $100 million for
1976 and open-ended funding for 1977;
subsequent   appropriations   would   be
limited to two-year periods.

Phillips   out,   OEO   in.   President
Nixon June 26, 1973 signaled the OEO's
extension by naming former OEO Deputy
Director Alvin J. Arnett to succeed Howard Phillips as OEO director. In the
announcement from the Western White
House in San Clemente, spokesman
Gerald L. Warren said the appointment
was an indication that the Administration
would await Congressional action on the
proposed dismantling of the OEO.

Phillips' attempts to break up the
agency by abolishing programs or transferring them to other agencies had been
stymied by a series of court decisions.
Reinforcing an April 11 decision barring
the breakup of OEO without Congressional approval, U.S. District Court
Judge William Jones ruled June 11 that
Phillips had been serving illegally and enjoined him from taking further action as
head of the agency.

Ruling in a suit filed by four Democratic senators, Jones said Phillips' nomination only as acting director and Nixon's failure to submit the nomination to the Senate for confirmation violated the law setting up the OEO.

Jones ruled that the President's power concerning interim appointments, "if it exists at all, exists only in emergency situations," and that Phillips' case did not involve such a situation.

The U.S. Court of Appeals June 22 declined to overturn the decision but directed Jones to consider amending the order if he found merit to Administration arguments that the OEO would suffer "irreparable injury" under his ruling. Judge Jones responded June 25 by ordering the OEO to submit the names of those authorized to spend funds already committed to OEO programs.

Despite the concession to Congress in the Arnett appointment, Warren noted that the Administration was still committed to the goal of eventual abolition of the agency. Arnett, who was executive director of the Appalachian Regional Commission before coming to the OEO, was quoted by an agency spokesman June 26 as saying "the poor won't miss a stroke or notice when OEO is gone," and that the only solution for the poor was to "directly supplement their income. In any social service program, it's the technicians who benefit, not the poor."

Proposals & Actions

Nixon's human resources message. President Nixon sent a "human resources" message to Congress March 1, 1973 and said he had dropped for the present a minimum family income plan.

Nixon said "the legislative outlook seems to preclude passage of an overall structural reform bill" for the welfare system. The House had twice passed versions of his minimum income plan, but disputes between Senate liberals and conservatives had killed the plan in 1972.

Nixon said he still believed that the welfare system was "a crazy quilt of injustice and contradiction," and said he would "work diligently" with Congress to obtain some reforms to improve management of

the program. Caspar Weinberger, secretary of health, education and welfare (HEW), told a White House news conference the same day that the Administration was considering flat grants to welfare families "to replace degrading investigations of family budgets," and might permit state administrative experiments.

Weinberger conceded that "many people in this Administration were never really comfortable" with the minimum income idea, and had become concerned that the plan would increase welfare rolls rather than reduce them.

Nixon defended his unsuccessful attempt to dismantle the OEO. Under his plan, the only OEO program that would not shift to other agencies was the community action program, which he called "no longer necessary or desirable." He said the Johnson Administration had made "sweeping, sometimes almost utopian commitments in one area of social concern after another," leading to "dismal failure" in "case after case." Weinberger charged that 80% of the community action budgets had gone to "overhead."

Nixon had explained his social programs in a nationwide radio address Feb. 24. He repeated earlier statements against "paternalism, social exploitation and waste" in federal programs, but noted that federal spending on all forms of social welfare activities, including Social Security, veterans, health and education programs, had nearly doubled under his Administration.

Nixon on welfare reform. In an impromptu news conference March 2, 1973, President Nixon told reporters he considered it essential that a new approach to welfare be developed "in which there is a bonus not for welfare but a bonus, if there is to be one, for work." He still considered his family assistance proposal "the best answer," but there was "no chance" to get the proposal through the Senate in acceptable form. So the Administration was developing an alternative program, which might include, he said, some form of family assistance.

HEW plans services cuts. The Department of Health, Education & Welfare Feb.

15, 1973 proposed rule changes in social services programs for welfare recipients and other poor people that would cut off federal funds for a variety of state and private programs. The changes would curb spending beyond the $2.5 billion limit set by Congress in 1972.

Under the program, the federal government provided 75% of funding for programs including day care, job training, meals for the aged, and services for the blind and mentally retarded, with the other 25% supplied by local governments or private agencies. The fiscal 1972 federal share came to $1.7 billion, but mushrooming costs and a lack of program or eligibility limits led to the $2.5 billion Congressional ceiling.

HEW Secretary Caspar Weinberger said the curbs were intended to "permit available resources to be used most effectively for those who need them most," in view of the ceiling, although observers believed the rules would limit spending to about $1.8 billion a year. Weinberger said the "unfocused nature" of the programs led to doubts about who they "were really benefitting" and to suspicions of major abuses. The new rules would tend to limit benefits to welfare recipients.

The most important change would bar matching funds to private programs. The proposal was criticized in a letter sent to Weinberger Feb. 15 by a bipartisan group of 46 senators, led by Sen. Walter F. Mondale (D, Minn.), who said the change "would seriously undermine the excellent private-public partnership approach to human problems that now exists." Weinberger said the private groups had not been adequately supervised by the government.

A number of services for welfare families, the aged and the blind which had been mandatory for states would become optional. Weinberger claimed the old rules provided "a very broad opening for states to provide services to people who may not have been in need at all." Block certification, under which residence in designated areas established eligibility for certain programs would be eliminated

Federal day care standards would be revised to allow double the number of children per adult. Since many day care programs were operated by private

groups, such services would be especially hard hit by the new rules.

Funds would be distributed only to expanded state activities, and states could not reorganize existing programs to qualify. HEW spokesmen said a large part of the recent rise in social services costs resulted from HEW paying for programs formerly financed by the states.

First retreat—Weinberger told the Senate Intergovernmental Relations Subcommittee March 14 that the Administration had decided to abandon one of the proposed rules changes in the state and local social services program, which would have barred private funds from being used as part of local 25% matching funds to qualify for federal aid.

Weinberger said objections to some of the other rule changes, which would limit eligibility for the day care, job training and other programs, would be reviewed "sympathetically" before action was taken. Furthermore, he said in response to a question by Sen. Lawton Chiles (D, Fla.) that although HEW had budgeted only $1.8 billion for the program in fiscal 1974, the department would be willing to reimburse the states up to the full $2.5 billion authorized by Congress if requested.

HEW compromises—After receiving more critical comments on the proposals, HEW issued final rules April 26 on eligibility and payments for social services programs designed to get or keep people off welfare. The new regulations were generally less restrictive than those proposed Feb. 15.

In a key concession, HEW said it would continue to allow donations by private agencies to be used as part of a state's 25% matching funds for federal aid, but with safeguards to prevent donors from deriving benefits. Under the final rule, a donating agency could specify a particular activity as long as it was not the sponsor or operator of such a program.

HEW also retreated on the income-cutoff level for free social services, granting eligibility to families earning up to 150% of a state's standard for receipt of welfare payments. The February proposal had set a ceiling of 133.3% of a state's actual welfare payments, which in some states were less than the standard.

Subsidized child care would be provided to families with incomes between 150% and 233.3% of a state's welfare standard, with recipients paying on a sliding scale to be determined by each state.

Among the rules retained from the February proposals: former welfare recipients could get social services aid for three months after leaving welfare rolls instead of two years, and potential recipients would be eligible for six months instead of five years; "block certifications," under which residence in designated poverty areas established eligibility for aid, would be eliminated; and payments for subsistence income maintenance and mental health services available under other programs would be stopped.

Although the new regulations were designed to meet a $2.5 billion annual spending ceiling for social services set by Congress, federal outlays would be held to as little as $1.6 billion, the Wall Street Journal reported April 27. Most rules were to become effective July 1, with all to be in effect by Jan. 1, 1974.

HEW not to withhold funds. Secretary of Health, Education & Welfare Caspar W. Weinberger said April 4, 1973 the government had decided not to go through with its plan to withhold an estimated $689 million over 18 months in matching welfare payments to states, the amount of money allegedly going to ineligibles or in overpayments. Instead, states would be given two years to reduce improper payments.

Weinberger said the states would have until June 30, 1975 to cut back ineligibles to 3% of the rolls and those receiving overpayments to 5% of recipients, to be checked by sample surveys, and to be reached in six month increments. HEW officials were reported April 4 to claim that the new rules would still produce about the same level of savings in fiscal 1974, because of actions already being taken in some states.

Welfare directors in 34 states and jurisdictions had taken joint legal action to oppose HEW's original Jan. 1, 1973 deadline for complete elimination of ineligibles and overpayments, first announced Dec. 4, 1972. HEW had also decided, it was reported April 4, to eliminate three rules imposed during the 1960s that limited local welfare officials' power to investigate eligibility, eliminate recipients from the rolls or recover overpayments.

Final rules—HEW Aug. 14 announced final rules on eligibility requirements, restrictions on individual hearings and recovery of overpayments.

The rules would allow states to reinstate secret investigations of welfare applicants and recipients. Under current rules, states could make outside inquiries only with a welfare client's permission. Responding to complaints from welfare organizations that the new rule might lead to harassment and invasion of privacy, HEW included a regulation which "restates that constitutional rights are to be observed and protected."

Another rule would allow states to develop their own regulations for recovering overpayments, with a one-year retroactive limit which would also apply to correction of underpayments. Under old rules, overpayments were recoverable only if they involved fraud, an error caused by the recipient or if the recipient was found to have sufficient financial resources.

Other new rules would extend from 30 to 45 days the time in which states must decide on welfare applications, extend from 60 to 90 days the deadline for acting on hearings and reduce from 15 to 10 days the period of advance notice for reduction or elimination of benefits.

The rules were to take effect Oct. 15 but could be implemented earlier if states needed no new legislation.

Social Security increase. Congress completed action Dec. 21 on a bill to increase Social Security benefits by 11%—7% in March 1974 and 4% in June 1974. The votes were 65–0 in the Senate and 301–13 in the House. The first increase would supersede a 5.9% cost-of-living increase enacted previously in 1973.

The payroll tax base for Social Security would rise to $13,200 in 1974.

Federal welfare payments to the aged, blind and disabled would rise in January 1974 from $130 a month for a single person to $140, from $195 for a couple to $210, followed in June by another $6 rise for one and $9 for couples. Their entitlement to food stamps and Medicaid benefits also was written into the bill.

The bill suspended until 1975 Department of Health, Education and Welfare regulations restricting use of federal welfare money by the states for social services. Unemployment compensation was extended an extra 13 weeks for states where the jobless rate exceeded 4%.

Separate consideration of many Senate amendments was held over for 1974 after the House delayed conference action on the bill until a day before adjournment. Among the provisions held over were a tax credit for low-income workers, Medicare and Medicaid modifications and increased child welfare and support programs.

Benefit inequities cited. A report prepared for the Congressional Joint Economic Committee by the General Accounting Office found that substantial inequities existed in the cumulative effect of about 100 different federal cash, commodity and service programs on poor people. Some jobless families were drawing multiple benefits totaling more than average wages in some areas, while other poor people were completely ignored, it was reported March 27, 1973.

The report was based on a survey of 1,-758 representative families in poverty sections of five cities and one rural area. About 60% of families in the areas received one or more benefits, while 11% received aid under five or more programs. In half the areas, nonjob income for multiple-benefit families averaged $426 a month, or $55 more than the median wage for women, less Social Security taxes, in those areas.

More than half the $100 billion annual expense in the 100 programs was for Social Security and Medicare, the rest for welfare, housing subsidies, food stamps, unemployment and veterans benefits, job training, school lunch and other programs.

Rep. Martha Griffiths (D, Mich.), who ordered the survey, said the findings showed the inadequacy of the total federal welfare effort, which she said should provide "a reasonable amount of aid to those who need it." She said that while some poor people were ignored by the government, the Census Bureau had been

"exaggerating the poverty in this country under the present system" by not counting non-cash benefits. She pointed to work disincentives in some of the programs, since small increases in earned income could cut several benefits for a family. Griffiths said some programs conflicted with each other, and said recent Social Security increases had left some families worse off by reducing benefits in other categories.

Guaranteed income test reported. According to a four-year study of the minimum income approach to welfare reform, the "work ethic" was not substantially affected by direct cash subsidies, it was reported Aug. 27. A guaranteed income plan had been part of the Nixon Administration's reform proposals which died in Congress in 1972.

The study had been conducted by University of Wisconsin researchers for the Office of Economic Opportunity. The project covered 1,357 poor families in New Jersey and Pennsylvania, 725 of whom received income guarantees ranging from $2,000–$5,000 for a family of four.

Preliminary results showed that some groups—women, elderly men and those in poor health—were inclined to work less or not at all with the income supplements. Other groups—blacks, the young and relatively well-educated and the healthy—tended to work more steadily under the grants and to seek higher-paying jobs.

Families were questioned periodically on psychological effects of the program: degrees of self-esteem and possible feelings of greater personal control of one's own destiny. Responses showed no significant differences in attitudes between those who received subsidies and those who did not.

A similar study in rural sections of North Carolina and Iowa found that the plan had little effect on family stability, marital happiness or aspirations of teenage children for education and jobs.

Education proposals. The Administration March 19, 1973 detailed a proposed "Better Schools Act of 1973," which would replace 32 federal programs that aid elementary and secondary education with five revenue sharing categories

The bill would provide a total of $2.8 billion for fiscal 1974, including $1.5 billion for aid to disadvantaged students. But the distribution formula for poverty aid would result in substantial redistributions among the states and reduce the number of benefitting students.

In the first year of the new plan's operation, each state and district would be guaranteed at least as much money in the poverty program as it received in fiscal 1973 under Title I of the Elementary and Secondary Education Act, which the new plan would abolish. But the new bill would eventually benefit only 5 million disadvantaged students, compared with 6.1 million currently, according to acting U.S. Education Commissioner John R. Ottina, testifying March 19 at the House general education subcommittee. Health Education and Welfare (HEW) Assistant Secretary Sidney P. Marland told the subcommittee that an average of $300 would be provided for each student, compared with $220 under the latest Title I appropriations.

The formula would result in more funds to poor rural states and reduced funds for large urban states, and some districts within each state, with small proportions of poor students, would lose current funding. 75% of the disadvantaged student funds would have to be spent on reading, writing and arithmetic. Noting that the Administration had defended revenue sharing as a means to revive local control of spending, Rep. Lloyd Means (D, Wash.) said the requirement would substitute "chains for strings."

The four other revenue sharing categories would be vocational education, schooling for handicapped children, aid to districts with large numbers of children of federal employes living on nontaxable federal property and assorted services such as textbooks and school lunches.

Sixteen parents from communities across the country, mostly representing local Title I parental advisory groups, testified before the subcommittee March 12 against educational revenue sharing, which they said would give excessive control over poverty funds to state and local officials. Further opposition was expressed to the subcommittee March 15 by a spokesman for the National School Boards Association, who said lumping programs into revenue sharing block grants might make them more liable to budget-cutting.

Carter scores revenue sharing—Gov. Jimmy Carter (D, Ga.) charged Feb. 9 that revenue sharing had proved to be a "cruel hoax" for Georgia that especially affected the poor and powerless. His state's first-year share of revenue sharing funds was $36.6 million, he said, while $57 million was lost in child care and social rehabilitation programs and another $174 million was expected to be lost because of Nixon's new budget and his impoundment of mandated funds.

Carter's comments came during a visit to Washington, where he addressed the National Press Club.

Title I alternative—The Health, Education & Welfare Department announced Aug. 17, 1973 a compromise under which 21 states and the District of Columbia would be allowed to spend more of their own funds on the education of poor children rather than refunding federal Title I grants allegedly misspent on general school aid in the years 1965–1969.

The plan gave states the option of raising state and local funds equal to the amounts challenged in Title I audits and spending the money within three years in schools that had been short-changed. The plan included controls to prevent repetition of abuses.

The alternative would be to repay the federal treasury, which—according to an HEW spokesman—would penalize disadvantaged children a second time.

Summer job funds offered. President Nixon said March 21, 1973 that $354 million would be provided to states and cities for summer youth jobs, but $300 million of the total would come from unspent money appropriated under the public service employment program for needy unemployed adults.

The announcement was criticized by Republican Sen. Jacob Javits (N.Y.), who called it a "breach of promise" that left local governments with the "Hobson's choice of firing the father in order to hire the son." Javits said the 776,000 job opportunities Nixon said would be provided with the funds "still falls short by 242,000 jobs of the 1,018,891 needed, according to a survey by the National League of Cities-U.S. Conference of Mayors," and would reduce the number of public service jobs available to "the returning veteran, the welfare recipient, the displaced aerospace engineer and other unemployed." The League-Conference itself issued a statement expressing "extreme dismay."

Nixon said an additional $70 million would be provided for summer recreation, transportation and food programs for youth, while $54 million of the $354 million total would come from direct federal hiring and Youth Conservation Corps jobs. The overall federal figure of $424 million would be only $3 million more than in 1972, when 812,000 jobs were financed. Nixon said the National Alliance of Businessmen planned to hire an additional 175,000 young people in 126 major metropolitan areas during the summer.

The $300 million would apparently come from $580 million in unspent funds in the public service job program under the Emergency Employment Assistance Act, which had been originally budgeted at $1.25 billion for fiscal 1973. Summer youth jobs had formerly been funded mostly through the Neighborhood Youth Corps since the urban riots of the 1960s. Nixon had asked for and been granted a $256.5 million 1973 fiscal year appropriation for the corps from Congress, before the $250 billion budget ceiling was imposed.

'Workfare' results reported. HEW reported April 19 that 82,075 welfare recipients were placed in private jobs during the first nine months of the "workfare" program, under which recipients in the aid to families with dependent children category were required to register for work or training.

Officials estimated that 60% of those placed would eventually be removed from welfare rolls and many others would have benefits reduced.

HEW and Labor Department figures showed that 1,023,083 were registered during the period, of which 256,678 were certified as able to work. In addition to those placed in private jobs, 146,359 were placed in federally funded training programs or in public work. About 18,000 could not be placed in jobs or training programs.

Manpower, jobs bill. A comprehensive manpower training and jobs bill was passed by both houses of Congress Dec. 20, 1973 and was signed by Nixon Dec. 28. The bill consolidated manpower programs enacted since 1962 and authorized needed funding, estimated at $1.8 billion in fiscal 1974.

The legislation represented a compromise of a protracted controversy between the Nixon Administration and Congress on revenue sharing and public service jobs. Comprehensive manpower services were folded into a special revenue sharing plan. Training and employment programs would be administered by states and units of local government exceeding 100,000 in population, which would be eligible for federal grants allocated on previous year funding and the number of unemployed and low-income families.

For public service employment—the other half of the compromise, normally opposed by the Administration—the bill earmarked $250 million in fiscal 1974 and $350 million in fiscal 1975 in areas where the jobless rate was 6.5% or more. Further spending if required by high unemployment was authorized.

Special assistance was authorized for certain hard-hit areas of the labor market—Indians, migrant and seasonal farm workers and youth.

The Job Corps program was extended and consolidated within the Labor Department.

GAO scores migrant programs. The General Accounting Office (GAO) reported to Congress that federal programs to aid migrant and other seasonal agricultural workers were underfunded and fragmented. In the study, reported Feb. 12, 1973, it said that despite a continuing decline in the number of farm jobs, retraining and job placement efforts were usually ineffective.

GAO said four federal agencies had responsibility for various migrant programs, and recommended that the Office of Management and Budget set up a farmworkers' council to coordinate and improve programs.

The report said some 800,000 farm jobs would be lost in the seven years ending in 1975, but no coordinated retraining plans had been made. Health care had improved, but policies were needed to provide continuity of service to migrating families.

Day care centers were "providing good care," but usually were too small to meet the demand. Local schools had made no special effort to help children of migrant workers. GAO said few homes were being built for farm workers despite shortages of decent housing.

Final Nixon State-of-Union message. In his last State-of-the-Union message, delivered in person before a joint session of Congress Jan. 30, 1974, President Nixon reiterated his calls for welfare reform. He said:

Many of those in this chamber tonight will recall that it was three years ago that I termed the nation's welfare system a monstrous consuming outrage, an outrage against the community, against the taxpayer, and particularly against the children that it is supposed to help. That system is still an outrage. By improving its administration we have been able to reduce some of the abuses.

As a result, last year for the first time in 18 years there has been a halt in the growth of the welfare caseload. But as a system, our welfare program still needs reform as urgently today as it did when I first proposed in 1969 that we completely replace it with a different system.

In these final three years of my Administration, I urge the Congress to join me in mounting a major new effort to replace the discredited present welfare system with one that works, one that is fair to those who need help or cannot help themselves, fair to the community and fair to the taxpayer. And let us have as our goal that there will be no government program which makes it more profitable to go on welfare than to go to work.

Final Nixon budget. President Nixon submitted his final budget to Congress Feb. 4, 1974. Among its proposals regarding the poor and welfare:

Welfare—A new Supplemental Security Income (SSI) program for the aged poor, disabled and blind was allotted $3.9 billion for fiscal 1975 for 5.6 million beneficiaries. The total of beneficiaries for the previous year was put at 3.4 million. The budget indicated the cost of the SSI program, which replaced state welfare programs for these recipients Jan. 1.

Draft legislation was being prepared to build the cost-of-living increase into the SSI benefit.

A $3.9 billion figure for fiscal 1975 also was attached to the program of Aid to Families with Dependent Children (AFDC). But this total was a $14 million drop from the previous year's anticipated total, which was a drastic reversal from the customary increases—up to 15%—of recent years. Little or no growth was forecast by officials for the next year and a closer watch for payments to ineligible recipients was given credit for the decline.

The Health, Education and Welfare Department (HEW), whose entire budget was up $14 billion to $111 billion, was currently campaigning against payments to ineligible recipients and overpayments. The ineligibility factor was said to consist of 10% of persons receiving welfare; overpayments were said to encompass 23% of the eligible recipients. The department wanted to reduce the ineligible factor to 3% and overpayments to 5% and set a deadline of June 30, 1975 for the states to reach these marks, using loss of federal welfare funds as inducement.

On the food programs, the Administration advocated HEW administration of $5.9 billion worth of welfare programs currently lodged in the Agriculture Department. These included the food stamp program, budgeted at $3.9 billion, up $900 million, and school lunch subsidies and nutrition education.

Nixon referred to his plan to revise the welfare system into one "that works," but the start-up goal was July 1976 and funding for it did not appear in the fiscal 1975 budget.

Health—Nixon mentioned his plan for "basic reform in the financing of medical care," to bring "comprehensive insurance protection against medical expenses within reach of all Americans." But the proposed date was January 1976 so there were no funds for it in the fiscal 1975 budget.

The budget was dominated by the Medicare and Medicaid programs providing health care for the aged and poor, which absorbed 60¢ of every health dollar. The increase alone in Medicare spending was massive—$2 billion—which took the program to the $14.2 billion level. Medicaid spending followed with a $736 million increase to $6.6 billion.

The Administration made several proposals to try to hold down these costs. It suggested eliminating payments under Medicaid for dental care, and it planned tighter admission procedure for Medicaid patients proposed for elective surgery and an attempt to shorten hospital stays.

Manpower—Manpower programs were funded at about the same level as in fiscal 1974, receiving $23 million more for a total of $4.8 billion in fiscal 1975. The programs included operation of state employment services, vocational rehabilitation, job training and child care related to jobs and veterans' programs.

The Comprehensive Manpower Assistance program, slated to begin July 1, was funded at $1.6 billion. Under it, state and local agencies would assume administration of many federal job aid and training programs funded with $1.4 billion in fiscal 1974. The total did not include the public service jobs program, which was put under the new setup after separate budgeting in previous years. It was expected to absorb $350 million of the new program's funding.

The Work Incentive Program to provide job training to recipients of Aid to Families with Dependent Children was maintained at the $300 million level, the same as in fiscal 1974.

Urban development—Spending by the Housing and Urban Development Department was projected at $5.6 billion for fiscal 1975, up from $5 billion. Payments to subsidize low- and moderate-income housing were allotted $2.3 billion, up from $1.9 billion.

Further uncertainty existed in projections for the subsidized housing area. The budget covered subsidy commitments for 300,000 leased units in fiscal 1975, but 225,000 of these would be projected as new units into the following fiscal year. The comparable totals for fiscal 1974 were 118,000 and a 68,000 carryover.

Subsidized starts in fiscal 1975 were estimated at 285,000 units, with leased units accounting for about half the total. The previous year figure was 187,000.

Health care plan presented. President Nixon submitted his national health insurance plan to Congress Feb. 6 and urged enactment "as soon as possible" so the program could begin in January 1976.

The plan called for a basic insurance program to be available to all full-time employes; federally subsidized coverage for the poor, the unemployed, the self-employed and those with high medical insurance risk; and a revised Medicare program for the aged. The President said the program would cover the costs of catastrophic illnesses.

The basic program would be paid for by employers and employes. The subsidized program, which would eventually replace Medicaid, would be financed largely by federal and state governments. The increased Medicare coverage would be offset with increased charges. Nixon estimated that the program would cost an additional $6.4 billion a year in federal funds, an additional $1 billion in state funds.

The program was predicated on maximum use of the private health insurance industry. "Let us not be led to an extreme program," he warned, "that would place the entire health care system under the dominion of social planners in Washington."

The plan for the unemployed and poor would replace most of the current Medicaid program. It would be operated under federal guidelines by the states, which would pay 25% of the increased costs of the program. The Medicaid program would be continued on an interim basis "to meet certain needs, primarily long-term institutional care," the President said. Eventually, it would be replaced with the "assisted health insurance" plan financed by the federal and state governments, contributions from employes and premium payments by patients.

Coverage would be extended to nonworking families with annual income below $7,500, all families with income below $5,000 and persons with high medical risk.

No premiums would be required for the families with income under $5,000 and individuals with income under $3,500, and their deductibles and copayments would be less than under the basic plan.

Medicare benefits would be expanded to cover outpatient drugs and mental health services.

In the program for the elderly, Medicare would be expanded to cover outpatient drugs and mental health services. A ceiling of $750 was set for the maximum annual cost to the individual, but the aged would have payments increased over the current program.

All three phases of his plan would be voluntary, Nixon told Congress, and one of the three would be available to every American and all would offer identical benefits.

Nixon proposes fund cuts; rolls down. President Nixon said March 30, 1974 that he would ask Congress to cut $800 million from welfare appropriations for the current fiscal year, citing the "first major drop in the nation's welfare rolls in a number of years."

Nixon noted that as of the end of 1973 there were 10.8 million recipients in the Aid to Families with Dependent Children category (AFDC)—the largest welfare program—a reduction of 255,000 in a year.

Although the welfare system was still "marred with inequities," Nixon said, the latest figures showed that "we are beginning to make some progress in solving the welfare mess." He cited better management as a "very significant" factor in reducing the AFDC rolls.

The AFDC statistics had been reported March 29 by Health, Education and Welfare Secretary Caspar W. Weinberger, who added that the reduction in the number of recipients had enabled 25 states to increase payments to those families remaining on the rolls.

Housing allowance plan criticized. The General Accounting Office (GAO) urged in a study April 2, 1974 that Congress delay nationwide implementation of the Administration's proposals for cash housing allowances for the poor until 1977. The report also said current experimental cash grant programs would yield insufficient data for an effective national program.

The report contended that the 11 test sites were unrepresentative of urban conditions because they were in areas of high-quality housing and low vacancy rates. Results of such tests, the GAO said, would be incomplete and could "adversely affect the benefits" derived from a na-

tional program. The report said the testing should be expanded to include at least two areas more typical of urban conditions.

Data from similar grant programs, according to GAO, suggested that cash allowances might have a widely adverse impact on the housing market: as cash payments rose, there was generally an increase in rents—for both poor and nonpoor—without a corresponding improvement in services.

Hunger & Food Aid

Food stamp rise. The Agriculture Department said March 26, 1973 that the 12 million recipients of food stamps would receive a 3.6% cost-of-living increase in allocations beginning July 1 to $116 per month for a family of four. The stamps were sold at varying rates to poor families depending on size and income.

Lag in food aid found. A Senate study released May 6, 1973 found that of the 25–30 million poor eligible for federal food assistance programs, only 15 million were participating and that none of the programs assured nutritional adequacy.

The report, prepared by the staff of the Select Committee on Nutrition and Human Needs, concluded that food programs enacted by Congress in the 1960s might have become unsuited to present conditions, especially the rapid increases in food prices. Some federal programs had been unable to buy meat, fruit and dairy products during March and April because of high prices, the study noted.

Nationwide, the committee's survey identified 263 "hunger counties" compared with 280 mostly different counties in 1968 and an increase from 5.4 million to 15 million recipients of food stamps, food aid in schools, day care and surplus food, at a total annual cost of $4 billion. Despite the overall deficiencies in the programs, the study found significant improvement in food assistance in Southern states in the same period. Midwestern states, however, continued to lag.

The report noted that the food stamp program provided less than $1 per person per day for a family of four, an amount

Poverty & Food Aid, 1973

Region/State	Number of population in poverty	Percent of population in poverty	Number receiving food assistance	Percent of poor receiving food assistance	Number in poverty not receiving food assistance	Percent of poor not receiving food assistance
REGION I	1, 033, 081	9. 0	646, 572	63	386, 511	37
Maine	131, 271	13. 6	102, 110	78	29, 161	22
Vermont	51, 621	12. 1	31, 659	61	19, 962	39
New Hampshire	64, 807	9. 1	28, 157	43	36, 650	57
Massachusetts	473, 200	8. 6	276, 333	58	196, 867	42
Connecticut	212, 185	7. 2	136, 124	64	76, 061	36
Rhode Island	99, 997	11. 0	72, 189	72	27, 808	28
REGION II	2, 559, 628	10. 3	1, 648, 198	64	911, 430	36
New York	1, 985, 954	11. 1	1, 311, 046	66	674, 908	34
New Jersey	573, 674	8. 1	337, 152	59	236, 522	41
REGION III	2, 866, 365	12. 6	1, 472, 632	51	1, 393, 733	49
Pennsylvania	1, 227, 794	10. 6	652, 030	53	575, 764	47
Delaware	58, 155	10. 9	24, 934	43	33, 212	57
Maryland	386, 579	10. 1	220, 708	57	165, 871	43
West Virginia	380, 113	22. 2	256, 102	67	124, 011	33
Virginia	690, 615	15. 5	209, 858	30	480, 757	70
District of Columbia	123, 109	17. 0	109, 000	89	24, 109	11
REGION IV	6, 705, 966	22. 1	2, 930, 769	44	3, 851, 536	56
Alabama	857, 248	25. 4	427, 155	50	430, 093	50
Tennessee	836, 405	21. 8	323, 386	39	513, 019	61
North Carolina	996, 309	20. 3	299, 589	30	696, 720	70
South Carolina	594, 938	23. 9	353, 255	59	241, 713	41
Georgia	924, 262	20. 7	395, 969	43	528, 293	57
Mississippi	759, 038	35. 4	382, 875	50	376, 163	50
Florida	1, 019, 453	17. 0	400, 493	39	618, 960	61
Kentucky	718, 313	22. 9	348, 047	48	370, 260	52
REGION V	4, 272, 192	9. 9	2, 533, 738	59	1, 750, 814	41
Ohio	1, 041, 348	10. 0	637, 983	61	403, 365	39
Indiana	493, 379	9. 7	227, 009	46	266, 370	54
Illinois	1, 112, 145	10. 2	727, 748	65	384, 397	35
Michigan	819, 438	9. 4	612, 515	75	206, 923	25
Wisconsin	415, 778	9. 7	154, 848	37	260, 930	63
Minnesota	390, 104	10. 6	173, 635	45	216, 469	55
REGION VI	4, 194, 284	21. 2	1, 738, 008	41	2, 456, 276	59
Arkansas	522, 969	27. 8	198, 003	38	324, 966	62
Louisiana	932, 671	26. 3	459, 392	49	473, 279	51
Oklahoma	464, 931	18. 8	232, 906	50	232, 025	50
Texas	2, 046, 593	18. 8	702, 189	34	1, 344, 404	66
New Mexico	227, 120	22. 8	145, 518	64	81, 602	36
REGION VII	1, 454, 429	13. 3	566, 767	41	817, 662	59
Kansas	275, 497	12. 7	66, 261	24	209, 238	76
Missouri	672, 092	14. 7	339, 464	51	332, 628	49
Iowa	318, 605	11. 6	108, 351	34	210, 254	66
Nebraska	188, 235	13. 1	52, 691	28	135, 544	72

(over)

(Poverty & Food Aid, 1973, continued)

Region/State	Number of population in poverty	Percent of population in poverty	Number receiving food assistance	Percent of poor receiving food assistance	Number in poverty not receiving food assistance	Percent of poor not receiving food assistance
REGION VIII	626, 375	12. 9	247, 530	40	476, 231	60
Colorado	263, 224	12. 3	117, 935	45	145, 289	55
Utah	118, 349	11. 4	47, 692	40	70, 657	60
Wyoming	33, 436	11. 5	9, 477	28	23, 959	72
Montana	53, 378	12. 7	23, 110	43	30, 268	57
South Dakota	87, 394	17. 0	28, 377	32	59, 012	68
North Dakota	70, 594	15. 0	20, 939	30	49, 655	70
REGION IX	2, 339, 778	11. 1	1, 756, 120	75	727, 395	25
Arizona	170, 259	13. 6	59, 521	35	110, 738	65
Nevada	43, 478	9. 1	13, 403	31	30, 075	69
California	2, 057, 498	11. 0	1, 644, 897	80	412, 601	20
Hawaii	68, 543	9. 3	38, 299	56	30, 244	44
REGION X	681, 720	11. 0	456, 724	67	224, 996	33
Idaho	75, 864	13. 2	27, 233	36	48, 631	64
Oregon	234, 848	11. 5	144, 410	61	90, 438	39
Washington	335, 597	10. 2	263, 371	78	72, 226	22
Alaska	35, 411	12. 6	21, 710	61	13, 701	39
Total U.S.	26,733,818	13. 7	13, 997, 058	52	12, 736, 760	48

From "Hunger—1973," prepared by the staff of the Senate Select Committee on Nutrition & Human Needs which failed to provide even the nationally-averaged foods on which the plan was based for recipients in high-cost urban areas. Recipients depending on surplus commodities distribution were provided food valued at 23¢ per person daily.

The Department of Agriculture was held responsible for many of the deficiencies of the programs, including poor administration and failure to increase benefits in line with changing conditions.

Ban on stamps to strikers loses. A compromise farm bill was passed by both houses of Congress Aug. 3, 1973 and signed by President Nixon Aug. 13 after the deletion of an amendment to bar food stamps for most strikers and their families.

As previously passed by the House July 19, the bill had carried the food stamp restriction as a floor amendment.

A House-Senate conference deadlocked over the amendment to bar food stamps for most strikers. Conferees conceded disagreement after five days of negotiations resolving 110 other provisions of the two bills.

The Senate then voted 87–7 July 31 to approve the bill in a compromise version eliminating the antistrike provision.

When the bill came up for clearance by the House Aug. 3, steps were taken to prevent reintroduction of the food stamp amendment and reopening of the controversy.

Nixon objected to one provision of the bill to extend the availability of food stamps to the aged, blind and disabled, who had been scheduled to lose the privilege Jan. 1, 1974 when they would receive extra Social Security payments. He did

---

Persons Receiving Food Stamps, 1973
(By Household Income Levels)

Annual cash income[1]	Thousands		Rate of participation (percent)[4]
	U.S. population[2]	Food stamp participants[3]	
Under $1,000	1,894	937	50.0
$1,000 to 1,999	2,651	2,338	88.0
$2,000 to 2,999	4,923	2,356	48.0
$3,000 to 3,999	6,627	2,602	39.0
$4,000 to 4,999	7,385	1,472	20.0
$5,000 to 5,999	7,764	1,236	16.8
$6,000 to 6,999	8,143	737	9.0
$7,000 to 7,999	8,711	401	5.0
$8,000 to 8,999	9,279	217	2.0
$9,000 to 9,999	9,089	311	3.0
$10,000 to 11,999	20,451	0	0
$12,000 to 14,999	28,972	0	0
$15,000 and over	73,471	0	0
Total	189,360	12,607	6.7
Cumulative:			
Under $1,000	1,894	937	50.0
$1,000 to 1,999	4,545	3,275	72.0
$2,000 to 2,999	9,468	5,631	60.0
$3,000 to 3,999	16,095	8,233	51.0
$4,000 to 4,999	23,480	9,705	41.0
$5,000 to 5,999	31,244	10,941	35.0
$6,000 to 6,999	39,387	11,678	30.0
$7,000 to 7,999	48,098	12,079	25.0
$8,000 to 8,999	57,377	12,296	21.0
$9,000 to 9,999	66,466	12,607	19.0
$10,000 to 11,999	86,917	0	0
$12,000 to 14,999	115,889	0	0
$15,000 and over	189,360	0	0

[1] The census income refers to income before taxes, and the food stamp program participants income refers to income after taxes.
[2] From census series P–60, No. 97, January 1975.
[3] Computed from the Chilton Survey of the food stamp program participants in November 1973 and expanded to the 12,600,000 participants in November 1973.
[4] Refers to percentage of stamp participants out of the total U.S. population in each specified income level. Thus, these rates are U.S. participation rates by income levels, not the participation rates of the eligibles.

not object to the privilege itself, but to the "highly undesirable" administrative procedure requiring, he said, states to maintain records and staff involved in the welfare system merely to determine eligibility for the food stamp program.

Food stamp program upheld. U.S. District Court Judge John H. Pratt ruled in Washington Dec. 12, 1973 that Agriculture Department operation of the food stamp program fulfilled legal requirements. In upholding the department, Pratt rejected arguments by a group of welfare recipients that the "economy food plan" for stamp allotments did not provide a nutritionally adequate diet.

The Supreme Court June 25 had upheld a lower-court decision that had invalidated a controversial requirement of the Food Stamp Act of 1964 that a household could not participate unless all its members were related to one another.

School lunch increase. President Nixon Nov. 7, 1973 signed a bill authorizing increases of about $220 million in federal aid to the school lunch program. The conference committee bill had been passed by voice votes in the Senate Oct. 23 and in the House Oct. 24.

In its final form, the measure increased the basic federal reimbursement per lunch from 8¢ to 10¢, the additional federal payment for each free lunch from 40¢ to 45¢, and the additional payment for each reduced-price lunch from 30¢ to 35¢.

Stamp raise. The Agriculture Department announced April 1, 1974 that food stamp recipients would get a cost-of-living increase in allocations from $142 a month for a family of four to $150, effective July 1.

The income cutoff level would be increased from $473 a month to $500 for low-income families not on welfare, also effective July 1.

Hunger, poverty found worsening. The Senate Select Committee on Nutrition & Human Needs was told at hearings June 19–21, 1974 that the nation's needy were getting hungrier and poorer and that government programs dealing with hunger were ineffective.

A report prepared for the committee by a panel of outside experts cited steeply rising food costs and inequities in federal food programs, particularly food stamps, as the major problems.

The panel noted that between December 1970 and March 1974, food stamp benefits for a family of four had increased 34% while the cost of foods in the Agriculture Department's "economy" food plan—the basis for food stamp allocations—had increased 42%.

With the cheapest foods having the sharpest price increases during that period (124% for rice, 256% for dried beans), the poor did not have the "spending down" option available to higher-income groups.

The report said only about 15 million of an estimated 37–50 million eligible persons were buying food stamps, and that many were not even aware of their eligibility. There were basic flaws in the program, according to the report, including an unfairly large monthly amount needed to purchase the stamps, the time-consuming "and frequently degrading" process of application and periodic recertification, and the exclusion of persons without kitchen facilities.

Among the report's recommendations were: easing of income-eligibility requirements and increased availability of free stamps; changes in the Agriculture Department's food classification system; and allowing the elderly, disabled and persons without kitchen facilities to use food stamps for restaurant or take-out meals.

A separate outside panel on nutrition and the consumer recommended that all food policy programs be centralized in one federal agency covering production, programs for the poor, safety and nutrition standards, and labeling and advertising.

Data on Jobs, Income, Poverty & Welfare

Federal grants to the states for the needy aged, blind and disabled were replaced Jan. 1, 1974 by the Supplemental Security Income (SSI) program created by the 1972 Social Security Act amendments. The new SSI program provided for (a) federal pay-

ments to the 50 states and the District of Columbia under uniform national standards and eligibility requirements plus (b) state supplementary payments under individual state rules.

Black incomes & jobs. Federal Reserve Board member Andrew F. Brimmer said in a lecture March 2, 1973 at the University of California at Los Angeles that while black income continued to rise in 1972, unemployment remained a major problem, especially among youths.

Brimmer said total income for blacks had increased to a record $51 billion in 1972, up from $46 billion in 1971, increasing the black proportion of total income from 6.6% to 6.7%. Blacks were 11.3% of the total population.

Blacks suffered disproportionately from the 1969–70 recession, Brimmer said, with sharply increased joblessness among women and youths, so that "blacks suffered all of the recession-induced decline in jobs, while whites made further net job gains." Unemployment among black youths had actually increased in the 1971–72 expansion, rising to 35.9% of the work force in the fourth quarter of 1972.

Among other points, Brimmer cited evidence that blacks earned as large a percentage of their income through jobs as whites, to refute charges of "excessive" dependence on welfare.

Reports on black migration, jobs. A Census Bureau study of six urban areas outside the South, released July 29, 1973, showed that southern-born black men in those areas were more likely to be in the labor force and more likely to be married and living with their spouses than northern-born blacks living in the same area.

Robert Hill, research director of the National Urban League, said the report refuted the widely-held view that "blacks migrate from the rural South to the North to get on welfare."

The study, based on 1970 data, showed that in the New York City area, for example, about 65% of the black men born in New York were in the labor force.

The figure rose to 78% for southern-born men who migrated by 1965 and to 82% for those who moved north after 1965.

In the Chicago area, the study found that 70% of southern-born men were married and living with their wives, compared with 51% of Illinois-born blacks.

Indian lag reported. A Census Bureau analysis of 1970 data showed that Indians continued to lag behind the rest of the nation in most economic and social areas, but had made significant advances in education since 1960. The report was released July 16, 1973.

The survey found that the 1969 median income for Indian families was $5,832, while the national median was $9,590. The 1970 census found 40% of Indian families living below the poverty level, compared with 14% of all families and about 32% of black families. While median Indian family income ranged as high as $10,000 a year in two urban areas (Washington and Detroit), the figure dropped to $2,500 on the Papago reservation in Arizona.

The report showed 95% of Indian children of ages 7–13 and more than half the Indians ages 3–34 were attending school in 1970. The number attending college had doubled since 1960.

Increase in some poor groups reported. While the overall number of poor families decreased 4% to 5.1 million families (9.1% of all households) from 1971 to 1972, the number of poor black families and the number of poor families headed by women increased during the period, the Census Bureau reported Dec. 27, 1973. The increases in certain poor groups paralleled an 8.1% rise to $11,120 in the median income for all U.S. families, an increase of 4.6% when adjusted for inflation.

(The official poverty level was defined as an annual income of $4,275 for a nonfarm family of four.)

The Census Bureau noted that the latest increase in the proportion of low-income families headed by women continued a steady, long-term trend, rising from 23% in 1959 to 43% in 1972. Of the 6.6 million female-headed households in 1972, 37% had incomes below $4,000, the report said, while only 8% of the 46.3

million husband-wife families earned less than $4,000.

Nearly 25 million persons, eight million of them black, were reported to be living on incomes below the poverty level. The number of low-income whites fell 9% from 1971 to 1972, but there was "some evidence," the report said, of an increase in the number of poor blacks, mostly in female-headed families.

Women & children first—in poverty. Dr. Heath Ross of the Urban Institute asserted at a welfare seminar sponsored by the institute for congressional and executive branch aides that while the number of poor persons had declined between 1960 and 1972, the percentage of poor families headed by women and/or with children had increased. She said (according to her text as inserted in the Congressional Record for Dec. 26, 1973 by Rep. Martha W. Griffiths, D, Mich.):

In 1960 there were 40 million poor persons. By 1972 this number had fallen to 24½ million poor persons. But virtually the entire decline was accounted for by persons in male-headed families. The number of poor persons in female-headed families rose by 867,000. This meant a substantial swing in the composition of poor families. In 1960, 29% of poor families were female-headed. By 1972, 43% were female-headed. If we focus further on families with children, the shift is even more dramatic. The majority of these families are now female-headed. And if we disaggregate further, by race, we find that 70% of nonwhite poor families with children are female-headed, while 43% of white poor families with children are female-headed.

Thus, the trend toward female-headed families is more pronounced in the nonwhite community, but it is nevertheless well underway in the white community as well. Table 1 should make the relationships a little clearer. It shows the proportion of poor families with children which are female-headed by race. Looking first at the left hand side, we see that about ¼ of poor white families with children were female-headed in 1960 and ¾ male-headed. Looking down the columns for subsequent years, we see that the proportion of female-headed increased steadily to 43% by 1972. Now looking at the right-hand side for nonwhite families, we see that about ⅓ of poor families with children were female-headed in 1960 and ⅔ male-headed. Again, reading down the columns, we find that almost 70% of these families were female-headed by 1972. Nonwhites have always had a higher proportion of poor families with children female-headed, as can easily be seen in the table. But, the pace at which the population of poor families with children has been tipping toward female-

headedness is almost as rapid for whites as for nonwhites. When plotted on a graph, the upward slopes of the two lines are not far from parallel. So the trend toward female-headed families at low income is not exclusively a black phenomenon as many seem to have believed, and as earlier treatments of the subject like the 1965 Moynihan report implied. . . .

TABLE 1.—POOR FAMILIES WITH CHILDREN BY RACE AND SEX OF HEAD, 1960-72

[In percent]

	White poor families with children>18		Nonwhite poor families with children>18	
	Female head	Male head	Female head	Male head
1960	24.5	75.5	34.9	65.1
1961	23.6	76.4	35.7	64.3
1962	24.7	75.3	39.5	60.5
1963	26.5	73.5	41.9	58.1
1964	25.4	74.6	39.9	60.1
1965	30.3	69.7	41.6	58.4
1966	33.5	66.5	45.5	54.5
1967	32.9	67.1	51.1	48.9
1968	36.4	63.6	57.0	43.0
1969	40.1	59.9	59.2	40.8
1970	40.1	59.9	62.3	37.7
1971	41.4	58.6	64.6	35.4
1972	43.3	56.7	69.0	31.0

TABLE 2.—TRENDS IN POVERTY, WELFARE, AND FEMALE FAMILY HEADSHIP, 1960-71

[Numbers in thousands]

	Number of poor female-headed families with children>18	Number of poor and near poor female-headed families with children>18	Total female-headed families with children>18	Annual female-headed family AFDC caseload
1960	1,476	1,742	2,621	692
1961	1,505	1,793	2,687	813
1962	1,613	1,874	2,701	844
1963	1,578	1,881	2,833	935
1964	1,439	1,776	2,895	1,020
1965	1,499	1,817	2,872	1,070
1966	1,410	1,756	2,993	1,139
1967	1,418	1,747	3,187	1,385
1968	1,469	1,842	3,271	1,509
1969	1,497	1,905	3,373	1,817
1970	1,680	2,067	3,814	2,460
1971	1,830	2,315	4,078	2,837

A few cautions are in order when interpreting the numbers in this table. First of all the family unit definitions for a welfare unit and for a female-headed family unit as measured by Census are different, with the former being broader than the latter. Secondly, the use of an annual caseload figure for AFDC gives a much higher caseload total than the monthly figure usually reported, since the annual number of units served is much higher than any average monthly total due to high caseload turnover. The figure does not mean that all poor and near poor female-headed families with children are presently receiving welfare....

There are three major factors to be cited in connection with this large welfare caseload growth. One is an increasing participation rate. The probability that a female-headed family with children which is eligible for welfare will actually be receiving it at any point in time has grown significantly, especially since 1967....

The second factor is increasing coverage of female-headed families with children through raised income eligibility ceilings. As states have raised their welfare benefit levels over the 1960's, the incomes at which families can establish eligibility for welfare have gone up correspondingly, so that welfare coverage has extended higher and higher up the income distribution of female-headed families with children. The third factor is simply increased formation of female-headed families with children at low income....

To sum up, what we have seen here is that female-headed families with children are on the increase at all income levels, with many more being formed who are nonpoor than are poor. But because the number of poor families who are male-headed has declined so significantly over the 1960's, the poverty population has come to be increasingly characterized by female-headed families. We have seen that this tipping toward female-headedness is going on almost as rapidly in the poor white community as in the poor black community....

These tables provide a context for asking the important question of what role the welfare system has played in the growth of female-headed families with children. By restricting its benefits for the most part to these kinds of families, has welfare encouraged their formation, and has it done so through illegitimacy, through family splitting, through undoubling of families, or how?

The first point to note is the magnitude of the financial incentive to become female-headed—that is, the dollar value associated with not living with the father of one's children and receiving welfare versus the value associated with living with him and forfeiting welfare. The trade-off between what low-skilled men can provide and what welfare can provide has been tipping over the last decade in favor of welfare, especially when the value of benefits tied to welfare status, such as medicaid coverage, are figured in too. It is relatively easy to calculate these trade-offs for different state welfare programs and different local labor markets, and this has been done recently by a number of analysts.

But determining the behavioral response to these trade-offs—that is, the way people actually act when confronted with these financial incentives—has proved very difficult. On illegitimacy, for example, some researchers have found that the birth rate is directly related to the size of available AFDC benefits for some groups of women. But most research has not found such a relationship, and no one has yet found statistical evidence that higher AFDC payments are related to higher illegitimacy, even though many people think this may be true.

On marital disruption the picture is also mixed. Some analysts have found that higher AFDC benefit levels mean higher proportions of ever-married women with children living as heads of households, and some have found that they do not. The bulk of the evidence supports the latter finding, but the most sophisticated recent work suggests the former.

It should be noted that in the case of both illegitimacy and marital disruption, welfare could contribute to the total number of female-headed families as well as by putting them in that status. This could occur if women failed to marry or to remarry due to concern for losing welfare benefits. This is a particularly interesting aspect of the effect of welfare on family organization right now because the rules of the game in this area have recently been changed.

In 1968 the Supreme Court invalidated the man-in-the-house rule, and in 1970 it further ruled that in the case of a man assuming the role of spouse, including a nonadopting stepfather, no presumption could be made that the man was contributing any of his resources to the support of children in the family. Documentation of an actual flow of resources of some particular amount from the man to the children would have to be made before any adjustment in benefits to the children could be carried out.

Thus, welfare no longer discriminates against married people: it discriminates against natural parents. A woman can marry a man who is not the father of her children without any necessary loss in her benefits. The potential for significant change in the living arrangements of welfare families is evident here. Women will be able to marry and continue welfare coverage of their children. If the poor are at all sensitive to financial incentives structured into government programs one would expect some response to this rule change, and indeed this seems to have occurred. Stepfather cases in AFDC have grown appreciably since the court rulings, and are currently increasing half again as fast as the overall caseload.

Finally, on the issue of living arrangements, it seems likely that welfare has contributed to the Census count of female-headed families with children by providing recipient units with the resources needed to establish their own households rather than doubling up with relatives. But again the empirical evidence to make this case and to measure the magnitude of it has not been assembled.

The message from this discussion of welfare effects on female-headed families with children is that little is known conclusively about what these effects are....

Welfare rolls drop, cost growth slows. Welfare rolls at the end of fiscal 1973 (June 30) totaled 14.8 million persons, a decrease of 1.7% from the previous year, HEW reported Oct. 30. It was the first decline in seven years. Total welfare-Medicaid payments in fiscal 1973 were $19.4 billion, a 6% increase over fiscal 1972, when payments rose 17.4% over 1971.

Most of the caseload reductions, HEW said, were among the aged, many of whom shifted off welfare when they began receiving higher Social Security payments, and among those on general assistance. The Aid to the Blind caseload also dropped.

The 10.9 million recipients of Aid to Families with Dependent Children included an increase of 5,000, considered statistically insignificant. This compared with a 1972 caseload increase of almost 700,000.

Cash welfare payments were $10.5 billion, and Medicaid spending was $8.8 billion.

Payment errors. HEW reported Dec. 20, 1973 that its recently adopted stepped-up "error control program" had found that in the April–September period 22.8% of welfare recipients in the Aid to Families with Dependent Children category (AFDC) were overpaid, 8.1% were underpaid and 10.2% were ineligible. The total error figure of 41.1% compared with 28% for all of 1972.

The department said that in 1973, erroneous payments would cost about $1.17 billion, or 15% of the federal-state AFDC budget. An HEW spokesman said that in order to enforce HEW orders for states to cut overpayment and ineligibility errors, federal grants to be made in January 1974 would be cut by a percentage equal to one-third of a state's error rate.

The General Accounting Office reported Jan. 11, 1974 on savings made by its efforts during fiscal 1973.

More than $5 million was in the health field, including almost $4 million in excessive payments to states for Medicaid and $440,000 for Medicare overpayments.

Recovery of $622,000 in overpayments for aid to dependent children was reported.

Poverty area unemployment. A report released by the Labor Department Aug. 29, 1974 showed that in 1973 the unemployment rate in metropolitan center poverty areas was almost twice that in non-metropolitan poverty areas: 9% vs. 4.7%. A "poverty area" was defined as a census tract in which at least one-fifth of the residents had incomes at or below the poverty level ($4,540 a year for a non-farm family of four).

The report also showed that 70% of the blacks living in poverty areas were in metropolitan centers. For blacks in all poverty areas, the unemployment rate was 10.8%, compared with 4.6% for whites. The rate for blacks outside the poverty areas was 4.7%, compared with 2.8% for whites.

Overall, the survey found 28,978,000 working-age persons living in poverty areas, with an unemployment rate of 6.5%.

11% live in poverty. A Census Bureau report published July 3, 1974 indicated that 11% of Americans lived in poverty. The poverty-stricken included 31% of all blacks, 8% of whites, 16% of the elderly, 40% of black children and 14.2% of all children.

The report, which was based on a survey conducted in March, also showed that the number of persons with income below the officially defined poverty level ($4,540 in 1973) fell by 1.5 million to about 23 million persons during 1973. (However, the statistics did not take into account the effect that soaring food prices had on the poor, indicating that the inflation adjustment for poor families was too small.)

The largest proportional decline in the numbers of the poor was among the elderly.

Court Decisions

Supreme Court on state welfare laws. The Supreme Court May 7, 1973 agreed to reverse a lower-court decision that upheld the validity of New Jersey's "working poor" welfare laws that denied benefits to families with illegitimate children.

In a 7-2 decision June 21, 1973, the court ruled that states were not precluded from requiring welfare recipients to work as a condition for receiving federally financed aid to families with dependent children.

Ruling Jan. 14, 1974, the high court upheld the right of New York State to conduct welfare programs requiring recipients to accept public service employment or face reduced benefits.

In an action of Feb. 26, 1974, the court, over the dissent of Justice William H. Rehnquist, struck down an Arizona law denying indigent health and hospital care to individuals who had not met the state's residency requirement of one year.

The court April 1, 1974 held invalid a Pennsylvania statute denying welfare benefits to otherwise eligible minors living with adults not on welfare and not their parents.

The court held April 23, 1974 that a State of Colorado welfare regulation requiring recipients to deduct a standard amount for work expenses, rather than actual work expenses, to determine continued eligibility was unconstitutional.

Ruling in a case involving a convicted criminal defendant who received free legal counsel at his trial because he was too poor to pay, the court May 20, 1974 upheld the validity of an Oregon law requiring the man to reimburse the county if, after his release from prison, he made enough money to do so.

Conn. illegitimacy law upheld. A three-judge federal panel in Hartford, Conn. Sept. 7, 1973 upheld a state law that unwed mothers receiving welfare payments could be required under court order to name the fathers of their children so that the state could collect support payments.

The current law requiring a court order for the naming of a father had replaced one declared unconstitutional in 1970 under which an unwed mother had to reveal the father simply on the request of welfare authorities.

Sterilization program curbed. U.S. District Court Judge Gerhard A. Gesell ruled in Washington March 15, 1974 that rules proposed by the Department of Health, Education and Welfare (HEW) to cover federally-financed sterilizations of poor persons were "arbitrary and unreasonable" and failed to give sufficient protection to minors and mentally incompetent persons.

HEW had been attempting to draw up regulations because of disclosures of sterilization of retarded minors in federally-aided clinics and, as Gesell noted in his decision, evidence that welfare recipients had been threatened with loss of benefits if they refused sterilization.

Proposed HEW rules, scheduled to go into effect March 18, provided that legally competent adults must give "informed consent" to sterilization, and that minors and mental incompetents must give written consent approved by a third party in their behalf.

Ruling in a suit filed by the National Welfare Rights Organization, Gesell said that neither minors nor mental incompetents could meet a standard of voluntary and truly informed consent, and that the "will of an unspecified representative" could not be imposed in a matter as serious as sterilization.

Gesell also said that the consent procedures involving competent adults must be amended to require that persons be informed that no federal benefits could be withdrawn because of a failure to accept sterilization.

Noting that in recent years 100,000–150,000 low-income persons had been sterilized annually in federal programs, Gesell said the matter was of major national significance. Government, including Congress, he said, should "move cautiously" to set regulations in "one of the most drastic methods of population control" which could irreversibly deprive unwilling or immature persons of their rights.

Pennsylvania abortion aid ban voided. A three-judge federal panel ruled in Pittsburgh that the Pennsylvania medical assistance program for welfare recipients unconstitutionally discriminated against recipients who chose to have abortions, it was reported May 8, 1974.

The ruling voided state regulations requiring agreement by two doctors that a woman's life would be endangered by giving birth, evidence of rape or incest, or evidence of potential infant deformity before a welfare recipient could receive state reimbursement for an abortion.

(The Supreme Court June 4, 1973 had unanimously upheld a lower court rejection of an argument that abortions should not be covered by Medicaid because they violated the rights of living but unborn children.)

The Ford Administration

Ford & the Welfare-Poverty Issue

Gerald R. Ford succeeded Richard M. Nixon Aug. 9, 1974 as President of the U.S. In the decade that his predecessors, Lyndon Johnson and Nixon, had sought to aid the poor, the number of Americans living in poverty had declined from 36.1 million (or 19% of the population) in 1964 to 24.8 million (11.6% of the population) in 1974. In the calendar year (1974) in which Ford became President, nearly 29 million Americans, or 13.6% of the nation, received public assistance. During his first fiscal year in office (fiscal 1975), federal expenditures on the various programs for aiding the poor totaled $27.8 billion (according to a Congressional Research Service report).

Ford bars OEO revival. In his first televised news conference as President, Ford indicated Aug. 28, 1974 that he did not intend to revive the Office of Economic Opportunity (OEO), whose existence then was in the process of being ended by Congressional action.

Ford pointed out that most OEO programs, except for the Community Action Program (CAP), had been transferred to established departments and that there was much duplication in CAP and the Model Cities program. Under new housing and urban development legislation,

Ford said, "local communities are given substantial sums to take a look at the Model Cities programs and related programs and they may be able to take up the slack of the ending of the Community Action Programs."

OEO replaced by CSA. A compromise bill ending the existence of the controversial Office of Economic Opportunity (OEO) but extending many of its programs through fiscal 1977 was passed by Senate voice vote Dec. 19, 1974 and 244-43 House vote Dec. 20. President Ford signed the measure Jan. 4, 1975.

The bill replaced the OEO with an independent Community Services Administration (CSA) immediately on enactment.

Programs continued through fiscal 1977 included local community action, community economic development, community food and nutrition, comprehensive health services, migrant workers, poverty research, native Americans, Head Start and Follow Through.

The Head Start, Follow Through, comprehensive health services and native Americans programs were transferred to the Health, Education & Welfare Department.

Budget for fiscal 1976. President Ford submitted his fiscal 1976 budget to Congress Feb. 3, 1975. Among its proposals in the poverty and welfare areas:

Income maintenance—Budget outlays for income maintenance, mainly Social Security payments, were scheduled to amount to $92.3 billion in fiscal 1976, a rise of $4 billion. The cost of Social Security was expected to rise 8.7% or $2.6 billion if Congress refused the President's request for a 5% limit in fiscal 1976 on benefit increases.

The President planned a reduction of public welfare payments by the federal government. Congress was asked to cut to 50% the 75% federal share of the cost of state-provided service programs for welfare recipients. The federal budget's outlays for public welfare payments would drop $300 million to $6.3 billion in fiscal 1976.

Federal welfare aid for the aged, blind and disabled was put at $4.6 billion for fiscal 1976, up $500 million despite the proposed 5% limit in benefit increases.

Food aid—Ford budgeted a cut in food programs. The programs, including stamps and child nutrition programs, were allocated $5.4 billion in fiscal 1976, a $411 million drop from the previous year. A proposed increase in the cost of food stamps, already evoking stiff resistance in both houses of Congress, was expected to save the government $215 million in fiscal 1975 and, combined with tightened eligibility rules, $650 million in fiscal 1976. Expenditures for the program were budgeted at $3.7 billion for fiscal 1975 and $3.6 billion in fiscal 1976.

Health—The Administration requested $27.3 billion for fiscal 1976 spending on health programs. The total was $1.5 billion above previous-year funding although the department's (Health, Education & Welfare) fiscal plans were being shaped by an intensive cost-control effort.

A 20% spending cut was imposed on direct service programs such as neighborhood health centers, maternal and child health and community mental health centers. The department expected state and local governments to provide the deleted funds. The spending reductions would hit migrant health care, family planning, drug abuse, alcohol control, immunization and venereal disease programs.

For Medicare, Congress was asked to endorse a cost-control plan to limit the rate of increase in average daily costs reimbursable to hospitals from the government. The Administration also was seeking legislation for authority to raise the monthly premium for Medicare paid by the aged as well as legislation to increase the non-premium, or out-of-pocket, payments by the aged for Medicare benefits, up to an annual ceiling of $1,500.

The Administration further requested legislation to reduce to 40% the current 50% federal share of Medicaid programs funded in cooperation with the states.

Recession delays welfare roll reduction. Caspar W. Weinberger, secretary of health, education and welfare (HEW), March 26, 1975 said that the federal effort to cut welfare costs by reducing administrative errors had been delayed by the current recession. "Because of the states' administrative commitments due to the current high rate of unemployment and the uncertain state of the economy, the department has decided to give the states an additional grace period to reduce their rates," he said.

Under HEW rules published in 1974, states had to meet certain targets in reducing the number of welfare overpayments, underpayments and payments to ineligible persons or lose part of the federal share of Aid to Families with Dependent Children (AFDC). In fiscal 1975, the federal government was to provide $4.2 of $8 billion due to be spent on AFDC.

By paring welfare rolls, HEW had hoped to save $514 million in overall welfare costs in fiscal 1975—$238 million by the federal government and $231 million by the states. However, the New York Times reported April 9 that the cost-cutting campaign was proceeding at a rate that would result in a $262-million saving for the fiscal year.

Errors were being made in 36.4% of all cases, compared with 41% at the outset, the Times reported. The Administration's goal for the end of the fiscal year was an incidence of error of 13%—3% ineligible families, 5% overpaid clients and 5% underpaid recipients.

New welfare rules. The Department of Health, Education & Welfare announced June 30, 1975 that in the future, adults and children on welfare would have to give their Social Security numbers to state agencies in order to receive benefits. The order was made in compliance with welfare services legislation signed Jan. 4 by President Ford.

All applications for Aid to Families With Dependent Children (AFDC), the nation's largest welfare program, were obliged to submit numbers from July 1, and persons already receiving benefits would have six months to do so. Medicaid recipients not on AFDC rolls would have to furnish their numbers if they lived in states that required them before Jan. 1 or if they were on the Supplemental Security Income rolls. An HEW spokesman said the object of the new rule was "to make sure these people and families are who they say they are when they apply."

In related developments, the Labor Department raised the minimum annual income figure below which it considered an urban family of four poor, according to the Wall Street Journal May 7. Effective April 30, the poverty level was increased to $5,050, a rise of 11% over the figure for the previous year, which had been $4,550. The poverty level for a single person was $2,590, up from $2,330 in 1974.

A federal judge in Washington temporarily blocked June 13 the application of new HEW guidelines that would have had the effect of reducing the number of people on welfare. The guidelines concerned changes in the means used by states to determine the eligibility of persons applying for assistance under the AFDC program, whose cost of benefits and administration was paid back to the states by the federal government. The blocked guidelines had reduced the amount of property a person could own before he became eligible for welfare.

In granting a temporary restraining order to the National Welfare Rights Organization, the Commonwealth of Pennsylvania and local welfare groups, Chief Judge George L. Hart Jr. of Federal District Court for the District of Columbia said the proposed guidelines "would throw the system of every state into chaos," especially if they were later ruled illegal.

John Svahn, an HEW spokesman, announced June 25 that states were being required to develop plans for locating an estimated 1.3 million absent parents of children living with the help of AFDC.

Svahn characterized the regulation, which would force parents to help support their children, as having the purpose of "making the states accountable to their citizens for the use of federal social services resources."

The Washington Post June 27 reported that HEW regulations would go into effect July 1 requiring all states to "sample scientifically" claims made under the Medicaid program in order to reduce the number of persons receiving free or low-cost medical care without being eligible for it.

Ford for welfare reform. President Ford discussed with New York Times reporters July 23, 1975 (in an interview published July 25) the developments of his first year in office. He said he would seek "something new" to replace the current welfare system, which continued to grow more costly "with too much going to people who don't deserve it and too little to the people who do deserve it." He disclosed that he had rejected, because of budget restraint, a 1974 cabinet proposal to supplant antipoverty programs with "outright cash" payments to the needy.

Ford rejects report on aged. President Ford July 24, 1975 dissociated himself from a report to Congress that chided the Administration for "apparent lack of consideration for the economic plight of the elderly." The report was by the Federal Council on Aging, established in 1973 to advise the president on the needs of the elderly.

"The report does not reflect the Administration's policies," Ford told Congress in submitting the council's recommendations to Congress.

The report protested "cutbacks in federal money for social services for the elderly and ceilings on benefit programs financed from social insurance trust funds" as "particularly burdensome" to the aged. It recommended "that the President reconsider the serious effect of these fiscal proposals on the elderly of this nation with their urgent humanitarian needs."

In his comments, Ford sympathized with the council's concern about the level of funding for programs to aid the aged but said he was "determined to reduce the burden of inflation on our older citizens and that effort demands that government's spending be limited." Curbing inflation "would be of particular benefit" to the elderly, he said.

Ford Nov. 29, 1975 signed a bill extending the 1965 Older Americans Act until the end of fiscal 1978. The bill had been passed by the House Nov. 19, by a 404–6 vote, and by the Senate Nov. 20, by a vote of 89–0.

As enacted, the measure authorized total expenditures of $1.7 billion, most of which were to go for grants to fund state and community programs aiding the elderly, for support of the community service jobs program for the elderly and for senior volunteer programs run by Action, the federal agency administering volunteer programs.

The bill revised basic grant programs by requiring states to set aside at least one-fifth of funding received for special programs designed to help the elderly remain out of institutions by making them more self-sufficient. In addition, the measure prohibited unreasonable discrimination on the basis of age in federally funded programs.

In signing the bill, the President said he was troubled by the amounts authorized "at a time when we are struggling to restrain growth in the federal budget."

'Real' family income fell in 1974. The average family's income increased 6.5% during 1974, but because of double-digit inflation, failed to keep pace with inflation, the Commerce Department reported July 23, 1975. Although 1974's median income was $12,840, compared with $12,051 in 1973, real income adjusted for price changes declined 4% from the 1973 level.

The number of persons with incomes below the poverty line increased by 1.3 million (5.6%) in 1974 to 24.3 million, despite an increase in the official poverty line for a nonfarm family of four to $5,038 from $4,540 in 1973. Those who were officially designated "poor" represented 11.6% of the population.

Whites accounted for 1.1 million out of the 1.3 million rise in the poverty population; 15.7% of all persons 65 and older were classified as poor in 1974, 8.9% of whites, 31.4% of blacks, 15.5% of all

children under 18, and 40.7% of all black children under 18.

Welfare rolls shrink. The number of families on welfare dropped .1% in July, 1975, the Health, Education & Welfare Department said Nov. 15. This continued a decline begun in May but left the total 8.9% above the 3.1 million families receiving aid in July, 1974. The May decrease had been the first in nearly a year. [See p. 649A3]

Despite the decline, welfare expenditures increased 20% to $22.6 billion in fiscal year 1975, the department reported. That total included $9.5 billion in direct money payments and almost $13 billion for medical care for the poor.

HEW said Aid to Families with Dependent Children reached a monthly average of 3.3 million families, or a record high 11,078,000 persons, during the year, 5.6% more than in fiscal 1974.

Housing aid. President Ford Aug. 22, 1974 signed an $11.1 billion compromise housing and community development bill containing broad revisions in the formulas for distribution of federal aid.

Most of the money ($8.6 billion over three years), as well as the major departure from previous programs, lay in provisions authorizing locally-administered block grants for community development to replace categorical aid plans such as Model Cities and urban renewal.

The funds would be allocated on the basis of population, degree of overcrowding and poverty (weighted double in the formula). During the three-year period, no community would receive less than the total previously granted under the categorical programs.

A separate provision established a $1.23 billion rent subsidy program for low-income families under which tenants would pay 15%–25% of gross income towards local fair market rentals, with the difference subsidized.

The bill also extended through fiscal 1976 two home ownership and rental assistance programs suspended in 1973, but with authorizations of only $75 million in new funds.

The omnibus measure authorized $800

million in loan subsidies for developers of housing for the aged and handicapped.

Housing & Urban Development aides said Jan. 20, 1975 that $900 million was being allocated for a rent subsidy program for the poor and $215 million was being released to finance low interest construction loans for housing projects for the elderly.

Carla Hills, secretary of housing and urban development, said the Administration would release the funds, beginning in 1976, over a two-year period to subsidize mortgages on 250,000 new and rehabilitated dwellings for families earning between $9,000 and $11,000 a year. Families qualifying for the HUD program, Hills said, would be able to obtain mortgages of $21,600 to $28,800 at a subsidized interest rate of 5%. (The interest rate for other government-backed mortgages was currently about 9%.)

Hills said that she had recommended reactivation of the program and that her decision had been an "economic" one. She conceded, however, that a General Accounting Office lawsuit seeking release of the funds "obviously was a factor" in President Ford's decision to begin the program again.

The GAO suit had stemmed from President Ford's refusal to spend congressionally appropriated funds for the HUD home ownership subsidy program, which the Nixon Administration had suspended in 1973 as too costly and unworkable.

Hills said that the new program would be restructured to avoid past problems, among them a foreclosure rate exceeding 10%. Thousands of homes had been abandoned after low-income buyers left them because of their inability to keep up with maintenance costs. By gearing the program to a higher income group than before and requiring participants to make at least 3%-down payments ($1,500 to $2,000), Hills said, HUD would be able to "decrease the chances of abandonment." (Under the previous program, home buyers with annual incomes of between $5,000 and $7,000 were able to obtain 1% subsidized mortgages and make down payments as small as $200.)

Homes owned by poor called unrealistic. HUD Secretary Hills said in a speech before the Washington Press Club Sept. 12 that "home ownership for the poor is probably an unrealistic goal in today's economy."

Past government programs to make homes available to the poor did not work, she asserted, because the poor were not prepared to deal with problems associated with owning homes. "When the plumbing backs up, when the heating acts up . . . these people do not have the wherewithal to deal with these problems," Hills said.

States for U.S. relief role. In a joint telegram to President Ford Jan. 2, 1976, the Democratic governors of New Jersey, New York and Pennsylvania called for a federal takeover of the current "patchwork" of federal, state and local welfare programs. They were joined in their request by Gov. Patrick J. Lucey of Wisconsin, also a Democrat.

The telegram, which requested a meeting with the President to present a plan for welfare reform, was initiated by Gov. Brendan T. Byrne (N.J.). It was also signed by Gov. Hugh L. Carey (N.Y.) and Gov. Milton J. Shapp (Pa.).

"It is time for a fundamental reordering of our approach to income maintenance," their telegram declared. "Mere tinkering with existing programs is not enough."

The existing welfare system, they argued, "tolerates unacceptable variations between different parts of the country, . . . encourages family instability and disintegration [and] . . . does too little to help the working poor while it permits excessive levels of ineligibility and fraud."

"The nation, and particularly state and local governments, cannot indefinitely bear excessive rates of growth in this sector," they said. (In all three states soaring welfare costs had been frequently cited as contributing factors to budget crises in recent years.)

The governors' wire proposed the following reforms:

■ Consolidation of all existing federal programs into a "single, federally financed cash system providing a floor to the income available to every family."

■ Uniform treatment of divided or fatherless families and united families.

■ Preservation of work incentives and a "fair level of assistance to the poor." (According to New Jersey officials who helped draft the proposals, a minimum income of about $4,000 a year should be guaranteed to a family of four.)

■ A uniform and simple benefit reduction schedule that would gradually reach a "zero point of no benefits and no income taxation" when actual family income reached about $7,500 a year.

■ Retention of state responsibility for a number of social services for the poor and the elderly.

■ Elimination of a means test for the elderly.

According to New Jersey officials, the cost of the total reform package for the federal government would be between $5 and $7 billion a year. They estimated the proposals would annually save New Jersey $116 million, New York $324 million and Pennsylvania $231 million.

Ford's Basic Programs

Gerald R. Ford's final full year as President was 1976. As the year started, Ford outlined his basic policies and programs in such mandatory communications to Congress as his State-of-the-Union and Budget messages.

1976 State-of-the-Union proposals. In his 1976 State of the Union message, delivered before a joint session of Congress Jan. 19, President Ford outlined proposals for dealing with unemployment and welfare. He said:

As we rebuild our economy, we have a continuing responsibility to provide a temporary cushion to the unemployed. At my request the Congress enacted two extensions and two expansions in unemployment insurance, which helped those who were jobless during 1975. These programs will continue in 1976.

In my fiscal year 1977 budget, I am also requesting funds to continue proven job training and employment opportunity programs for millions of other Americans.

Compassion and a sence of community—two of America's greatest strengths through our history—tell us we must take care of our neighbors who cannot take care of themselves. The host of federal programs in this field reflect our generosity as a people.

But everyone realizes that when it comes to welfare, government at all levels is not doing the job well. Too many of our welfare programs are inequitable and invite abuse. Too many of our welfare programs have problems from beginning to end. Worse, we are wasting badly needed resources without reaching many of the truly needy.

Complex welfare programs cannot be reformed overnight. Surely we cannot simply dump welfare into the laps of the 50 states, their local taxpayers or private charities, and just walk away from it. Nor is it the right time for massive and sweeping changes while we are still recovering from the recession.

Nevertheless, there are still plenty of improvements that we can make. I will ask Congress for Presidential authority to tighten up the rules for eligibility and benefits.

Last year I twice sought long-over-due reform of the scandal-riddled food stamp program. This year I say again: Let's give food stamps to those most in need. Let's not give any to those who don't need them. . . .

Using resources now available, I propose improving the Medicare and other federal health programs to help those who really need protection: older people and the poor. To help states and local governments give better health care to the poor I propose that we combine 16 existing Federal programs including Medicaid into a single $10 billion Federal grant.

Funds would be divided among the states under a new formula which provides a larger share of federal money to those states that have a larger share of low income families. . . .

Shapp scores Ford's proposals—Gov. Milton Shapp (Pa.), seeking the Democratic presidential nomination, criticized Ford's State of the Union address Jan. 20 as a "little Reagan plan" that would put one million more Americans out of work.

Campaigning in Florida, Shapp said Ford's program would "cause great hardship to people all over the nation." The proposals for block grants to states for social welfare programs, he said, "will lead to some states raising taxes to support the needs of the poor and others reducing payments to the needy. History shows that the net result of this kind of program would be the migration of the poor to states that give more and would create additional burdens there."

Fiscal 1977 budget plans. President Ford Jan. 21, 1976 submitted his budget for fiscal 1977. In it he proposed reducing expenditures for Social Security, Medicare, food stamps, housing subsidies and child nutrition. Among his proposals:

Health—Ford proposed major revisions of the Medicare program.

Under new "catastrophe" insurance coverage, cash costs to a beneficiary would be limited to $500 a year for hospitals and $250 for doctors. This would result in additional benefits of $538 million a year for the recipients. But another new provision to raise the fee of Medicare coverage would reduce benefits $1.9 billion.

Still another new proposal was to limit fee increases under Medicare to 7% a year for hospitals and to 4% for doctors. The estimated federal savings for this were $909 million in fiscal 1977 and more than twice as much the following year.

As a result of the changes, Medicare outlays were budgeted at $19.6 billion, $2.2 billion more than in fiscal 1976 but $2.2 billion less than they would be without the revision.

A major innovation also was planned in other health areas, where the Administration wanted to provide $10 billion in a "block grant" formulation to the states to replace funds currently channeled into 16 separate programs, including Medicaid, health planning, community health and mental health centers.

This would result in an initial budget increase of $1 billion for Medicaid, but funding of most of the other health programs would decline. The Administration extended a budgetary guarantee for fiscal 1977 against any decrease in these programs. Beyond that, however, a new distribution would be applied to the states under a formula involving the number of poor people, per capita income and "relative tax effort." The formula was expected to favor the rural South and West at the expense of the industrial states. After the first year, a state could be cut back as much as 5% from its previous funding level.

Welfare—In another block-grant proposal, the budget called for $2.5 billion for a variety of social services such as day care centers, aid to senior citizens, foster care, homemakers' care and family planning. A 25% state matching requirement was eliminated and the states were given more flexibility in disbursement.

Outlays for aid to families with dependent children were up $100 million to $6 billion. Outlays for the Supplemental Security Income program for the aged, blind and disabled were up $700 million to $5.2 billion.

In both these and other welfare programs, the Administration planned a drive to enforce and review eligibility requirements.

In a fourth block-grant area, President Ford called for consolidation of 15 child nutrition programs into one $2.4 billion budgetary unit.

Income maintenance—The proposed .6% increase in the Social Security payroll tax, effective Jan. 1, 1977, was expected to add $3.3 billion to the trust fund revenues in fiscal 1977. Split between the employer and employe, it would raise the combined rate to 12.3%. Without the increase, the fund would be depleted by the early 1980s, it was estimated, because of the increase in beneficiaries, higher earned benefits and cost-of-living increments. A cost-of-living adjustment due in July was estimated by the Administration at 6.7%, another in July 1977 at 5.9%.

Ford suggested reductions estimated to total $826 million in fiscal 1977. One of them was to phase out benefits paid to students aged 18 to 22. Other aid was available, the administration pointed out, such as the Basic Opportunity Grants for college students. Other suggestions were to eliminate retroactive payments on initial application for Social Security benefits and to apply an annual instead of a monthly test of outside earnings to reduce benefits.

On a longer-range basis, partly because the Social Security trust fund was facing a dwindling proportion of workers to support the retired, the administration proposed another financing change, to tie initial benefits only to rising wage levels rather than to the combination of wages and prices. The goal was to stabilize at current levels the proportion of a worker's wages to benefits received upon full retirement.

Food aid—A $1.3 billion reduction was made in food-aid programs, which were budgeted at $7.1 billion. Reduction of the food-stamp program, proposed in 1975 but not enacted by Congress, accounted for $900 million of the fund scaleback. The change, pegging eligibility to the poverty-level income ($6,550 for a family of four), would drop 3.4 million persons as food stamp beneficiaries.

A proposed consolidation of other food programs, also broached without avail to Congress in 1975, accounted for the other $400 million reduction in food programs. These programs currently supplied cash or food to subsidize school cafeteria operations, summer meals for needy children and supplementary diets for infants and pregnant women. The Administration proposal was to consolidate these

15 programs into one block grant to the states for administration and to limit eligibility to poverty-level families. This was expected to eliminate 10 million children from the school meal program. The Administration also wanted to end the 25¢ subsidy to all school lunches and to eliminate a supplemental milk program.

Unemployment aid—Predicated on the Administration's forecast of a 1.6% drop in the unemployment rate from calendar 1976 to 1977, $15.4 billion was budgeted for unemployment compensation in fiscal 1977 (9.6 million recipients), a drop from $18.2 billion in fiscal 1976 (11.5 million recipients).

The budget also reflected the administration's ($1.3 billion) recommendation that Congress let two emergency jobless-benefit extensions expire as scheduled March 31, 1977.

The $15.4 billion for jobless compensation included $5.7 billion to replenish the states that exhausted their unemployment insurance trust funds, an occurrence in 18 states that was expected in 10 to 12 more by June.

A rapid diminution was scheduled in the budget for public service jobs programs—from $3.2 billion level in fiscal 1976 to $1.6 billion the following year. The President planned to ask for $1.7 billion in a supplemental budget request in fiscal 1976 to maintain the current program at the 330,000 jobs level until Jan. 1, 1977, but he also wanted the funds applied only to areas with over 6.5% unemployment and to jobs paying no more than $7,000 a year.

Other jobs and training programs also were due for budget reductions. The special program to provide summer jobs for youths was put down for $400 million (670,000 jobs), down from $440 million (740,000 jobs) for the summer of 1976 in the current fiscal year. Training programs operated by states and cities were slotted for $2 billion, down from $2.5 billion in fiscal 1976.

Housing programs—The Ford Administration budgeted $7.2 billion for the Housing & Urban Development Department (HUD). That level of activity was consistent with that of fiscal 1976. Going into fiscal 1977, the department planned more emphasis on community develop-

ment grants to local governments and on housing subsidies and less emphasis on older programs, such as urban renewal.

On programs to aid housing by purchase of home mortgages made at below-market interest rates, the budget assumed "that there will no longer be a need for these temporary programs . . . as conditions in the mortgage market return to normal." Despite the same assumption in the previous budget, HUD had injected $8 billion into the housing market in 1975 to buy mortgages in an attempt to spur the market.

In HUD's apartment-subsidy program, under which rent aid was provided for low-income families, the Administration projected subsidies for 400,000 units. The department planned to use part of the funding to ease the problem of defaults on government-insured mortgages by apartment projects. The apartment subsidies were to be applied in both fiscal 1976 and 1977 to up to 110,000 units in apartment projects near default or owned by HUD as a result of default.

Programs Under Attack

Federal health, welfare programs faulted. Supplemental income and health programs administered by the Department of Health, Education & Welfare (HEW) were criticized in January and February 1976 by Congress as well as by government officials for the misuse or waste of funds. The department of agriculture, during the same period, reported various irregularities in the operation of the food stamp program.

Health programs—The New York Times reported Jan. 7 that a General Accounting Office (GAO) audit of HEW records revealed that HEW had failed to require states to file plans for enforcing HEW regulations on the length of hospital stays by Medicaid patients. Of 14 states reporting to the two HEW offices checked by the GAO, only one had filed plans for all the quarters since the regulation went into effect. The HEW regulation did not set an absolute limit on the length of time a Medicaid patient could stay in a hospital, but it did require states to have doctors justify hospital stays longer than the average time for a disease. The determination of the average length of a hospital stay for a particular disease was left to the state.

The GAO audit was requested by Rep. John E. Moss (D, Calif.), chairman of the Oversight and Investigations Subcommittee of the Interstate and Foreign Commerce Committee. The subcommittee report, released Jan. 25, criticized HEW for allowing unneeded surgery to be performed on Medicaid and Medicare patients. Such surgery, the report said, "wastes lives and dollars." The report went on to say that "to the extent that HEW has failed to implement cost control procedures mandated by Congress, it can be said HEW is responsible for waste of more than $1 billion." (In 1974, according to the report, there were in all 2.38 million unnecessary operations, causing 11,900 deaths, and costing $3.92 billion.)

HEW Secretary David Mathews acknowledged Jan. 26 that the federal health programs had wasted money, but said that the solution was to shift health care responsibilities to state governments.

The New York Times reported Feb. 2 that officials of the Social Security Administration (a division of HEW) had confirmed reports that millions of dollars were being wasted by renting medical equipment for Medicare patients when purchasing it would have been more economical. Among other examples, the article noted the rental of a wheel chair for 72 months at a cost of $1,080, and of a hospital bed for 58 months for $1,654.20. To purchase, the wheel chair would have cost $168 and the bed $283.50.

Under law, Medicare patients had the choice of purchasing or renting, with Medicare funds defraying 80% of the expenses. Patients often rented because the cash outlay for purchasing was impossible for them (the government's 80% contribution came in monthly installments; also, reimbursement stopped if the patient recovered and no longer needed the equipment). Renting also ensured the maintenance of the equipment (while purchase did not) and was psychologically more acceptable to some patients (because it implied that the disability was only temporary).

According to the Times article, Social Security Administration officials doubted that the waste could be checked without Congressional revision of the Medicare law.

The New York Times reported Feb. 16 that Senate investigators had discovered that kickbacks and other illegitimate costs had accounted for nearly $45 million out of the $213 million paid under Medicare and Medicaid to clinical laboratories. Val J. Halamandaris, the associate counsel of the subcommittee looking into the matter, said: "The greater the kickback offered [to the doctor treating the Medicaid patient], the more likely the lab will be to obtain Medicaid business." He said that the kickbacks averaged about 30% of the total payment to the lab for Medicaid services. The kickbacks were usually disguised as rent for part of the doctor's office space (often far in excess of the total rent for the office) or as salary for an assistant, who in fact worked for the doctor.

Supplemental income—James B. Cardwell, commissioner of the Social Security Administration, reported to Congress Jan. 20 that, in its first two years of operation, the Supplemental Security Income (SSI) program had made overpayments estimated at $547 million. A total of $419 million still had not been returned, and Cardwell said that "recovery of this amount is expected to be limited." Figures on the latest six-month period available showed that 11% of the recipients were overpaid, 5.7% underpaid, and 7.7% ineligible. Cardwell said that a "significant improvement" in reducing inaccurate payments was anticipated, through the use of computer controls and by visiting recipients more frequently than once a year.

A government study, described in the Jan. 27 Wall Street Journal, which looked into ways to improve SSI's "effectiveness and fiscal accountability," recommended that the federal cash grants be increased, but also urged that more precautions be employed to prevent mispayments or abuse of the program. The study urged that the cash grants (at present $157.70 a month for individuals and $236.60 for couples) be increased to parity with the government determined poverty levels ($2,352 a year for individuals and $2,958 for couples).

The study also called for eliminating the variation within states in supplemental payments (currently afforded by 31 states) to the SSI payment. The practice of states' offering different allowances for different classes of recipients was seen as responsible for much of the difficulty currently experienced by the federal agency in administering the program. (Although the state supplemental payments came from state funds, they were disbursed by the Social Security Administration). The study was carried out by a group formed in April 1975 by then HEW Secretary Caspar Weinberger.

(A Jan. 7 United Press International release said that government statistics indicated that people were shifting from unemployment pay to welfare. The shift was predicted by HEW in 1975 after the U.S. Supreme Court ruled that a person could choose between welfare or unemployment pay. In most states, welfare benefits amounted to more than unemployment compensation.)

Fraud—A subcommittee of the House government operations committee charged in a report issued Jan. 26 that the resources of HEW for detecting fraud were "rediculously inadequate." The report said that at present HEW employed, in the Office of Investigation and Security, only 10 investigators, although the total fulltime payroll of the agency was over 129,-000. "HEW's operations" were exposed to an "unparalleled danger through fraud and program abuse" the report said. In December 1975 the department had announced the creation of a fraud and abuse unit, which would eventually raise the number of investigators to 74. A subcommittee spokesman called the unit a "step in the right direction," but said it was far from a complete solution.

In a report to Congress, HEW said Jan. 28 that its vulnerability to fraud was probably an inescapable consequence of several factors: the multiplicity of its programs, the great number of people participating in the programs, many of whom were functionally illiterate, the amount of money involved (the HEW annual budget was in excess of $100 billion), and the fragmentation of authority and responsibility between federal and state governments.

Food stamps—The Agriculture Department charged that money paid for food stamps had been returned late, or not at all, to the department, and that the stamps had been made available to ineligible persons.

An Agriculture Department spokesman told the Senate agriculture committee Jan. 21 that $6.69 million in federal food stamp funds was missing. This was part of a total of nearly $17.5 million that the Agriculture Department had found to be missing or deposited late, since it began a special audit last fall. (Food stamps were distributed by the department to local venders, who sold them to eligible persons for about 30% of their exchange value. The venders' receipts were supposed to be deposited immediately with federal reserve banks.) By depositing stamp receipts late, venders in effect gained interest-free loans, while the federal government lost the interest the money would have earned.

The Agriculture Department said Jan. 22 that it contemplated withholding administrative funds for the food stamp program from states in which a "large enough" proportion of the receipts were late or missing. What a "large enough" proportion would be was not specified.

A Washington, D.C. official responsible for that city's food stamp program said Feb. 12 that already more than half of the funds the Agriculture Department had claimed were missing for that city had been found. An Agriculture Department official had said Feb. 11 that $3.2 million was missing in Washington, D.C., remarking that, "It's a nationwide audit, but the District seems to be the culprit so far."

Controversy also arose over an Agriculture Department report released Feb. 11 on misallocation of food stamps received by "non-public-assistance households" (a household in which at least one member is not receiving public assistance). Such households accounted for "approximately 55% of the total program." The report said that nationally, for the period covered, January–June 1975, 8.9% of households receiving food-stamps were ineligible by "basic program criteria," another 10.1% were ineligible on procedural grounds and 7.7% had paid too much or received fewer stamps than they were entitled to.

Certain states were reported as having ineligibility rates well above the national average: In Rhode Island 57.2% of the recipients studied were termed ineligible, in Massachusetts, 52%, and in Delaware, 35.3%.

Officials of those states claimed Feb. 12 that the Agriculture Department report was misleading. They said that heavy workloads had at times prevented the states from following all the administrative procedures, but that by the basic financial criteria the great majority of food stamp recipients were eligible.

The Agriculture Department favored administrative reforms which would, according to the Feb. 13 Washington Post, reduce the $5 billion food stamp program by $1.2 billion, and take 1.5 million people off the food stamp rolls. The number of persons receiving food stamps currently was 18.6 million.

Federal welfare overpayments reported. Aged, blind and disabled recipients of Supplemental Security Income benefits received $403 million in overpayments in the first 18 months of the program, Social Security officials had conceded Aug. 15, 1975. Of the amount overpaid, they said, $115 million had been recovered or written off and $285 million remained to be collected.

Robert P. Bynum, assistant commissioner for Social Security program operations, said most of the overpayments were the result of human errors and occurred shortly after SSI went into effect in January 1974. At that time, the Social Security Administration took over case loads of 1,200 state and local welfare agencies.

Bynum and other officials blamed the overpayments on erroneous or missing data supplied by state and local agencies at the time of the transfer. The officials also admitted that the SSI program had been understaffed and its staff not adequately trained.

In a related development, U.S. District Court Judge William B. Jones ruled Aug. 29 that the federal government could not halt overpayments of SSI without first notifying recipients in advance, stating the reason and giving them time to appeal. Jones ordered the Department of Health, Education and Welfare to inform all SSI recipients of their new procedural rights.

The $403-million overpayment of SSI had also caused the Social Security Administration to become involved in a dispute with at least 27 state welfare agencies, the Washington Star reported Aug. 18. The state agencies, which were withholding from the Social Security Administration $206 million in supplemental SSI payments, claimed that the Social Security was chronically overpaying persons enrolled in the SSI program. In addition, the state agencies were questioning the accuracy of the Social Security Administration's accounting methods.

The dispute involved supplemental payments by some states beyond the SSI benefits paid by the federal government. To save money, the federal government had agreed to lump the states' supplemental payments into the individual recipients' monthly SSI check and then bill the states later.

When the SSI program started, the states began contributing $119 million each month to the federal payments. For the 1.8 million persons receiving state supplements, the average state increment was $70.

According to the Star, the states blamed the overpayments on errors by Social Security computer key punch operators, as well as on poor record keeping. To get around the problems and others, the states simply were not paying all of the bill Social Security sent them each month, the Star said.

HEW tries to counter Medicaid losses. David Mathews, Secretary of Health, Education & Welfare, March 26, 1976 announced a major effort to check fraud and abuse of the Medicaid program, at present costing the government an estimated $750 million annually (out of annual program expenditures of approximately $15 billion).

The new effort would team an expanded force of HEW investigators with state officials. The investigations would center on nursing homes, doctors, druggists and clinical laboratories receiving Medicaid funds. Mathews said the campaign would be launched in June in Ohio and Massachusetts (both states were among the ten largest users of Medicaid).

Mathews noted that the new effort would be partially staffed by 108 investigators working in the HEW fraud and abuse unit. At present, officials said, there were only five persons working in that area, and there had been only one part-time person in the summer of 1975.

HEW, Labor funds enacted over veto. Both chambers of Congress Sept. 30

mustered well over the required two-thirds majorities and overrode President Ford's veto the previous day of legislation appropriating $56.6 billion in fiscal 1977 for the Labor and Health, Education and Welfare Departments. The House vote was 312–93, with 65 Republicans supporting the override motion. The Senate vote was 67–15, with 19 Republicans voting against the President.

The bill appropriated almost exactly $4 billion more than Ford had requested in his budget proposal. It also contained a controversial provision—of which Ford had expressed approval in his veto message—barring use of federal funds that were disbursed through Medicaid for most abortions.

In his Sept. 29 veto, Ford had charged that the Democratic Congress had a "partisan political purpose" in approving the legislation. That purpose, Ford said, was to confront him with the dilemma of having to either veto the bill—and thereby appear "heedless of the human needs which these federal programs were intended to meet"—or sign the bill at the cost of demonstrating "inconsistency with my previous anti-inflationary vetoes. . . ."

Ford said that the veto (his 59th) was based purely on "the issue of fiscal integrity." He said he could not agree to legislation that provided large spending increases over his budget without incorporating financial reforms in the programs being funded.

House Speaker Carl Albert charged Sept. 29 that "the veto underscores his [Ford's] total lack of compassion for the most vulnerable members of our society."

The legislation had cleared Congress Sept. 17 when the Senate approved, 47–21, a compromise version of the abortion provision. The House had finished its action on the bill the previous day by approving the abortion provision, 256–114.

Both chambers had approved the bill's spending levels in August. The bill had not cleared Congress then because the House and Senate had disagreed on abortion. The House wanted a provision barring outright the use of the bill's funds to pay for or promote abortions; the Senate would not agree to such a provision. The final version incorporated a provision, worked out in a House-Senate conference committee, that barred use of the funds to

pay for abortions "except where the life of the mother would be endangered if the fetus were carried to term."

Opponents of the abortion curb charged that it was discriminatory and unconstitutional because it would effectively deprive poor women of the right to an abortion. Supporters of the curb contended that the government should not fund operations that were considered immoral by a substantial percentage of citizens. (The New York Times Sept. 16 cited official HEW figures which showed that in 1975 between 250,000 and 300,000 women had received abortions that were paid for by Medicaid.)

Most of the bill's funding, $45.12 billion, was allocated to HEW. The Labor Department received $10.13 billion and various related agencies $1.36 billion. Within HEW, the bill allocated $5.016 billion for health, $5.935 billion for education and $34.171 billion for welfare.

Revenue-sharing attacked. A study conducted over 2½ years by four public-interest groups attacked the federal revenue-sharing program for not insuring that funds were directed where most needed. The study, made public March 2, 1976, was done by the League of Women Voters Education Fund, the National Urban Coalition, the Center for Community Change and the Center for National Policy Review.

The revenue-sharing program, with funding of $30.2 billion, was initiated in 1972 and was due to expire at the end of 1976. President Ford had proposed a 5¾-year, $39.85 billion extension of the program.

The study charged that the "averaging of per-capita income within a jurisdiction [on which basis federal funds were allocated] may conceal substantial pockets of poverty and need." The distribution of funding, the study said, "allowed cities to get blacker and poorer and the suburbs whiter and richer by perpetuating [the] status quo with no requirements to share the wealth."

The study also charged that the Office of Revenue Sharing had allowed some governments to use the funds in a racially discriminatory manner, and that there was little accountability or public knowledge concerning how the funds were eventually spent by the state and local governments.

Priscilla Crane, a spokesman for the Office of Revenue Sharing, acknowledged March 2 that some governments receiving revenue-sharing funds had engaged in racial discrimination, but said that enforcement "initiatives" of the office had recently won court orders against discrimination. She cited court orders against employment discrimination issued in Miami, Fla. and East Providence, R.I.

John Gunther, executive director of the U.S. Conference of Mayors, criticized the study for attacking a program essential to the well-being of cities. He said March 2: "With these kinds of 'friends' of the cities, who needs enemies?"

Employment Programs & Unemployment Aid

1974 jobs & jobless aid bills. Congress cleared in the final days of the 1974 session a package of bills to authorize an emergency public service jobs program and to extend unemployment compensation coverage.

A bill adopted Dec. 18 by a 346–58 House vote and Senate voice vote authorized $2.5 billion in fiscal 1975 for state and local governments to hire jobless workers for community service work in education, health, sanitation, day care, recreation and similar programs. The same bill extended jobless compensation to about 12 million workers not currently covered, primarily farm workers, domestics and state and local government workers. The extension was on a one-year basis and would provide eligibility for up to 26 weeks of compensation in areas of high unemployment.

A $500 million authorization in the bill was designed for acceleration of federal public works projects.

Companion legislation was prepared to provide an additional 13 weeks of emergency unemployment compensation benefits for unemployed workers who had exhausted their regular benefits. The Senate approved the final form of the bill by an 84–0 vote Dec. 16. The House cleared the bill for the President Dec. 19.

A bill to appropriate $4 billion in fiscal 1975 to fund the emergency programs was passed by both houses Dec. 19. More than $2 billion of it was allocated for the jobless compensation provisions. States and communities would receive $875 million for the public service jobs aspect. Another $125 million was channeled for stimulation of public works projects in depressed areas.

President Ford signed the legislation Dec. 31.

1975 jobs bill vetoed. A $5.3 billion jobs-producing bill was vetoed by President Ford May 29, 1975 as "not an effective response to the unemployment problem."

Noting that the bill authorized spending $3.3 billion above his budget request, almost half of that in fiscal 1976, Ford said the bill "would exacerbate both budgetary and economic pressures and its chief impact would be felt long after our current unemployment problems are expected to subside."

"Economic recovery is expected to be well under way by the end of 1975," Ford said in his veto message, "and the accelerative influences of this bill would come much too late to give impetus to this recovery."

The President urged Congress to act quickly on a bill to provide funds for "immediate and temporary employment through the public sector and summer youth jobs." The vetoed bill contained such provisions, but it also had "a host of provisions of questionable value," according to Ford.

Among the vetoed bill's provisions:

The President's request for $1.625 billion for 180,000 public service jobs was approved. In addition, the measure allocated $119 million for part-time jobs for college students, $458 million for summer jobs for youth and $30 million for community service employment for the aged. Funds would also have been appropriated to create jobs by speeding work on federal public works and other construction projects. Another section of the final measure contained funds for the purchase of 21,000 automobiles. The House version had provided for the buying of 121,000 vehicles to stimulate the ailing automobile industry.

Veto sustained by House—The veto was sustained by the House June 4. A vote to override was 277–145, five short of the two-thirds majority of those present and voting required to carry. The totals included 22 Democrats voting to uphold the veto and 19 Republicans voting to override. The latter contrasted with 48 Republicans voting for passage originally.

Party lobbying before the vote was intense. President Ford telephoned several members—some Southern Democrats as well as Republicans, whose votes were uncertain—from the Presidential plane. House Speaker Carl Albert (D) made a rare appearance in a floor debate to plead with the House to override "to show we are a legislative body."

House Democratic Leader Thomas P. O'Neill Jr. (Mass.) told the House Democrats at a caucus June 4 "we will not be faced again this session with so clear a confrontation between the philosophy and ideals of the Republican and Democratic parties."

On the floor later, O'Neill rebutted Ford's budgetary argument for veto, that the bill was $3.3 billion more than his budget, by claiming Ford's economic policies had "cost the government $56 billion" in eight months of office. This was based on the increase in the unemployment rate since Ford took office of 3.5%, from 5.4% to 8.9%. House Appropriations Committee chairman George H. Mahon (D, Tex.), floor manager of the override vote, had said that each 1% increase in unemployment increased the federal deficit $16 billion—$14 billion in lost income tax revenue and $2 billion paid out in unemployment benefits.

On the other side, House Republican Leader John J. Rhodes (Ariz.), attributing the current economic condition to the Democrats, who controlled the last two Congresses, referred to the "93rd and 94th Congressional recession."

Summer job funds approved—The Senate June 12, by voice vote, passed and sent to the White House legislation appropriating $473 million for summer jobs for 840,000 economically disadvantaged youths. The House June 10 had cleared the bill, 408–8. Originally part of the $5.3 billion jobs bill vetoed by President Ford May 29, the measure was rushed through Congress in four days because of the need of local communities to plan summer work programs. Ford signed the bill June 16.

Congress clears jobless aid plan. Legislation to extend and modify the unemployment compensation program was approved by both houses of Congress and sent to the White House June 26. President Ford signed it June 30.

The unemployment benefits were extended from June 30 to the end of the year for a maximum of 65 weeks' duration. The maximum would be available in states having a jobless rate exceeding 6% of the workers covered by unemployment insurance. In states having a 5%–6% jobless rate among insured workers, the jobless would be eligible for 52 weeks of benefits, and 39 weeks would be available in states where the jobless trigger was less than 5%. Under the previous law, the extended benefits were available when either the national unemployment rate or a particular state's rate exceeded 4.5% of the work force.

The legislation required those who had received 39 weeks of compensation to apply for state occupational training to be eligible for further benefits. The state was to decide on an individual's need for it.

Special unemployment assistance for some workers, such as domestics and farm workers, outside the coverage of the regular federal-state jobless compensation system, would be expanded from 26 weeks to 39 weeks.

1976 works bill vetoed. President Ford vetoed a $6.1 million public works employment bill Feb. 13, 1976 as "little more than an election year pork barrel."

He said that the bill "would do little to create jobs for the unemployed" and that the most effective way to create new jobs was "to pursue balanced economic policies that encourage the growth of the private sector without risking a new round of inflation."

In his argument against the bill, Ford said it would create only 250,000 jobs at most, instead of the 600,000 to 800,000 jobs advertised for it, and almost none of them immediately when they were needed but in late 1977 and early 1978. He said the cost of producing the jobs would be "intolerably high, perhaps in excess of $25,000 per job."

He found some merit in the bill's "counter-cyclical" provisions, or revenue-sharing grants to states and cities to areas of high unemployment, but he criticized the section for tying the aid to the spending levels of the state and local governments, which he thought would encourage waste.

The veto was sustained Feb. 19 when the Senate vote to override (63–35) fell three votes short of the two-thirds majority needed to cancel a veto.

In the House, the vote was 319–98 (263 D & 56 R vs. 82 R & 16 D). This was 41 more than the required two-thirds.

Public works, service bills cleared. The Senate gave final congressional approval by voice votes Sept. 22 to two key bills that would help achieve the Democrats' goal of creating more jobs. One bill was an appropriations measure that provided $3.7 billion through Sept. 30, 1977 for public works, "counter-cyclical" aid to state and local governments and construction of water-treatment plants. The other bill extended through fiscal 1977 a program providing federal grants to state and local governments to allow them to hire people for public service jobs in the government.

Both bills passed the House Sept. 17. The vote on the public works bill was 263–53; on the public service extension bill it was 295–9.

The public works bill funded programs that had been authorized by Congress over President Ford's veto. The measure allocated $2 billion to public works projects, $1.25 billion in counter-cyclical aid and $480 million for the water pollution control plants.

The other bill provided for an expansion, as well as the extension, of the public service jobs program. The number of new jobs created would depend on the level of funding, which was to be decided in a separate appropriations measure. The bill also required that any new jobs created by the program should be filled by low-income persons who had been jobless for 15 weeks or more or were on welfare. The same group would fill half of the program's existing jobs as vacancies occurred.

The legislation nullified a Labor Department regulation limiting to 10% the proportion of jobs funded by the program that could be filled by rehiring government employes who had been laid off for bona fide budgetary reasons.

Jobless-benefits revision. Congress Oct. 1, 1976 gave final approval to a bill extending the coverage of the regular unemployment compensation system and revising the system's financing to cope with unemployment trust-fund deficits. Both chambers passed the bill Oct. 1, the House, 272–97, the Senate by voice vote. President Ford signed the bill Oct. 20.

The extension of the program chiefly involved non-elected state and local government workers, who had been covered by the Special Unemployment Assistance (SUA) program. Some farm and domestic workers would also be covered, and the Virgin Islands would be brought within the system. The changes would take effect Jan. 1, 1978. The SUA was extended through 1977.

In its financing provisions, the bill raised the taxable wage base (levied on employers) from $4,200 to $6,000, and increased the federal unemployment compensation tax rate by two-tenths of one percent. The tax-rate increase, which would take effect Jan. 1, 1977, would be rescinded when the unemployment trust fund had repaid its borrowings from general federal revenues. The bill also:

■ Barred jobless benefits for teachers during school vacation periods and for professional athletes during the off-season. Benefits for illegal aliens were also prohibited.

■ Provided that, effective Jan. 1, 1979, benefits for pension recipients would be reduced by the amount of the pension.

■ Described conditions—related to jobless rates—under which extended unemployment benefits would be triggered. The Department of Labor predicted that the national economic condition would trigger the extended benefits at least through 1977.

■ Barred the denial of jobless benefits merely on the basis of pregnancy.

■ Set up a 13-member commission to

examine the unemployment system and to report to Congress by Jan. 1, 1979.

■ Required unemployed fathers to apply for jobless benefits before seeking welfare benefits. When individuals qualified for both kinds of aid, the bill ordered states to bring jobless benefits up to welfare aid levels.

Food Aid

Food stamp fund ordered spent. Judge Miles Lord of federal court in Minneapolis Oct. 13, 1974 ordered the Agriculture Department to spend $278 million remaining in 1973 funds for the food stamp program rather than return the money to the Treasury Department.

A suit brought on behalf of the National Welfare Rights Organization and three Minnesota plaintiffs accused the department and Agriculture Secretary Earl Butz of inadequately administering the $2.5 billion food stamp funds allocated by Congress for the 1973 fiscal year. Judge Lord agreed with the charge, ruling that the department and Butz had violated the law in refusing to spend money to implement the Food Stamp Act's "outreach" program. The program was designed to inform low income persons of their rights to food stamps. According to a plaintiff's lawyer, an estimated 37 million persons were eligible for assistance, but only 14 million persons were receiving food stamps. Suits recently filed in 17 states also charged state officials with failing to implement outreach programs.

Food stamp benefits for a low income family of four would be increased $4 a month to $150 a month beginning Jan. 1, 1975, the Agriculture Department announced Oct. 14. The adjustment was based on new calculations of food costs for an "economy" menu, showing it cost $35.40 a week to feed a family of four, including two school age children.

Ford backs higher stamp cost. At his press conference Jan. 21, 1975, President Ford defended his decision to raise the cost of federal food stamps. Recipients, who currently paid about 23%

of their net income to obtain food relief, would be required to pay 30% on March 1.

Congress revokes stamp price raise— Ford's decision to raise the cost of food stamps was voted down overwhelmingly by Congress. The House Feb. 4 approved by 374–38 vote a bill blocking food stamp price increases for the remainder of 1975. The Senate followed suit Feb. 5, passing an identical bill 76–8.

The Administration had proposed the increase as part of its effort to stem the rapid growth in the cost of social programs. Under the proposal, the cost of a month's allocation of food stamps would have increased from an average of 23% of recipient families' net income to 30%. The Administration had hoped to realize annual savings of about $650 million. (About 17.1 million poor and elderly persons participated in the program, administered by the Agriculture Department.)

Congressional opponents of the increase argued that it would worsen the plight of the poor and elderly during a time of recession and inflation.

In testimony before the House Agriculture Committee Jan. 30, Edward Hekman, administrator of the Food and Nutrition Service of the Agriculture Department, had defended the proposed increase. Calling it a means of slowing the growth rate of federal expenditures, Hekman asserted the increase would make the program more equitable because "everybody would pay the same thing for food." Hekman, who claimed to have suggested the increase, also said that poor people paid a lower percentage of income for food than the rest of the population.

McGovern scores food stamp red tape. Sen. George S. McGovern (D, S.D.) called on the Agriculture Department to simplify procedures for applying for food stamps. "What we need," McGovern told applicants at a Miami Beach stamp distribution center March 4, 1975 "is a form on which a person simply declares a need for stamps, a form that can be picked up an any post office or bank."

McGovern, chairman of the Senate Select Committee on Nutrition and Human Needs, had come to center to glean opinions of the food stamp program from its participants. Generally, he heard complaints that registration forms were too complicated, that too many receipts for such things as rent and medical bills were required and that clerks often regarded applicants as second-class citizens. Afterward, McGovern urged that a simple form, widely available, replace the current procedure. He said that if Agriculture Secretary Earl Butz were worried that a shortened form would not detect fraud, a system of spot checks, similar to that of the Internal Revenue Service, could be instituted.

McGovern's committee issued a staff report March 3 that also criticized the program. While the number of persons receiving food stamps had risen almost four million to 17.9 million in less than six months, the report said, the program continued to fall behind in taking care of those eligible. Moreover, the report pointed out that in 1972, 52% of those eligible had been given federal food stamps, but in September 1974 only 38% of those eligible were given assistance.

Committee investigators found, the study said, that although the law required the processing of applications in 30 days or less, "the most conservative estimates indicate that in mid-February at least 85,-000 people were waiting longer than 30 days." The 50-50 state-federal formula for paying for state administrative costs was no longer sufficient to meet the rapid rise in applications, the report said. In addition, the report asserted that the Agriculture Department had failed to encourage states to vigorously seek out and register potential recipients. It did note, however, Atlanta, Georgia's effort to reduce application backlogs by opening centers on weekends, and using volunteers.

Among the recommendations of the staff report: food stamps should be sold in post offices, as a means of compensating for short hours and long lines at banks; certification of eligibility on a simple form, with random checks for fraud, should be instituted; Congress should appoint an advisory council, which included poor people; and food stamp benefits should be boosted, because they provided for a diet plan that Agriculture Department nutritionists said was not conducive to good health over a long period of time.

Other reports criticize program—Separate reports by the Agriculture Department and the General Accounting Office (GAO), made public March 1, expressed criticism of the food stamp program.

The Agriculture Department survey said that a sample audit of the program showed that errors in payment had been made in 56.1% of the cases studied. The survey also determined that among the recipients sampled, 23.2% of the bonus dollars—the difference between what participants paid as their purchase requirement and the amount of food stamps they were alloted—had been overissued. As was the case with the investigation by the Senate select committee, the Agriculture Department survey found little abuse of the food stamp program. It reported losses that amounted to 14 cents for each $1,000 worth of food stamps issued during the first nine months of fiscal 1973.

The report by the GAO, the accounting arm of Congress, urged simplification of the procedure for certifying eligible recipients and improvement in the states' quality control programs. It pointed out that about one in five participants did not meet eligibility requirements, that a "significant number"—7% of the cases sampled—of applicants were turned down improperly and that about two of every five participants paid the wrong amount for their food stamps.

Ford not to veto food stamp freeze—President Ford announced Feb. 13 that he would allow a bill barring an increase in the cost of food stamps through 1975 to become law without his signature. Ford said he would not fight "the clear will of Congress" on the bill, which passed by large margins in both houses.

The President expressed disappointment that Congress not only rejected his plan but failed "to advance a constructive proposal of its own." If Congress continued such practice "an unthinkable [budget] deficit will result and there will be no mistaking where the responsibility lies," Ford said.

The President's decision was announced as a federal court considered two suits filed against the increase. Judge William B. Jones had said Feb. 11 he would issue a temporary injunction against the increase unless informed by Feb. 13 the bill would not be vetoed. The suits, brought by

Consumers Union and the Food Research & Action Center of New York, were dismissed after Ford's announcement.

Stamp allotments raised. The Agriculture Department announced April 8, 1975 that food stamp allotments would rise 5.2% effective July 1. A family of four that currently paid $25 for $154 worth of stamps would receive $162 in stamps for the same amount of money.

Department officials said that because of increased benefits and the quantum leap in the number of persons qualifying, the total cost of the program would be $5 billion in the fiscal year ending June 30 and $6 billion in fiscal 1976.

Meanwhile, the department reported March 31 that the number of persons receiving stamps had increased by 500,000 in February, bringing current total enrollment to 18.4 million persons.

In a July 25 message to Congress, in which he requested $3.8 billion in additional funds for the program for fiscal 1976, President Ford called the food stamp program "another massive, multibillion dollar program, almost uncontrolled and fully supported by federal taxpayers." Ford asked for tighter controls over eligibility.

The Agriculture Department Nov. 26 again raised food-stamp allotments—to $166 a month for a family of four, effective Jan. 1, 1976. The maximum eligible income for a family of four was raised from $540 a month to $553.

Stamp allotment plan invalid. The three-judge U.S. Circuit Court of Appeals in Washington ruled unanimously June 12, 1975 that the formula under which allotments were made in the Agriculture Department's food stamp program was illegal. The court gave the department 120 days to devise a new allotment system for the estimated 19.6 million persons receiving food stamps.

The case, Rodway v. U.S. Department of Agriculture, was four years in litigation and had been brought by the Food Research and Action Center, a New York-based public interest law firm, on behalf of nine food stamp recipients—three each from New York, Connecticut and Pennsylvania. Other plaintiffs in the suit were

the City of New York, the Commonwealth of Pennsylvania and the National Welfare Rights Organization.

In their decision, the judges did not actually say the allotment formula failed to provide a nutritionally adequate diet. However, they concluded that it failed to insure such a diet and that its benefits were too low even for the department's economy plan diet. Judge J. Skelly Wright, in handing down the opinion, criticized the practice of distributing food stamp benefits on the basis of family size, saying that the allotment formula ought to take into account such factors as varying needs in a family, the age and sex of its members and the area of the country in which they lived. "For a family that needs a loaf of bread, the offer of a slice is poor comfort," Wright said. Referring to what it said was a defense of the allotment formula that had been made by the Secretary of Agriculture on grounds of "administrative necessity," the court declared it did "not think that justifies automatically ignoring easily generalized, easily quantified, and easily verified differences among recipients under the rubric of administrative necessity." Wright added: "We think it plain that the Food Stamp [Reform] Act requires the secretary to distribute the food-stamp coupons in such a way that all, or virtually all, recipients are given the 'opportunity to obtain a nutritionally adequate diet'." The court also found the department in violation of the Administrative Procedure Act for not promulgating food stamp regulations before applying them and for not soliciting and considering public reaction to its allotment practices.

In a related development, the Agriculture Department June 30, in a 150-page document, criticized its method of distributing food stamps but said the June 12 court decision "needs to be resolved before changes in eligibility and benefit levels are advanced."

Food stamp enrollment declines. The number of persons enrolled in the federal government's food stamp program in July declined 100,000 from the month before to 19.1 million, the Agriculture Department reported Aug. 29. According to the department, the number of recipients was the lowest since February.

In testimony before the Senate Select Committee on Nutrition and Human Needs July 31, Assistant Secretary of Agriculture Richard L. Feltner had said that the number of persons eligible for food stamps was growing and that it was "not inconceivable" that it might go as high as half the U.S. population.

Continuing down, enrollment in the stamp program dropped in September to 18.5 million persons, the lowest number since January, the department said Oct. 31. Officials attributed at least part of the decline to normal seasonal factors.

Food stamp data said to be suppressed. Sen. George McGovern (D, S.D.) said Aug. 6, 1975 that the Administration had suppressed portions of an Agriculture Department report to the Senate that failed to support the Administration's contention that the food stamp program was growing at a dangerously uncontrolled rate and needed to be scaled down.

The suppressed material, made public by McGovern, said that the number of food stamp recipients would decline by 1980, that the program's cost in constant dollars would remain the same through 1980 and the program stimulated the economy by providing jobs, farm income, retail sales and tax revenues above administrative costs. The deleted portions assumed that the nation's unemployment rate would fall to 4.5%, that disposable income would rise 12% a year and that food costs would increase at 4% a year.

However, McGovern, in releasing the suppressed material, characterized the food stamp program as "the best social program we've got on the books, with the exception of Social Security.... These sections [that were deleted] refute current scare charges about food stamp trends," he said.

Simon criticizes food stamp program— Treasury Secretary William E. Simon, in a speech in Bloomington, Ind. Aug. 12, criticized the Agriculture Department's food stamp program. "We begin with the best of intentions, but wind up with social programs that are spinning out of control," he said.

"The food stamp program began as a small $14-million experiment in 1962. By 1976 it will cost $6.6 billion a year. That is a 47,000 per cent increase, and it is a well-known haven for the chiselers and rip-off artists," Simon said.

Studies show food stamp errors. Of an average 15.2 million persons enrolled in the food stamp program during the latter half of 1974, about 653,000, or 4.3%, should not have received stamps, an Agriculture Department quality control study, reported Sept. 11, 1975, said. The study showed that 8.8% of recipients not on welfare were not eligible on the basis of need. (Welfare recipients were automatically eligible and accounted for 45% of those in the program.)

Overpayments to eligible and ineligible nonwelfare families during the six-month period totaled $160 million. Meanwhile, eligible recipients were shortchanged by roughly $20 million.

Total enrollment in the program rose 25% and 41% among families not on public assistance. Department officials attributed the increase to the effects of the recession.

The program's overall rate of error, including both substantive and administrative mistakes, dropped to 17.3% from 18.2% for the first half of 1974 and 21.6% for 1973. The report said that 43% of the errors could be blamed on state processing agencies rather than on individual applicants.

A Treasury Department study released Oct. 28 also charged that "lax administration" by the states was apparently the primary reason for the high error factor. The Treasury study indicated that about two out of five stamp recipients were getting too many and that one of every six recipients was not eligible for the program.

Stamp cutback urged. President Ford sent Congress Oct. 20, 1975 a plan that would limit participation in the foodstamp program, generally, to persons whose incomes were below the poverty level. The Administration presented the plan as one that would save taxpayers $1.2 billion a year and remove 3.4 million persons from the program, which currently cost the government $6 billion a year and served 18.8 million persons.

The numerous deductions, currently permitted in the program to bring a family's income down to eligibility at the poverty level, would be eliminated under the Ford plan. Instead, a $100-a-month deduction would be permitted per household, or $125 if a person over 60 years old was in the family. For a family of four, where the poverty level was calculated by the government at $5,050 annual income, the total income it could have under the Ford plan and still qualify for food stamps was $6,250 or $6,550, after adding on the only monthly deductions allowed.

The Ford plan would figure family income, in determining eligibility, on the basis of the average income during the 90 days prior to application for food stamps. Currently, income was figured on the basis of a family's estimate of earnings in the coming month.

A uniform charge was proposed for the food stamps—30% of net income after the standard $100 or $125 monthly deduction. The charge currently varied with a family's income.

The Administration also proposed to tighten eligibility of students and strikers for the program. Students would have to show that their parents were not claiming them as dependents on income-tax returns. The strikers would have to give proof that they looked for other employment before receiving the stamps.

The Administration proposed to increase the federal share of costs of investigating and prosecuting fraudulent food-stamp claims.

Sen. James Buckley (R-Conservative, N.Y.) and Rep. Bob Michel (R, Ill.), who were sponsoring a bill for even more drastic cutback of the food-stamp program, endorsed the Administration proposal. But it was criticized Oct. 20 by Sens. George McGovern (D, S.D.) and Robert Dole (R, Kan.), sponsors of a more moderate revision. McGovern accused the Administration of "gutting" the food-stamp program; Dole charged a political tilt to the right to curry favor with conservatives.

Reform promulgated—The Agriculture Department promulgated a food-stamp reform program Feb. 26, 1976. The proposal, designed to save $1.2 billion a year, would eliminate five million of the current

19 million beneficiaries. Benefits would be reduced for five million and increased for another five million recipients.

The proposals were requested by President Ford, who had informed Congress Feb. 20 of his intention to take administrative action for "the reforms needed" rather than wait for legislation. "While statutory changes by the Congress would be the most desirable course of action," he said then, "we can no longer afford to wait."

Regulations to put the reforms into effect were announced by the Agriculture Department May 4.

The cutoff point would be a take-home pay of $6,700 a year for a family of four. The new rules granted a standard deduction of $100 a month ($125 for persons over 65 years old).

A family also would be required to pay about 30% of its income in cash for the monthly stamp allocation, which was valued at $166 for a family of four. On an annual basis this would mean that such a family at the top of the income scale would pay $1,650 a year for $1,992 in stamps. Under the old rules a cash outlay averaging 24% was required.

In another change, eligibility would be based on income for the 90 days prior to application instead of on income at the time of application.

Courts block reforms—The proposed food-stamp reforms were blocked May 28 when U.S. District Judge Howard F. Corcoran issued a temporary restraining order. The regulations—scheduled to go into effect June 1—had been challenged in a suit filed May 26 by a diverse assortment of plaintiffs, including 26 states, the U.S. Conference of Mayors, 73 families who were receiving food stamps, labor unions and church, civic and civil rights groups.

The suit—filed in U.S. District Court in Washington, D.C.—alleged that the revisions would violate the Food Stamp Act. That law, the suit said, established the right of all poor families to an adequate diet. The suit also charged that the new regulations would impose excessive paperwork and operating expenses on the local governments that administered the program.

The Agriculture Department had estimated that the proposed regulations would save the federal government $1.2 billion by cutting 5.3 million persons from the food-stamp program and reducing benefits for an additional 5.8 million.

At a June 15 hearing on the suit, the Agriculture Department modified its estimates of the impact of the proposed regulations. It said then that only 4.14 million persons would be dropped from the program, and that 4.42 million would have their benefits reduced. The savings estimate was lowered to $1 billion. The department also increased its estimate of the number of persons who would benefit from the revised regulations; the new figure was given as 6.89 million, a 24.7% increase from the previous estimate.

At that hearing, with U.S. District Judge John Lewis Smith Jr. presiding, the temporary restraining order was renewed.

The food-stamp reforms were put under indefinite suspension by a preliminary injunction issued June 19 by U.S. District Judge John Lewis Smith Jr.

Smith said that the Agriculture Department had "exceeded its congressional mandate" by revising the regulations and that "enormous administrative burdens" would come with their implementation. The "hunger and deprivation" that might result, he said, "could hardly be cured through any retroactive relief the court or defendants would provide."

"There is no indication that USDA was authorized to totally restructure the eligibility and purchase price criteria . . . on its initiative," Smith said. It was apparent, he said, "that substantive food stamp reform was intended to take place through ordinary congressional channels, not through appropriations measures or administrative action."

Funds for elderly released. The Department of Health, Education & Welfare announced April 2, 1976 that the full $187.5 million appropriated by Congress for meals for the elderly would be released.

A suit had been filed against HEW by the Food Research and Action Center, an anti-hunger organization based in New York, charging that the agency was illegally impounding the funds.

An HEW official said that, because of the normal lag in implementing programs,

the states would probably not spend all of the funds in the current fiscal year.

Court Decisions

Divorce aid denied. The New York State Court of Appeals May 1, 1975 ruled, 4–3, that a poor person wanting a divorce was not entitled to legal representation paid for by public funds.

In handing down the majority decision, Chief Judge Charles D. Breitel said that although counsel was "always desirable, and in complicated matrimonial litigation would be essential," it was not "a legal condition to access to the courts." In 1963, in Gideon v. Wainwright, the U.S. Supreme Court had held that a defendant charged with a felony was constitutionally entitled to the services of a lawyer. Judge Breitel declared in his opinion, however, that "no similar constitutional or statutory provision applies to private litigation."

Rent rule invalid. The Supreme Court May 19, 1965 invalidated New York State welfare regulations that reduced the rent allowance for a family with needy children when a parent allowed a person with no legal responsibility for support of the children to live in the house. The rules wrongly assumed that the lodger always contributed to the welfare of the children, the court said.

Rulings on abortion payments. Federal District Court Judge George H. Barlow Jan. 16, 1976 blocked implementation of a New Jersey law that would have banned the use of Medicaid funds for abortions. Barlow issued the order in Trenton in response to a suit filed by the American Civil Liberties Union of New Jersey charging that the law was unconstitutional. The ACLU contended that the law discriminated against poor women.

The ban, which prohibited use of Medicaid funds for abortions except in cases where the mother's life was in danger, was signed into law in December 1975.

A three-judge panel of U.S. District Court in Brooklyn March 10 reaffirmed a decision it had handed down in 1972 barring New York State from denying Medicaid reimbursements for voluntary abortions.

The state Social Services Department had appealed the district court's 1972 ruling to the U.S. Supreme Court, which had sent the case back to the lower court for reconsideration.

The lower court's 1972 ruling had been limited to the question of indigent women. The 1976 ruling broadened the issue to include all women, regardless of economic status. Also, for the first time, the state was prevented from withholding Medicaid reimbursements from women having abortions for other than health reasons.

The U.S. Supreme Court refused April 26 to stay the District Court decision.

The Supreme Court Nov. 8 again refused to stay a lower-court order barring the federal government from withholding Medicaid funds for elective abortions. The lower-court order—issued Oct. 22 by Judge John F. Dooling Jr. in U.S. District Court in Brooklyn, N.Y.—had been sought by Planned Parenthood, the New York City Health and Hospitals Corp. and other parties. They had brought suit after Congress incorporated a ban on Medicaid funding for abortions in the fiscal-1977 appropriations bill for the Department of Health, Education and Welfare.

The stay, which would have barred the use of Medicaid funds for abortions while the case was under appeal, had been requested by Sen. James L. Buckley (R-Cons., N.Y.), Rep. Henry J. Hyde (R, Ill.) and others. Hyde was the sponsor of the aid-cutoff amendment to the HEW funding bill.

The Planned Parenthood suit had contended that the cut off on abortion funds discriminated against poor women by effectively denying them their constitutional right to an abortion.

HEW and the Justice Department had defended the law but did not endorse the request for a stay. In a communication to the Supreme Court concerning the request for the stay, the departments said they believed Dooling's ruling was "erroneous and [would] be reversed on appeal."

The Supreme Court ruling did not touch on the basic question of whether the Hyde amendment was constitutional. However, the ruling insured that federal Medicaid funding for abortions would continue until, or unless, the district court ruling was overturned on appeal.

1976 Presidential Campaign

Former Gov. Jimmy Carter of Georgia was elected President of the United States Nov. 2, 1976 for a term beginning in January 1977. Carter, the Democratic candidate, defeated Republican incumbent Gerald R. Ford after a campaign in which welfare and the poor were major but not decisive issues.

Reagan on welfare & poverty. Former Gov. Ronald Reagan of California was President Ford's strongest challenger, although an unsuccessful one, for the Republican Presidential nomination. In a speech in Chicago Sept. 26, 1975, Reagan had proposed transferring various services and programs from the federal government to the states. These activities included food stamps, public assistance and child nutrition.

In Bloomington, Ill. Jan. 12, 1976, Reagan declared that such programs as welfare, Medicaid, subsidies of education, food stamps, housing and community development were "signal failures" under federal administration and they "belong back at the level of government closest to the people."

In southern New Hampshire Jan. 16, Reagan conceded that his federal budget proposal, for a shift of social welfare programs to state administration, might lead to abandonment of some of the programs by some states and a migration of those dependent upon the programs from those states.

Carter stresses commitment to poor. Carter spoke of his background and commitments in an informal chat with reporters during a flight back to Georgia from Texas the night of June 14. He had attended a fund-raising banquet in Dallas.

The commitments Carter stressed were to push forward on civil rights, to eliminate racial discrimination and to alleviate poverty, hunger and inadequate housing. The country was "resilient," he said, and "we can start again. I believe it can be done and I mean to do it."

Carter said there was a significant change in the government's attitude in 1968 with the election of Richard M. Nixon as president "and the people who lost were the blacks, the elderly, the illiterate, the sick."

"It changed when Johnson and Kennedy went out and Nixon came in," he asserted. "Another thing is, the policymakers, Kennedy and Johnson, in my opinion, didn't do enough to bring blacks into the policy-making positions in government.

"I think Johnson had a much greater feel for it than Kennedy did. Kennedy was not one of them. He didn't understand their special needs."

Carter said he felt he did understand because of his long relationship with poor people. "That's where I came from," he said. "That's where I lived. Those are my people, not only whites but particularly blacks."

Carter felt that Johnson "did an excellent job" on social programs but he "was never accepted by the liberal Eastern establishment." Carter suggested he could be accepted in such circles because "I'm sure of myself. I'm not sure Johnson was ever sure of himself when he was president."

Governors for national plan. A national welfare program with a minimum level of payment was the major recommendation emerging from the 68th annual meeting of the National Governors Conference in Hershey, Pa. July 5–6, 1976.

On the political side, the Democratic governors conferred their endorsement on Jimmy Carter for president.

The welfare proposal was based on a two-year study conducted by a governors' task force headed by Gov. Daniel J. Evans (R, Wash.).

As adopted July 6, the governors' plan called for a national minimum welfare payment with regional differences on the cost of living. Welfare recipients would be required to register for work and to accept available jobs.

The governors stipulated that their proposal was not an endorsement of any form of a guaranteed annual income.

The governors recommended that the federal government pay the full cost of the minimum benefits, 75% of a state's supplemental welfare payments and 75% of a state's administration costs for the program.

Carter attended a breakfast meeting of the Democratic governors July 6. A resolution pledging "our support and united effort" for his election was read to him by Gov. Marvin Mandel (Md.).

It was backed by 29 of the 30 Democratic governors attending the conference.

At a news conference afterwards, Carter said he favored a unified welfare payment for "those who cannot work." "I would press for one payment in all states, that should vary only with the cost of living," he said. As for financing the system, he said only that he "would try" to reduce gradually the share paid by the states and work toward a gradual federal takeover of the costs.

Carter repeated at the news conference his support of a plan not favored by the governors. It would bypass the states in revenue-sharing and provide the aid directly to local governments.

Carter did hold out some prospect of relief. He "would guess over a period of time," he said, that if elected "my administration would see a substantial reduction" in the states' share of costs for social programs.

1976 party platforms. The Democratic National Convention nominated Carter for President, and the Republican National Convention renominated President Ford. Both conventions also adopted platforms that included detailed statements on welfare and poverty.

Democratic platform—The Democratic platform's statements on the welfare and poverty issues included the following:

Today, millions of people are unemployed. Unemployment represents mental anxiety, fear of harassment over unpaid bills, idle hours, loss of self-esteem, strained family relationships, deprivation of children and youth, alcoholism, drug abuse and crime. A job is a key measure of a person's place in society—whether as a full-fledged participant or on the outside. Jobs are the solution to poverty, hunger and other basic needs of workers and their families. Jobs enable a person to translate legal rights of equality into reality.

Our industrial capacity is also wastefully underutilized. There are houses to build, urban centers to rebuild, roads and railroads to construct and repair, rivers to clean, and new sources of energy to develop. Something is wrong when there is work to be done, and the people who are willing to do it are without jobs. What we have lacked is leadership. . . .

Ten million people are unemployed right now, and twenty to thirty million were jobless at some time in each of the last two years. For major groups in the labor force—minorities, women, youth, older workers, farm, factory and construction workers—unemployment has been, and remains, at depression levels.

The rising cost of food, clothing, housing, energy and health care has eroded the income of the average American family, and has pushed persons on fixed incomes to the brink of economic disaster. Since 1970, the annual rate of inflation has averaged more than 6 percent and is projected by the Ford Administration to continue at an unprecedented peacetime rate of 6 to 7 percent until 1978.

The depressed production and high unemployment rates of the Nixon-Ford Administrations have produced federal deficits totalling $242 billion. Those who should be working and paying taxes are collecting unemployment compensation or other welfare payments in order to survive. For every one percent increase in the unemployment rate—for every one million Americans out of work—we all pay $3 billion more in unemployment compensation and $2 billion in welfare and related costs, and lose $14 billion in taxes. In fiscal 1976, $76 billion was lost to the federal government through increased recession-related expenditures and lost revenues. In addition, state and local governments lost $27 billion in revenues. A return to full employment will eliminate such deficits. With prudent management of existing programs, full employment revenues will permit the financing of national Democratic initiatives.

For millions of Americans, the Republican Party has substituted welfare for work. Huge sums will be spent on food stamps and medical care for families of the unemployed. Social insurance costs are greatly increased. This year alone the federal government will spend nearly $20 billion on unemployment compensation. In contrast, spending on job development is only $2½ billion. The goal of the new Democratic administration will be to turn unemployment checks into pay checks. . . .

In contrast to the record of Republican mismanagement, the most recent eight years of Democratic leadership, under John F. Kennedy and Lyndon B. Johnson, produced economic growth that was virtually uninterrupted. The unemployment rate dropped from 6.7 percent in 1961 to 3.6 percent in 1968, and most segments of the population benefited. Inflation increased at an average annual rate of only 2 percent, and the purchasing power of the average family steadily increased. In 1960, about 40 billion people were living in poverty. Over the next eight years, 14½ million people moved out of poverty because of training opportunities, increased jobs and higher incomes. Since 1968, the number of persons living in poverty has remained virtually unchanged.

We have met the goals of full employment with stable prices in the past and can do it again. The Democratic Party is committed to the right of all adult Americans willing, able and seeking work to have opportunities for useful jobs at living wages. To make that commitment meaningful, we pledge ourselves to the support of legislation that will make every responsible effort to reduce adult unemployment to 3 percent within 4 years. . . .

There are people who will be especially difficult to employ. Special means for training and locating jobs for these people in the private sector, and, to the extent required, in public employment, should be established. Every effort should be made to create jobs in the private sector. Clearly, useful public jobs are far superior to welfare and unemployment payments. The federal government has the responsibility to ensure that all Americans able, willing and seeking work are provided opportunities for useful jobs.

The American people are demanding that their national government act more efficiently and effectively in those areas of urgent human needs such as welfare reform, health care and education.

However, beyond these strong national initiatives, state and local governments must be given an increased, permanent role in administering social programs. The federal government's role should be the constructive one of establishing standards and goals with increased state and local participation. . . .

In 1975, national health expenditures averaged $547 per person—an almost 40 percent increase in four years. Inflation and recession have combined to erode the effectiveness of the Medicare and Medicaid programs.

An increasingly high proportion of health costs have been shifted back to the elderly. An increasing Republican emphasis on restricting eligibility and services is emasculating basic medical care for older citizens who cannot meet the rising costs of good health.

We need a comprehensive national health insurance system with universal and mandatory coverage. . . .

Welfare Reform

Fundamental welfare reform is necessary. The problems with our current chaotic and inequitable system of public assistance are notorious. Existing welfare programs encourage family instability. They have few meaningful work incentives. They do little or nothing for the working poor on substandard incomes. The patchwork of federal, state and local programs encourages unfair variations in benefit levels among the states, and benefits in many states are well below the standards for even lowest-income budgets.

Of the current programs, only Food Stamps give universal coverage to all Americans in financial need. Cash assistance, housing aid and health care subsidies divide recipients into arbitrary categories. People with real needs who do not fit existing categories are ignored altogether.

The current complexity of the welfare structure requires armies of bureaucrats at all levels of government. Food Stamps, Aid to Families with Dependent Children, and Medicaid are burdened by unbelievably complex regulations, statutes and court orders. Both the recipients of these benefits, and the citizen who pays for them, suffer as a result. The fact that our current system is administered and funded at different levels of government makes it difficult to take initiatives to improve the status of the poor.

We should move toward replacement of our existing inadequate and wasteful system with a simplified system of income maintenance, substantially financed by the federal government, which includes a requirement that those able to work be provided with appropriate available jobs or job training opportunities. Those persons who are physically able to work (other than mothers with dependent children) should be required to accept appropriate available jobs or job training. This maintenance system should embody certain basic principles. First and most important, it should provide an income floor both for the working poor and the poor not in the labor market. It must treat stable and broken families equally. It must incorporate a simple schedule of work incentives that guarantees equitable levels of assistance to the working poor. This reform may require an initial additional investment, but it offers the prospect of stabilization of welfare costs over the long run, and the assurance that the objectives of this expenditure will be accomplished.

As an interim step, and as a means of providing immediate federal fiscal relief to state and local governments, local governments should no longer be required to bear the burden of welfare costs. Further, there should be a phased reduction in the states' share of welfare costs. . . .

Older Citizens

The Democratic Party has always emphasized that adequate income and health care for senior citizens are basic federal government responsibilities. The recent failure of government to reduce unemployment and alleviate the impact of the rising costs of food, housing and energy have placed a heavy burden on those who live on fixed and limited incomes, especially the elderly. Our other platform proposals in these areas are designed to help achieve an adequate income level for the elderly.

We will not permit an erosion of social security benefits, and while our ultimate goal is a health security system ensuring comprehensive and quality care for all Americans, health costs paid by senior citizens under the present system must be reduced.

We believe that Medicare should be made available to Americans abroad who are eligible for Social Security.

Democrats strongly support employment programs and the liberalization of the allowable earnings limitation under Social Security for older Americans who wish to continue working and living as productive citizens. We will put an end to delay in implementation of nutrition programs for the elderly and give high priority to a transportation policy for senior citizens under the Older Americans Act. . . .

Housing

In the past eight Republican years, housing has become a necessity priced as a luxury. Housing prices have nearly doubled in the past six years and housing starts have dropped by almost one-quarter. The effect is that over three-fourths of American families cannot afford to buy an average-priced home. The basic national goal of providing decent housing and available shelter has been sacrificed to misguided tax, spending and credit policies which were supposed to achieve price stability but have failed to meet that goal. As a result, we do not have decent housing or price stability. The vision of the Housing Act of 1968, the result of three decades of enlightened Democratic housing policy, has been lost. The Democratic Party reasserts those goals, and pledges to achieve them. . . .

We support direct federal subsidies and low interest loans to encourage the construction of low-and moderate-income housing. Such subsidies shall not result in unreasonable profit for builders, developers or credit institutions.

We support the expansion of the highly successful programs of direct federal subsidies to provide housing for the elderly. . . .

Rural Development

The problems of rural America are closely linked to those of our cities. Rural poor and the rural elderly suffer under the same economic pressures and have at least as many social needs as their counterparts in the cities. The absence of rural jobs and rural vitality and the continuing demise of the family farm have promoted a migration to our cities which is beyond the capacity of the cities to absorb. Over 20 million Americans moved to urban areas between 1940 and 1960 alone. We pledge to develop programs to make the family farm economically healthy again so as to be attractive to young people.

To that end, the Democratic Party pledges to strengthen the economy and thereby create jobs in our great agricultural and rural areas by the full implementation and funding of the Rural Development Act of 1972 and by the adoption of an agricultural policy which recognizes that our capacity to produce food and fiber is one of our greatest assets.

While it is bad enough to be poor, or old, or alone in the city, it is worse in the country. We are therefore committed to overcome the problems of rural as well as urban isolation and poverty by insuring the existence of adequate health facilities, critically-needed community facilities such as water supply and sewage disposal systems, decent housing, adequate educational opportunity and needed transportation throughout rural America. . . .

Republican platform—The Republican platform made the following statements on the welfare and poverty issues:

Jobs and Inflation

We believe it is of paramount importance that the American people understand that the number-one destroyer of jobs is inflation. We wish to stress that the number-one cause of inflation is the government's expansion of the nation's supply of money and credit needed to pay for deficit spending. It is above all else deficit spending by the federal government which erodes the purchasing power of the dollar. Most Republicans in Congress seem to understand this fundamental cause-and-effect relationship and their support in sustaining over 40 presidential vetoes in the past two years has prevented over $13 billion in federal spending. It is clear that most of the Democrats do not understand this vital principle, or, if they do, they simply don't care.

Inflation is the direct responsibility of a spendthrift, Democrat-controlled Congress that has been unwilling to discipline itself to live within our means. The temptation to spend and deficit-spend for political reasons has simply been too great for most of our elected politicians to resist. Individuals, families, companies and most local and state governments must live within a budget. Why not Congress?

Republicans hope every American realizes that if we are permanently to eliminate high unemployment, it is essential to protect the integrity of our money. That means putting an end to deficit spending. The danger, sooner or later, is runaway inflation. . . .

Massive, federally-funded public-employment programs, such as the Humphrey-Hawkins bill currently embraced by the new national platform of the Democrat Party, will cost billions and can only be financed either through very large tax increases or through ever-increasing levels of deficit spending. Although such government "make-work" programs usually provide a temporary stimulus to the economy, "quick-fix" solutions of this sort—like all narcotics—lead to addiction, larger and larger doses, and ultimately the destruction of far more jobs than they create. Sound job creation can only be accomplished in the private sector of the economy. Americans must not be fooled into accepting government as the employer of last resort. . . .

In order to be able to provide more jobs, businesses must be able to expand; yet in order to build and expand, they must be profitable and able to borrow funds (savings) that someone else has been willing to part with on a temporary basis. In the long run, inflation discourages thrift, encourages debt and destroys the incentive to save which is the mainspring of capital formation. When our government—through deficit spending and debasement of the currency—destroys the incentive to save and to invest, it destroys the very well-spring of American productivity. Obviously, when production falls, the number of jobs declines.

The American people are beginning to understand that no government can ever add real wealth (purchasing power) to an economy by simply turning on the printing presses or by creating credit out of thin air. All government can do is confiscate and redistribute wealth. No nation can spend its way into prosperity; a nation can only spend its way into bankruptcy. . . .

Health

Every American should have access to quality health care at an affordable price.

The possibility of an extended illness in a family is a frightening prospect, but, if it does happen, a person should at least be protected from having it wipe out lifetime savings. Catastrophic expenses incurred from major illnesses and accidents affect only a small percentage of Americans each year, but for those people, the financial burden can be devastating. We support extension of catastrophic-illness protection to all who cannot obtain it. We should utilize our private health-insurance system to assure adequate protection for those who do not have it. Such an approach will eliminate the red tape and high bureaucratic costs inevitable in a comprehensive national program.

The Republican Party opposes compulsory national health insurance.

Americans should know that the Democrat platform, which offers a government-operated and financed "comprehensive national health-insurance system with universal and mandatory coverage," will increase federal government spending by more than $70 billion in its first full year. Such a plan could require a personal income-tax increase of approximately 20%. We oppose this huge, new health-insurance tax. Moreover, we do not believe that the federal government can administer effectively the Democrats' cradle-to-grave proposal.

The most effective, efficient and economical method to improve health care and extend its availability to all is to build on the present health delivery and insurance system, which covers nine out of every ten Americans.

A coordinated effort should be mounted immediately to contain the rapid increase in health-care costs by all available means, such as development of healthier life-styles through education, improved preventive care, better distribution of medical manpower, emphasis on out-of-hospital services and elimination of wasteful duplication of medical services.

We oppose excessive intrusions from Washington in the delivery of health care. We believe in preserving the privacy that should exist between a patient and a physician, particularly in regard to the confidentiality of medical records.

Federal health programs should be consolidated into a single grant to each state, where possible, thereby allowing much greater flexibility in setting local priorities. Our rural areas, for example, have different health-care delivery needs than our cities. Federal laws and regulations should respect these differences and make it possible to respond differently to differing needs. Fraud in Medicare and Medicaid programs should be exposed and eliminated. . . .

Child Nutrition

Every child should have enough to eat. Good nutrition is a prerequisite of a healthy life. We must focus our resources on feeding *needy* children. The present school-lunch programs provide a 20% subsidy to underwrite the meals of children from middle- and upper-income families.

The existing 15 child-nutrition programs should be consolidated into one program, administered by the states, and concentrated on those children truly in need. Other federal programs should insure that low-income people will be able to purchase a nutritionally adequate food supply. . . .

Welfare Reform

The work of all Americans contributes to the strength of our nation, and all who are able to contribute should be encouraged to do so.

In every society there will be some who cannot work, often through no fault of their own. The measure of a country's compassion is how it treats the least fortunate.

We appreciate the magnificent variety of private charitable institutions which have developed in the United States.

The Democrat-controlled Congress has produced a jumble of degrading, dehumanizing, wasteful, overlapping and inefficient programs failing to assist the needy poor. A systematic and complete overhaul of the welfare system should be initiated immediately.

The following goals should govern the reform of the welfare system: (1) Provide adequate living standards for the truly needy; (2) End welfare fraud and prevent it in the future with emphasis on removing ineligible recipients from the welfare rolls, tightening food-stamp eligibility requirements, and ending aid to illegal aliens and the voluntarily unemployed; (3) Strengthen work requirements, particularly those directed at the productive involvement of able-bodied persons in useful community work projects; (4) Provide educational and vocational incentives to allow recipients to become self-supporting; (5) Better coordinate federal efforts with local and state social-welfare agencies and strengthen local and state administrative functions. We oppose federalizing the welfare system; local levels of government are most aware of the needs of their communities. Consideration should be given to a range of options in financing the programs to assure that state and local responsibilities are met. We also oppose the guaranteed annual income concept or any programs that reduce the incentive to work.

Those features of the present law, particularly the food stamp program, that draw into assistance programs people who are capable of paying for their own needs should be corrected. The humanitarian purpose of such programs must not be corrupted by eligibility loopholes. Food-stamp-program reforms proposed by Republicans in Congress would accomplish the twin goals of directing resources to those most in need and streamlining administration.

We must never forget that unemployment compensation is insurance, not a welfare program. It should be redesigned to assure that working is always more beneficial than collecting unemployment benefits. The benefits should help most the hard-core unemployed. Major efforts must be encouraged through the private sector to speed up the process of finding jobs for those temporarily out of work.

Older Americans

Older Americans constitute one of our most valuable resources.

Families should be supported in trying to take care of their elderly. Too often government laws and policies contribute to the deterioration of family life. Our tax laws, for example, permit a deduction to the taxpayer who gives a contribution to a charitable institution that might care for an elderly parent, but offer little or no incentive to provide care in the home. If an elderly parent relinquishes certain assets and enters a nursing home, the parent may qualify for full Medicaid coverage, but if parents live with their children, any Supplemental Security Income benefit for which they are eligible may be reduced. Incentives must be written into law to encourage families to care for their older members.

Along with loneliness and ill health, older Americans are deeply threatened by inflation. The costs of the basic necessities of life—food, shelter, clothing, health care—have risen so drastically as to reduce the ability of many older persons to subsist with any measure of dignity. In addition to our program for protecting against excessive costs of long-term illness, nothing will be as beneficial to the elderly as the effect of this platform's proposals on curbing inflation.

The Social Security benefits are of inestimable importance to the well-being and financial peace-of-mind of most older Americans. We will not let the Social Security system fail. We will work to make the Social Security system actuarily sound. The Social Security program must not be turned into a welfare system, based on need rather than contributions. The cost to employers for Social Security contributions must not be raised to the point where they will be unable to afford contributions to employees' private pension programs. We will work for an increase in the earned-income ceiling or its elimination so that, as people live longer, there will not be the present penalty on work. We will also seek to correct those provisions of the system that now discriminate against women and married couples.

Such programs as Foster Grandparents and Senior Companions, which provide income exempt from Social Security limitations, should be continued and extended to encourage senior citizens to continue to be active and involved in society. Appropriate domiciliary care programs should be developed to enable senior citizens to receive such care without losing other benefits to which they may be entitled. . . .

The Medicare program must be improved to help control inflation in health-care costs triggered by present regulations.

Other areas of concern to the elderly that need increased attention are home and outpatient care, adequate transportation, nutrition, day care and homemaker care as an alternative to costly institutional treatment. . . .

Panels brief Carter. Experts from all over the country converged on Plains, Ga. Aug. 16–18 as Carter held successive one-day sessions at which he was briefed on domestic social issues, energy and international economics.

Carter said Aug. 16 that a consensus at the meeting on social issues supported restructuring of government as a key measure in improving social programs. Carter castigated the present government structure as a "bureaucratic mess" that made change virtually impossible.

Carter said that his aim of helping those capable of working to find jobs, rather than leaving them on welfare rolls was shared by other briefing participants.

Carter favors work over welfare. Carter formally opened his election campaign Sept. 6 with a speech in Warm Springs, Ga. in which he said that "when there is a choice between welfare and work, let's go to work." Repeating this theme at a suburban Birmingham, Ala. shopping center Sept. 13, he said, "We Southerners believe in work, not welfare."

TV debates. A feature of the 1976 Presidential election campaign was a series of three televised debates between the two major-party Presidential candidates. Among welfare-poverty related issues at the opening debate Sept. 23:

On handling unemployment—Asked to state, "in specific terms," what he would do to reduce unemployment, Carter said it was "a top priority" and "ought to be done primarily by strong leadership in the White House, the inspiration of our people, the tapping of business, agriculture, industry, labor and government at all levels to work on this project." Carter continued:

"There are several things that can be done specifically that are not now being done.

"First of all to channel research and development funds into areas that will provide large numbers of jobs. Secondly, we need to have a commitment in the private sector to cooperate with government in matters like housing, for a small investment of taxpayers' money in the housing field can bring large numbers of extra jobs and the guarantee of mortgage loans and the putting forward of 202 programs for housing for all the people and so forth to cut down the roughly 20% unemployment that now exists in the construction industry.

"Another thing is to deal with our needs in the central cities where the unemployment rate is extremely high, sometimes among minority groups, or those who don't speak English, or are black or young people. . . .

"Here a C.C.C. type program would be appropriate to channel money into the sharing with private sector and also local and state government to employ young people who are now out of work.

"Another very important aspect of our economy would be to increase production in every way possible to hold down taxes on individuals and to shift the tax burden on to those who have avoided paying taxes in the past."

Another need was for "a good relationship" between management and labor, Carter said. In areas of high unemployment, he said, "We might channel specific targeted jobs . . . by paying part of the salary."

Carter said that he was confident that by the end of the first year of the next presidential term, the jobless rate for adults would be down to 3%, inflation would be under control and there would be a "balanced growth" for a "balanced budget."

What about wage and price controls? he was asked. Carter replied:

"We now have such a low utilization of productive capacity—about 73%. I think it's about the lowest since the Great Depression years—and such a high unemployment rate now—7.9%—that we have a long way to go in getting to work before we have the inflationary pressures.

"And I think this would be easy to accomplish, to get jobs done, without having strong inflationary pressures that would be necessary, I would not favor the payment of a given fixed income to people and not say they're not able to work. But with tax incentives for the low-income group, we can build up their income levels above the poverty level and not make welfare more profitable than work."

Ford replied that he didn't think Carter had been "any more specific in this case than he has been on many other instances." Ford continued:

"I notice particularly that he didn't endorse the Humphrey-Hawkins bill which he has on occasion and which is included as a part of the Democratic platform. That legislation allegedly would help our unemployment, but we all know that it would have controlled our economy, it would have added $10 to $30 billion each year in additional expenditures by the federal government. It would have called for export controls on agricultural products.

"In my judgment the best way to get jobs is to expand the private sector, where five out of six jobs today exist in our economy. We can do that by reducing federal taxes as I proposed about a year ago when I called for a tax reduction of $28 billion—three quarters of it to go to private taxpayers and one quarter to the business sector. We could add to jobs in the major metropolitan areas by a proposal that I recommended that would give tax incentives to business to move into the inner cities and to expand or to build new plants so that they would take a plant or expand a plant where people are and people are currently unemployed."

Young people, Ford said, could be given "an opportunity to work and learn at the same time, just like we give money to young people who are going to college."

On vetoes of jobs bills—In reference to his opposition to jobs bills, Ford was asked, "Why do you think it is better to pay out unemployment compensation to idle people than to put them to work in public service jobs?"

Ford said each job under the jobs bills would cost taxpayers $25,000 and that the jobs would not be available for from nine to 18 months. He added:

"The immediate problem we have is to stimulate our economy now so that we can get rid of unemployment. What we have done is to hold the lid on spending in an effort to reduce the rate of inflation. And we have proven, I think very conclusively, that you can reduce the rate of inflation and increase jobs.

"For example, as I have said, we have added some four million jobs in the last 17 months. We have now employed 88 million people in America, the largest number in the history of the United States.

"We've added 500,000 jobs in the last two months. Inflation is the quickest way to destroy jobs. And by holding the lid on federal spending we have been able to do a good job, an affirmative job in inflation and as the result have added to the jobs in this country.

"I think it's also appropriate to point out that through our tax policies we have stimulated added employment throughout the country, the investment tax credit, tax incentives for expansion and modernization of our industrial capacity.

"It's my opinion that the private sector, where five out of the six jobs are, where you have permanent jobs with the opportunity for advancement, is a better place than make-work jobs under the program recommended by the Congress."

Carter, citing unemployment data, said it was "a terrible tragedy." Ford, Carter said, "doesn't seem to put into perspective the fact ... that this touches human beings." Carter said:

"This affects human beings. And his insensitivity in providing those people a chance to work has made this a welfare administration, and not a work administration.

"He hasn't saved $9 billion with his vetoes. There's only been a net saving of $4 billion. And the cost in unemployment compensation, welfare compensation and lost revenues has increased $23 billion in the last two years. This is a typical attitude that really causes havoc in people's lives, and then it's covered over by saying that our country has naturally got a 6% unemployment rate, or 7% unemployment rate and a 6% inflation. It's a travesty. It shows a lack of leadership."

Oct. 22 debate—In the Oct. 22 debate, Carter assailed Ford's alleged lack of an urban policy.

Congress had passed legislation in home-ownership, crime control, health care, education and other areas, Carter said, adding:

"Those programs were designed to help those who need it most. And quite often this has been for very poor people and neighborhoods in the downtown urban centers. Because of the greatly advantaged persons who live in the suburbs—better education, better organization, more articulate, more aware of what the laws are—quite often this money has been channeled out of the downtown centers where it is needed."

Carter said he favored: using all revenue-sharing money for local government and removal of prohibitions against use of such funds to improve education and health care; shifting welfare costs away from the local governments altogether, and, in time, a move by the federal government to absorb part of the monies now paid by state governments.

His last point was "that the major thrust has got to be to put people back to work."

Ford replied that his Administration "does have a very comprehensive program to help our major metropolitan areas." He said he "fought for" a general revenue-sharing program and "a major mass-transit program." He cited $3.3 billion made available to cities for community development. "We have a good housing program," he asserted. Ford said his tax program, to provide "an incentive for industry to move into our major metropolitan areas, into the inner cities, will bring jobs where people are and help to revitalize those cities as they can be."

Index